Becoming Your Sun Sign

The Journey from
Your Moon to Your Sun

Pamela Gallagher

LightPath, Inc.

Published by LightPath, Inc.
6507 Stewart Road
Cincinnati, OH 45236
www.midwestschoolofastrology.com
www.pamelagallagher.com
pam1gallagher@gmail.com

ISBN: 978-0-578-51275-4

Library of Congress Control Number: 2019910325

Editing by Karol Mackey and Tom Tenaglia
Cover and Book design by Lyza Fontana of www.CreativeHowTo.com
All Images Used By Permission
Cover and Interior Photos © www.istockphoto.com and © www.shutterstock.com
Additional Photos via www.pixabay.com

PRINTED IN THE UNITED STATES OF AMERICA

Dedication

Much appreciation and grateful thanks to all of the fathers and mothers of this book.

This includes all of my students and clients over the years who have supported my vision to take astrology to a larger audience. In particular, I must first thank my daughter, Mindy, who has read and reread these pages and continues to work with me.

Next, I appreciate my grandchildren Hugh, Logan, and Phoebe, who have been my inspiration to keep moving and creating.

special thanks to Karol Mackey, John Marani, his wife enaglia and Deanne Hernandez for reading, editing ught for the completion of this book. The design cover, edits and layout of this book have been artfully completed by Lyza Fontana of CreativeHowTo.com.

I would like to thank Fei and David Cochrane, owners and developers of Cosmic Patterns Software, for their collaboration with astrology charts. The service uses their Kepler/Sirius program to produce these charts.

And so it is!

About the Author

Pam Gallagher has over 40 years of experience practicing, studying and teaching astrology as well as being an Ordained interfaith minister with an Independent Unity Organization. She specializes in relationship counseling, forecasting and spiritual development.

After Pam completed her studies at the University of Cincinnati, she found her passion and life purpose in the world of astrology. She has traveled the world on her own quest to further her knowledge and understanding of metaphysics.

Pam completed her Masters in Theology after she returned to astrology upon retiring from corporate America as International Sales/ Marketing Training Director.

As an internationally recognized speaker, Pam shares her perspectives on astrology and its interaction with life on earth.

After teaching astrology for many years, Pam opened the Midwest School of Astrology in 2009 where she encourages students of all ages to learn and explore the mysteries of astrology.

She currently sits on the board of the Avalon School of Astrology and has lectured at the Kepler Institute of Astrology in Belgrade, Serbia, as well as many astrology groups.

Foreword

As a teacher of energy and empowerment with a 28th generation lineage from Hawai'i, I have been sharing knowledge with tens of thousands of students since the 1990s. In the workshops that I conduct, I teach various techniques to help people become more empowered on their path. In some of our events, we teach communication skills and how to do specific release work for negative emotions and limiting beliefs. In our Huna workshop that we run on the Island of Hawai'i, we teach how to do energy work with others and what is referred to in Hawai'i as ho'omana (empowerment).

With my advanced Huna students, some of whom have been with me for well over a decade, I teach them to start with simplicity and pay attention to the Moon. First, notice when you are more comfortable with your emotions based on the Moon phase. Next, begin to notice what sign it is in starting with the elements. For example, when the Moon is in a fiery sign like Aries or Leo, how do you feel? Make note of that and as you gain awareness, you gain empowerment.

Then, when my students are ready, we delve into the exploration of astrology.

I start with this explanation: Imagine for a moment you have a picture of you and the placement of all the planets and stars in the sky at the time of your birth. This can be considered a snapshot of how you are energetically hardwired. Now, imagine for a moment, based on the Law of Correspondence that how the stars and planets in the sky relate to each other was a picture of how your energy is naturally wired in your personal consciousness. That is astrology.

For example, as Pam explains: "The Sun, the central energy in the solar system, drives your vitality, growth, and life purpose in a masculine form." Where the Sun is at in your chart and what sign it is in teaches you how and where you like to shine—it's where you're most comfortable and feel at home in expressing your unique talents and special gifts. Naturally, finding where you like to shine will enhance your ability to drive you forward into your purpose.

A further reason why astrology is so useful is that it provides insight into the journey of your soul. Just as Pam describes, "The Moon is the other 'light'; it reflects your soul's emotions, moods, reactions, instincts, and soul history in a feminine form." When a person has an awareness of this, they gain a better understanding of their karmic patterns and lessons. Since we are all here to acquire new learnings and deeper lessons, and just as your purpose can be discovered in your chart, so can your soul's karmic patterns over lifetimes.

Let's start from the beginning to understand our purpose.

From the moment we as a species gained awareness, we looked up to the Sun, Moon and stars with wonder and awe. We marveled at their beauty and became increasingly curious as to what they mean and more importantly, what they represent to us as individuals.

Equally powerful is the drive for an individual to find their path and know their purpose. This is a subject that I have studied for the bulk of my life and after having taught tens of thousands of people, I have found that most individuals just want to know who they are. The students I see at my events want to gain insight as to why they are here and specifically they want to know who they are meant to be.

The problem is that our society, for the most part, teaches us how to discover who we are in a very backwards way.

Most people in this world, were taught to spend time focusing on having things as a means to bring happiness and joy into their lives; have the car, have the house, have the new gadget. And, while that may work for a while, most begin to wake up and wonder why the house, the car, or any of the material things didn't create any lasting happiness.

The individuals that wake from that trance of collecting and having things realize that the goal in life might be more about figuring out what they're meant to do with their lives. They sprint down different paths attempting to find one that fits. They explore different career paths, and different forms of personal growth or spirituality in an attempt to find out who they are. Unfortunately, our path is not about figuring out what to do, it is about finding deeper purpose and who we are meant to be.

That is because we are not human *havings* and we are not human *doings* – we are human *beings*.

There are several tools that you could use to discover who you are meant to be, where you are heading and what you are meant to do. And for me, astrology is one of the more powerful tools for discovering this.

For the most part, ancient cultures did not believe that the stars and planets in the sky did anything to them. People that studied astrology knew of the Law of Correspondence, which simply states that "as above, so below". The two most visible objects in the sky, the Sun and the Moon, have a connection to the cycles we experience within our physiology as well as the cycles we go through over the course of our lifetime.

For example, in the Hawaiian culture it was believed that the Moon represented an emotional cycle that we all progress through. At a full Moon, emotions were "lit up" and exposed, as if a light were shining on them. During a new Moon, things were darker and less emotional, and it seemed more of a time to draw our energy inward. Some people have an easier time with a full Moon, while others have an easier time with a new Moon.

The word lunatic comes from the term lunar because early psychologists noticed that some people became crazier during a full Moon. However, it is not that the Moon does anything to you, rather it represents a cycle that you go through.

The well-known earlier psychologist, Carl Jung, would look at a patient's astrological chart if he was having difficulty understanding how they interpreted their reality based on energy. Jung is someone who I have studied extensively in my career and one of the primary tools he utilized was astrology to not only understand how a person perceives reality, but also how they could connect with a deeper purpose.

For many years, Pam has been a guest educator at the advanced levels of my Huna workshop in Hawai'i, where students come to learn about the ancient wisdom of the Hawaiian culture. When it is time for my upper level students to embark on the path of astrology and understanding their own natal chart, there is only one person I trust.

Pam Gallagher is the most gifted astrologer I have ever met. This is because of her depth of knowledge, her 40 plus years in the field, and most importantly for me, because of her ability to teach from the heart and help people understand the value of being able to take action in life based on their astrological chart.

I entrust Pam with the higher-level astrological teachings with my students, many who have been with me for well over 20 years. I call upon her expertise when looking at the charts of my personal clients, and I look to her for guidance as a father in how best to approach my children based on their charts. After reading *Becoming Your Sun Sign*, I am in awe of how she has simplified the concepts and put it into a format that I have never seen before.

The way Pam wrote this book and the way she presents the information makes other astrology books pale in comparison. When I read it, my first thought was, "Finally! Someone did it the way people need to learn it!"

As you navigate *Becoming Your Sun Sign, The Journey from the Moon to the Sun*, your purpose and your soul's journey will become more evident and, regardless of your background in astrology, you will walk away with a greater depth of knowledge of who you are meant to be and how you are meant to shine.

Matt James, PhD,
Doctor of Integrative Psychology and Author of *Mental and Emotional Release* and *Ho'oponopono: Your Path to True Forgiveness*

A Note from the Author

Since childhood, I have been searching for answers to major Life questions. "Why are we here?" What is this all for?" "Why is there so much pain for everyone?" The biggest question for me has always been "What is my life purpose here on earth?"

My journey has taken me through many Christian churches and spiritual groups. Having started out in the Southern Baptist church, my early training brought me structure as well as the hidden message not to question church tradition. In 1969 as I was rummaging through a bookstore, I came across a numerology book which talked about higher destiny and divine synchronicity. These were new words to me from a spiritual perspective. Immediately, my thoughts began to take off in new directions. What if God had a higher plan for each one of us...what if there really was a time and a season for all things under the Sun...what if....what if....the search was on.

There is a famous eastern saying "when the student is ready, the teacher appears." So, not long after that, I met a woman who was studying astrology. Again, she opened many new doors of thought and questioning. By the end of that year, I had joined my first astrology class and was studying feverishly to find the missing links in my spiritual understanding. I desperately tried to prove that astrology did not work because it totally challenged the traditional teachings; but, every time I put the numerological mystical system to the test it did not fail. My search for higher truth continues to drive my life but I no longer challenge the universe; instead, I seek to understand its message. The zodiac and its twelve signs symbolize the path back to God. These symbols vibrate higher than religious dogma. I have learned to accept that truth reigns higher than religion.

Now, with more than forty years of practice, I do astrological consulting and teaching about God's higher plan for each of us. By working with individuals and their birth charts, I aspire to help them see their personal soul journey more clearly. There are many ways to travel from the mountains of Virginia to the California shores. We can walk, skateboard, bicycle, or drive a car. We can follow the Sun westward, wander in the desert, follow the main highways or choose to learn to read the road map. I prefer to use God's celestial road map which allows us more time to focus and enjoy the journey.

My highest intention with this book is to inspire all seekers and searchers to connect with their astrological road map, their electromagnetic energy field, that guides them along their unique spiritual road map back to the wholeness of God – the Supreme One.

For the sake of clarity and cosmic balance I will use "he" in my discussion on the masculine signs which are Aries, Gemini, Leo, Libra, Sagittarius, and Aquarius. I will use "she" when working with the feminine signs which are Taurus, Cancer, Virgo, Scorpio, Capricorn, and Pisces.

It takes courage to be willing to look deeper into one's behavior and then be called to change the pattern of response to allow for soul growth and enlightenment. Enjoy learning about your personal spiritual path by studying your astrological road map!

Godspeed on your journey!

- Pam Gallagher

Table of Contents

To learn more, get an astrological reading, or ask a question, email us at: pam1gallagher@gmail.com.

Universal Symbols & Keywords in Astrology

Sign		Ruling Planet		Attributes
Aries	♈	Mars	♂	Physical energy, Self, Action, Dominant
Taurus	♉	Venus	♀	Love, Money, Values, Talents, Resources
Gemini	♊	Mercury	☿	Mind, Communication, Thinking, Learning
Cancer	♋	Moon	☽	Soul, Emotions, Mother, Home, Reactions
Leo	♌	Sun	☉	Spirit, Self, Creativity, Ego, Children
Virgo	♍	Mercury	☿	Mind, Work, Analysis, Service, Health
Libra	♎	Venus	♀	Marriage, Balance, Relationships, Harmony
Scorpio	♏	Pluto	♇	Intensity, Investments, Courage, Death, Sex, Focus
Sagittarius	♐	Jupiter	♃	Expansion, Philosophy, Higher Education, Travel
Capricorn	♑	Saturn	♄	Contraction, Responsibility, Father, Career, Control
Aquarius	♒	Uranus	♅	Independence, Originality, Destiny, Friends, New Age
Pisces	♓	Neptune	♆	Compassion, Fear, Confusion, Spirituality, Psychic

The 4 Elements Used in Astrology

Element	Signs	Characteristics
Fire	Aries, Leo, Sagittarius	Energy/Spirit
Earth	Taurus, Virgo, Capricorn	Manifesting/Physical
Air	Gemini, Libra, Aquarius	Social/Mental
Water	Cancer, Scorpio, Pisces	Feeling/Emotions

How to Use This Book

The Sun and the Moon are the two lights in our solar system and they show the flow of energy that describes your growth pattern throughout your lifetime.

To get started, you will need to know your Sun and Moon signs from your Natal Birth Chart. *(If you already know your Sun and Moon signs, you have what you need. If you don't know your Sun and Moon signs, there are instructions on page 5 to obtain a FREE Natal Birth Chart.)*

First, find your Sun sign in the list below. Your Sun Sign is based on the date of your birth. These dates may change slightly from year to year. If you were born on the first or last day of a sign, then you were born "on the cusp" and you will need to verify your Sun Sign.

<u>Sun Signs</u>

Aries
March 19th to April 19th

Taurus
April 19th to May 20th

Gemini
May 20th to June 20th

Cancer
June 20th to July 22nd

Leo
July 22nd to August 22nd

Virgo
August 22nd to September 22nd

Libra
September 22nd to October 22nd

Scorpio
October 22nd to November 21st

Sagittarius
November 21st to December 21st

Capricorn
December 21st to January 20th

Aquarius
January 20th to February 18th/19th

Pisces
February 19th to March 19th

To find your Moon Sign, you will need a copy of your birth chart. There are many ways to obtain a copy of the individual birth chart, also known as the natal horoscope. The information needed to calculate the chart the birth date (day, month, year); the birth location (town/city/state/country, or longitude and latitude); and the birth time, which may be listed on your birth certificate. If the exact time is not known, it is important to inquire within the family to establish an approximate time frame of morning, afternoon, or evening. If the information is not available, the chart should be calculated for a 12:00pm (noon) birth time. Also, knowing which part of the day that the birth occurred helps to establish the Moon sign accurately.

In years past, someone who had the reference books would have had to calculate the chart by hand. Times have changed; it is very easy to use the Internet to create an accurate birth chart when the correct birth data is available.

Obtaining Your Natal Birth Chart

For a FREE astrological chart, go to my website at: www.midwestschoolofastrology.com. Go to interpretations and look for "Free Chart Wheel". Once you have entered your data correctly, you can print the chart and use the symbol list at the beginning of this book to find the placement of the Sun, Moon, nodes, plus the other planets.

If no internet is available, you can get an accurate Natal chart by sending the name, birthdate, birth time, and place of birth, with a self-addressed stamped envelope, along with $5 (check or money order), to Pamela Gallagher, Astrologer, 6507 Stewart Rd, Cincinnati, OH 45236.

If you're having difficulty obtaining a copy of your chart, which will have the Sun and Moon, please email us at pam1gallagher@gmail.com.

What Does an Astrological Chart Look Like?

The chart will appear as a circle, with each planet and sign shown as symbols around the center. A number of degrees will appear next to each symbol. Look earlier in this book to find the sign symbol to discover where the Moon was when you were born. That is your Moon sign.

When you have no birth time, if the degree of the Moon is between 0 – 5 degrees of any sign, read both that sign and the one before it. If the degree of the Moon is between 25-29 degree, then read both that sign and the sign that follows it. You should be able to recognize the description of how you handle your emotions or how you acted as a child.

The journey begins in earnest when your personality joins with the unconscious memories of past patterns that need to be worked on in this lifetime. Once you understand these patterns, you can focus on overcoming challenges, dissolving blockages, and using your soul's talents. This information is all registered in the person's birth (natal) chart.

The relationship of the Moon to the Sun is the primary indicator of the life path or life purpose; this is supported by all of the other planets, fixed stars, asteroids, and sensitive points relating to your unique astrological picture. The birth chart represents your spiritual DNA, or your distinct astrological "fingerprint" for this time on earth.

When you are ready to understand more about your life purpose, contact Pam Gallagher and the Midwest School of Astrology for a thorough birth chart reading (midwestschoolofastrology.com).

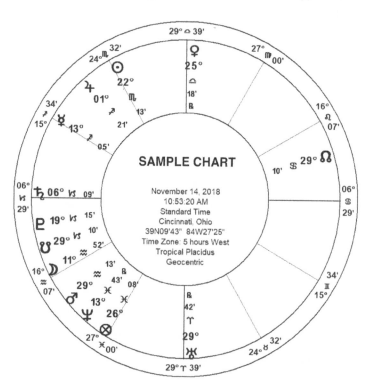

SAMPLE CHART

November 14, 2018
10:53:20 AM
Standard Time
Cincinnati, Ohio
39N09'43" 84W27'25"
Time Zone: 5 hours West
Tropical Placidus
Geocentric

Welcome to Your Life Path

When you sit back and observe life on earth, there seems to be a system of order that prevails over the events of life in dependable cycles. The ancients called it astrology, "the message of the stars." Each spring on March 20-21st, the Sun returns to the equator to start the new astrological year as it begins its journey through Aries. In reality, it is the earth that is rotating around the Sun. In astrology, the constantly changing planetary positions, projected against the zodiac from earth, reflect moments that are captured in astrological charts.

Back in the 1950s, a book was published called Linda Goodman's Sun Signs. It depicted the characteristics of each of the twelve zodiac signs with humor and depth. To expand on that theme of Sun sign personalities, let us journey back in time to the ancient astrologers who always considered the mystical feminine Moon sign to be as significant as the Sun's masculine position. In studying the spiritual connection between all living bodies in our universe, we can deepen our understanding by showing that the souls of children actually act out more of the Moon sign traits than the Sun sign traits.

The ancients referred to the Moon as the symbol of the soul. Why? Because the Moon has no light of its own; therefore, it reflects the light from the Sun, the life giver. As such, children reflect their circumstances because they have few choices of their own. Mythically, the Moon is feminine and absorbs energy to which it then responds. It has been called "the soul envelope" or the accumulator of all the experiences the soul has collected in its many lifetimes on its journey back to spiritual Oneness. This old behavior pattern is most commonly known as the personality.

In order to embrace the idea of a continuing life journey, you must first accept the premise that the soul is eternal. By observing nature, it becomes apparent that there is a time and a season for all things. There are trees still growing that are hundreds of years old and have budded, bloomed, grown and shed leaves, and then gone dormant in the fall every year, only to come back to new life in the spring of the next year. Nature provides a mirror of the natural cycles of the Divine Plan.

Even the Moon in its monthly movement consistently repeats an eightfold cycle. Once each month when the Moon meets the Sun, it becomes new. Then as it begins to grow in its unconscious state, it becomes crescent, first quarter, gibbous, and then full. After it crests at full, it becomes conscious of itself and begins its decreasing journey back to darkness. From full face, it declines to disseminating, last quarter, and then to balsamic, the period of completion where the soul pulls back into itself.

In a particular life cycle, the soul may excel in some areas such as art and music, but may not perform so well in relationships and social exchange. So relationships and socialization will be at the top of the list of required assignments in the growth experience. In this particular case, the soul might choose a chart where the Moon is in Pisces, and the Sun is in Libra or Aquarius, the social signs.

The evolving soul, represented by the reflective Moon, expresses itself instinctually until it stops reacting to life and begins to take action. When the Sun activates, it becomes purposeful and powerful as the soul takes on the characteristics of the Sun sign. If both the Sun and the Moon are in the same sign at birth, the message of the sign archetype continues to repeat throughout the life. During mature times of strength and deliberate action, the Sun sign energies are obvious and notable.

When life becomes difficult and emotional, however, the Moon behavior takes over in instinctual fashion. Moon sign behavior dominates in a crisis time because emotion is ruling, both in a child or an adult. Since experience is always the best teacher, action should override reaction. Until the soul stops instinctively reacting and starts deliberately acting, there is no forward movement; the soul continues to circle on the same track. When an individual consciously chooses to act in accordance with their Sun sign pattern, energy begins to move and change occurs. Spiritual growth manifests as a result of the new experiences and risk.

People who are concerned about spiritual growth often talk about karma, the law of cause and effect. The word "karma" comes from Eastern religious systems, but it still describes a universal law of balance. Most belief systems include the concept about the "circle" of life. Jesus said, "Cast your bread upon the waters. They will return to you." He also said, "As ye sow, so shall ye reap." Both of these Christian teachings reinforce the law of completion: In the Buddhist and Hindu traditions, they teach that what goes out from your energy must return to you.

God's universe is not a punishing universe. If a person sends out anger, sooner or later that soul must experience the return of that anger. It is not a punishment; it is a learning experience. The spiritual test comes when the anger returns. If the soul responds again with anger, then the test will return repeatedly until the soul consciously chooses to respond differently. When the personality chooses the more positive qualities of their Sun sign, the power of free will can override negative behavior patterns.

All living things are growing toward the light. The grass, the flowers, the plants, the trees, the crystals, and the soul of man is also reaching for that Light. God provided us with this celestial map to aid us on our journey back to wholeness.

The purpose for knowing your astrological birth chart is to put you on the path to making better life choices. It allows the soul to experience the spiritual growth that it incarnated to initiate. Identifying the flow of each planet by its astrological sign helps to direct the energy.

The ancients divided the twelve zodiac signs into four basic elements: Fire, Earth, Air, and Water. Each element is associated with a common temperament and includes three of the twelve zodiac signs. Our emphasis for this study will be the positions of the Moon and the

Sun, and each of the ten planets in our system are associated with a particular element and sign at any given time.

The Elements

The Fire element:
Includes Aries, Leo and Sagittarius, is known for its high-spirited enthusiasm and its vitality.

The Earth element:
Includes Taurus, Virgo, and Capricorn, projects a solid, grounded, practical reality.

The Air element:
Includes Gemini, Libra, and Aquarius, communicates with logic, reason, rational thought processes through interaction.

The Water element:
Includes Cancer, Scorpio, and Pisces, emits deep, passionate, intuitive, feeling responses to life's experiences.

The soul's behavior pattern should shift from the Moon energy toward the Sun energy with age and experience. Once you achieve a reasonable balance between the soul and spirit responses, expansion of your life purpose can occur. To focus on the growth path, the soul needs to be consciously aware of its life choices and deliberately choose to take the high road.

Understanding the Message of the Moon

Imagine a giant mirror reflecting past actions and experiences. According to mythology, the sign that the Moon was in at the time of your birth explains our soul's response in this lifetime. Understanding how the Moon's energy impacts your behavior and emotional reactions is key to understanding your hidden soul pattern and personal timing. You are the center of your own universe and the creator of your own destiny, so you need to understand your gifts and future goals. The eternal questions of the soul are: "Where have I come from?" and "Where am I going?" The most important question, of course, is "Why am I here?"

There appears to be a relationship between the macrocosm—the universe—and the microcosm—the human body. The Earth is approximately 75% water, which equates to the same approximate percentage of water that is found in the human body. This is not a coincidence. This analogy which ties all energy together relates to another correlation that the Moon's pull on Earth controls the daily tidal movement of Earth's bodies of water. So it could be concluded that the same force that controls universal cycles also influences the fluids within the human body.

Astrologers historically have identified all of the planetary patterns as sub-personalities acting in a person's birth chart to describe their actions and desires.

The Sun, the central energy in the solar system, drives your vitality, growth, and life purpose in a masculine form;

The Moon, the other "light", reflects your soul's emotions, moods, reactions, instincts, and soul history in a feminine form.

In the metaphysical world, masculine and positive relate to the out-flowing of universal energy, while feminine and negative relate to the inflow of that same energy. These terms represent the flow of electrical current, not a state of mind. The soul is evolving back to unite with the universal energy through growth. If the Moon represents that collection of past experiences, then a soul just arriving on Earth embodies the archetypal behavior of the Moon's sign.

The Moon Phases

"Astrology can be defined as a technique for the study of life-cycles. Its main purpose (is to establish) the existence of regular patterns in the sequence of events constituting man's inner and outer experience; then, to use the knowledge of these patterns in order to control or give meaning to these experiences...Indeed, the study of cycles—that is, of periodical activities in nature, human and otherwise—is the root of all significant knowledge, be it scientific or philosophical. And the study of cycles is a study of time."

- Dane Rudhyar, *The Lunation Cycle*

Astrology is based on the premise that the soul is here to grow in a structured pattern and that pattern is shown in the birth (natal) chart.

The Moon's dance around the Sun was used to track time as well as the seasons. Sailors used the position of the Moon to navigate vast seas when there was no land to mark their way, while farmers used it to plan their planting and harvesting cycles. Others observed the cycle of the Moon and Sun to anticipate human behavior.

There are 8 measurable cycles of the Moon phases as the Moon moves around the Sun every 28 days. In fact, the word Moon forms the basis of the word month. Rudhyar wrote much about the cycles of life, growth, and time. They can be applied to the growth of the personality during this life cycle that we are experiencing in our present.

You should now have a copy of your birth chart using any of the resources referenced in the "How to Use This Book" chapter. Use the Moon Phase chart below to identify your Moon phase and your place in the evolutionary cycle of your soul. Place the Sun at the 0 point of this diagram, then count forward however many degrees your Moon is from the Sun. Then us the Moon Phase circle to calculate where the Moon is in reference to the birth Sun.

Remembering that there are 30 degrees in a sign, count forward by sign to measure the angular distance between the lights.

New Moon   instantaneously pushing forward

Crescent Moon   pushing upward without thought

First Quarter Moon   struggle through difficulties to move onward

Gibbous Moon   the urge to learn and excel at life tasks

Full Moon   a time of blossoming and joining

Disseminating Moon   the action of spreading gifts and information

Last Quarter Moon   the need to shed and clear away whatever is not necessary for growth

Balsamic Moon   the closing period of review of soul patterns to distill values

We will begin this book with the Aries Moon in combination with each Sun sign and continue through the zodiac. We will describe the potential soul growth pattern through to each Sun sign aiming for the highest and best use of that energy.

Moon Phase Chart

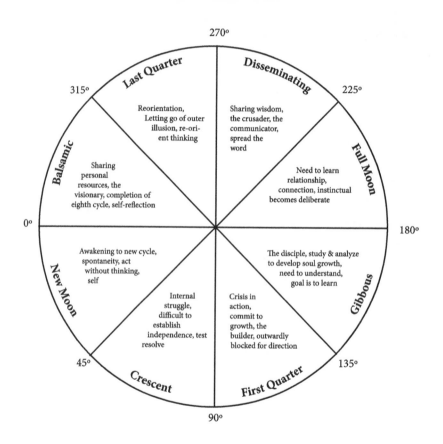

Moon in Aries

Moon in Aries (with all signs)

Each chapter begins with a description of the Moon's purpose for those readers who will want to go straight to a specific Moon/Sun combination.

Imagine a giant mirror reflecting past actions and experiences. According to mythology, the sign that the Moon was in at the time of your birth explains your soul response's in this lifetime. Understanding how the Moon's energy impacts your behavior and emotional reactions is key to understanding your hidden soul pattern and personal timing. You are the center of your own universe and the creator of your own destiny, so you need to understand your gifts and future goals. The eternal questions of the soul are: "Where have I come from?" and "Where am I going?" The most important eternal question, of course, is "Why am I here?"

Moon in Aries - Fire

The energy in Aries comes from the Fire element, known for its high vitality, quick action, and spirited passion. The Aries infant personality, with a strong tendency toward impulsive movement and self-reliance, has a little trouble being totally dependent upon its hovering parents and caring family members. This little one will probably take charge before the parents even realize what has happened to them.

There will be no question as to what the Aries Moon child likes to eat and when they like to sleep. Most of these energetic people do not require a lot of sleep. This child will want to feed himself or herself without any help and may walk earlier than most. When crossing the street, this little person will not want anyone to hold their hand or tell them when they can go. It is important to keep sharp knives and hot pots out of their reach because they move very quickly.

Their impatience will show up early as a quick temper, but the good news is it acts like a flash fire, burning out almost as rapidly as it starts. In the early years, it can show up as frustration when all does not go together smoothly. They may often throw toys against the wall, for example.

On the positive side, Aries loves a challenge, so the parents should always have new toys, puzzles, and other independent projects. They will enjoy having a wide variety of choices and lots of freedom. Their fast reactions will help keep them out of trouble.

As this Mars-ruled sign begins to grow up, a competitive spirit will begin to emerge. Aries loves to be first in every activity—they enjoy being first in line or first at bat. In school, the Aries Moon student does best in challenging academic settings. If they do not feel positively motivated, they may become impatient, agitated, or irritated. They work best alone because they feel that no one else moves as fast as they do.

Remember they do not like to be kept waiting. Allow Aries to lead and take risks, and everyone will be happy. For fun, this Mars energy will like fast-moving activities; they love being busy and on the move.

The hope is that the Aries Moon personality will always keep that fast-paced, independent spirit as they move toward their Sun sign energy. It is the blending of these energies that should bring the greatest growth and joy.

Sun in Aries (Fire) with Moon in Aries (Fire)

*"From a fiery, free-spirited child
to a brave, focused warrior."*

When both luminaries (Sun and Moon) fall in the same sign, the Moon phase may be either New or Balsamic in phase, and both of these call for much self reflection and self-motivation with the keyword being "Self". With the Sun and Moon in Aries together, the life journey is going toward the same energy that they came from because they are coming from Aries, and still focusing on Aries in this lifetime. Another way to understand this is to know that the goal is the evolution of the soul toward the light. When both lights are in the same sign—Aries— and the same element—Fire—the message is to integrate the more basic self-centered energy with the higher, more subtle message of the brave Mars warrior.

This young spunky Ram will want their independence straight from the crib so, a playpen is not a good choice. They will want to do everything on their own with no help. When this one gets tired or frustrated, watch for flying toys and tempers. They can easily entertain themselves and are happy playing alone.

This strong, initiating adult needs to be the one to start events, but not the one who maintains and manages them. These people are best when they act as initiators and then move on to another project. The double Aries moves fast and burns out quickly. This is definitely "Do It Now" energy; their nature wants to be direct and get straight to the point. Aries becomes more self-reliant as they age. Anger, frustration, and arrogance begin to fall away. The self-reliant, self-focused, independent leader steps forward to take charge and keep activities moving. To make a Ram happy, let them lead, let them do it their way, and let them figure it out for themselves.

If the Aries/Aries combination of energy gets out of balance or is not flowing smoothly, a self-centered attitude can lead this impatient soul into selfish actions that override the best interests of loved ones. Their need to push forward can alienate friends and family. Instant or impulsive financial decisions may put them and their families at risk. Also, the Aries warrior may attract difficult life lessons, including accidents and emotional outbursts where they fly off the handle.

The soul lesson of the Moon and Sun in Aries is to channel, control, and maintain the instinctive Fire energy. They need to stand as the brave, strong example of the committed warrior with a dynamic spiritual call to lead where destiny has placed them.

Keep moving, Aries Moon and Sun, in a smooth steady flow of divine energy, standing strong in your beliefs, with the courage to go first.

Sun in Taurus (Earth) with Moon in Aries (Fire)

*"From a fiery, free-spirited child
to a practical, purposeful, leader."*

When the Moon is in Aries and the Sun is in Taurus, the soul is moving from the active Fire element into the grounded Earth element. The soul chooses to enter this lifetime with the Moon placed behind the Sun by sign. The Aries infant personality functions in the integration cycle of spiritual development. The sign of Taurus is a fixed Earth essence with the icon of the bull. Its highest expression moves at a consistent, tranquil, determined pace to create security and stability in life. While Aries—the masculine, positive Fire energy—strikes out with speed, Taurus—the feminine, negative Earth energy—moves slowly and steadily to ground and manifest.

The restless, athletic Mars child will probably become much more of an observer than an athlete as she gets older. Early Aries impatience will be toned down by the caution of Taurus, who loves comfortable and beautiful surroundings. If the Aries Moon child is not worried about saving money and providing for a comfortable retirement, the well-developed Taurus Sun adult will be.

Venus is the ruling planet of Taurus, and she seeks more comfort, style, and ease the older she gets. If the soul is making progress in moving down the road of life, then Venus' love of pleasure will begin to override Mars' need for challenge as maturity sets in. Tenacity and perseverance is one of the greatest assets of the adult bull. A successful image is part of the positive Taurus identity, even though fast-moving Aries never stops pushing ahead. Hopefully, that speedy Fire energy becomes grounded and consistent without being smothered by the density of the slow moving Earth energy. If the bull can keep the fiery warrior grounded, she can complete many tasks experience great success through finance and management.

If the Aries/Taurus combination gets out of balance, a quick-tempered, strong-willed, stubborn bull may be unleashed. Then it becomes very difficult to get her attention because she has already made up her mind. In this way, immature Aries impatience may block Taurus from manifesting her long-term goals. If the Aries drive is stalled, give it something new to do to get the fixed Earth energy moving again.

The soul lesson of the Moon in Aries and Sun in Taurus is to channel the fast-paced movement into a steady long-term life plan. Acquiring and accumulating possessions is part of the Earth journey this time, but the Aries must not become selfish or self-righteous about its accomplishments. Doing, acting, completing, and planning are all part of the anchoring energy of Fire and Earth.

Keep moving, Aries Moon and Taurus Sun, in a smooth steady flow of divine energy, directing your personal reactions and strong determination to acquire much needed security over time.

Sun in Gemini (Air) with Moon in Aries (Fire)

*"From a fiery, free-spirited child
to a fast-paced, mentally-quick achiever."*

When the Moon is in Aries and the Sun is in Gemini, the soul's purpose is to blend the Fire and Air elements. This connection flows easily, because both Fire and Air energies are positive and masculine. The Moon cycle is waning—a state of integration—in this balsamic phase. Fiery Aries Moon expresses independence and strong will, motivated to take immediate action with a natural awareness of their surroundings.

This particular Moon child not only moves fast, but also thinks and talks fast. This combination tends to talk quickly and to change topics frequently, which may cause some burnout from over-stimulation. Aries is usually in a hurry and when associated with Gemini, the mental sign, there is little patience for slow thinkers or slow talkers. This Aries Moon child loves to learn by doing, but may become bored very quickly. In school, this Gemini Air element operates in the mental arena and is active in relationships; its theme is interaction. They will challenge their parents and teachers because they know that they are quick learners.

Just as Mars rules the Aries Ram, Mercury rules the Gemini Twins nature. Mercury, the winged messenger, delivers ideas, thoughts, and lots of communication. With the combination of these two restless energies, changing thoughts may come across too assertively or judgmentally. This logical mind will quickly analyze the social setting, learning when to speak and when to remain silent. This is one of Gemini's hardest lessons when coupled with any sign, but when it is paired with a Fire sign it may speak out of turn. One way to calm the Aries/Gemini combination is to introduce new ideas or a new topic into the conversation. Gemini loves to learn, whether it is from a teacher or from reading. Books are always a good diversion for the older Air sign; however, when young, the Aries Moon probably does not have the patience to read for very long. This Gemini will find success using their quick mind and communications skills in any career that involves negotiation. These people make good students and good teachers if they can master the lesson of patience with those who are not as quick to understand and learn.

If the Aries/Gemini combination of energy gets out of balance, there may be nervous problems, or the tendency to live in one's head and not be grounded. Erratic behavior may manifest under stress. Anxiety may cause a lack of self-control that causes the young Gemini to act without thinking. They may also speak before considering the impact of their words. This combination needs to learn the axiom that "Thoughts are Things" and once spoken, they cannot be retrieved.

The soul lesson of the Moon in Aries and Sun in Gemini is to channel the quick mental energy into a positive intellectual and academic outcome. They need to keep experiencing and learning or else they can become restless and unhappy. It is important for them to develop a quick wit instead of a sharp tongue, and to use their knowledge to inspire others to learn and to do.

Keep moving, Aries Moon and Gemini Sun, in a smooth steady flow of divine energy, directing your high enthusiasm toward learning, communicating and teaching.

Sun in Cancer (Water) with Moon in Aries (Fire)

*"From a fiery, free-spirited child
to a nurturing, kind, decision-maker."*

When the Moon is in Aries and the Sun is in Cancer, the Moon cycle is waning, and in the last quarter. Since Aries is Fire, and Cancer is Water, there is a challenge for the soul to integrate action with the emotional nature. These energies block one another and resist any flow. Fire expresses as positive and masculine, while Water expresses as negative and feminine. When these two elements join together there can be a great partnership; but if they resist each other, it can cause stress and internal struggle.

The Aries Moon child is still impatient and fast-moving, but the Cancer part of the soul tends to hold back because of the fear of being hurt. The Aries Ram still wants independence, but the emotional Cancer Crab is afraid to take a risk. In the young child, this may be experienced as a dilemma. Sometimes the child is highly self-absorbed and runs out into the world alone, only to look around and realize that no family member is there. Then the Cancer returns to the protective family nest. While the soul is still youthful, mood swings and emotional reactions seem quite normal. The parents usually receive the full measure of Aries child's impatience.

As the Aries Moon matures, emotional sensitivity to the problems of others can be a great asset; however, emotional extremes are not as acceptable. The warrior Moon can act in a self-centered way, while the Cancer Crab worries that their behavior could negatively impact the whole family. These people have the innate ability to achieve success through public affairs because people like them. Fame follows this dynamic energy when it is applied intellectually as well as intuitively.

If the Aries/Cancer combination of energy gets out of balance in the adult, a quick temper combined with emotional storms might arise. Because this personality is willing to take action to make things happen, the individual needs to remain focused so that the strong will does not override good judgment. This Fire and Water combination can get worked up into quite a head of steam if there is nowhere for all the energy to go. Steam has great power to move projects forward, but it can build up and explode, causing long-lasting damage.

The soul lesson of the Moon in Aries and Sun Cancer is to integrate high energy with a sensitive, feeling nature. This can be a very compassionate combination that is sensitive to the actions needed, along with a willingness to do what is necessary. When a positive Mars drives this nurturing Moon, it can help accomplish anything.

Keep moving, Aries Moon and Cancer Sun, in a smooth steady flow of divine energy, directing your quick-response energy into leadership positions within the network of home and family.

Sun in Leo (Fire) with Moon in Aries (Fire)

*"From a fiery, free-spirited child
to a fast-paced, outgoing leader."*

When the Moon is in Aries and the Sun is in Leo, both are in the Fire element, which brings tremendous energy to your soul. Fire symbolizes vitality and spirit, so when there is strong access to this dynamic energy, determination and action are ever-present. The phase of the Moon is full to disseminating, which calls for integration in relationships.

Strong impulsiveness, courage, and love of adventure may lead this high-energy soul into some risky situations during their younger years. In fact, this young person may come across as too rash, direct, or arrogant until they learn to control the ego-centered drive for recognition. The young Aries warrior may jump into a fight a little too quickly, but the strategic Lion slows the process and chooses only the worthy battles. Even as an adult, this playful combination can lighten up a room or create a scene if they are being ignored.

There is no shortage of ambition here. This enthusiast is capable of handling executive positions through strong leadership skills. The Warrior and Lion icons combine to create a true defender of right and wrong. Since Fire is both masculine and positive, this combination needs some feminine and negative energy to balance itself. Taking action may be easy, and stopping long enough to receive the lesson will be more of a challenge. Mars always charges ahead, but even the warrior must take his lead from the great Sun, the center of our system. The Sun-fueled Leo lion remains in charge at all times, whether they show it or not. They make a natural sales person.

If the Aries/Leo combination of Fire energy gets out of balance, there can be unpredictable actions and responses. To keep interactions with the Lion positive, always show him respect and never embarrass him in public. If he feels ignored, his dramatic ego will flare, and he may lash out. Once the Lion is wounded, it may take a very long time for this warrior to allow anyone close again. His intensity and drive can become pushy when pressured from the outside. One way to calm the intense Fire energy is to show appreciation and to praise them. Emphasize the positive and stroke the Lion's ego until they calm and respond to your soft smile and Sunny attitude.

The soul lesson of the Moon in Aries and Sun in Leo is to control the strong, fiery, ever present energy flow. There is a need not only to initiate action, but also to learn to maintain a consistent pattern that leads to the completion of tasks and projects. Leo's job is to master the process of follow-through without procrastination.

Keep moving, Aries Moon and Leo Sun, in a smooth steady flow of divine energy, initiating, planning, and completing your projects with joy and creativity.

Sun in Virgo (Earth) with Moon in Aries (Fire)

*"From a fiery, free-spirited child
to a grounded, analytical, problem solver."*

When the Moon is in Aries and the Sun is in Virgo, the Fire and Earth elements will need to blend the fiery masculine, positive energy with the more grounded, feminine, negative force of Earth. The Moon phase is Full Moon to disseminating, and it remains in a waning cycle. It calls for integrating oneself into relationships with others. Spiritual growth needs to be analyzed, processed, and organized. The fast-moving Aries Ram integrates with the Virgo Virgin, who brings a purity of mind and simplicity to the execution of Divine Will. The two parts of this soul will need to make major adjustments during this lifetime. Virgo's ruler, Mercury, brings a clear mind with strong analytical skills that need to learn to get along with Mars and his charging, freedom-loving nature.

The restless Aries child may lead the more timid and shy Virgo part of the personality into situations where the critical thinker is not comfortable. This little independent person will be neat and tidy with all the small pieces of their toys. A game of tug-o-war occurs between the instinctive fiery rebel and the purposeful, practical Earth worker.

As conscientious and clever as this Virgo becomes as they get older, the impulsive imp still lives within and shows up at the most unexpected times. Since their loner nature keeps this person standing back in an observation mode, personal health and routine seems to take up more of their time than romance and dreaminess. This health-conscious, practical Earth energy makes a dependable employee or independent businessperson because they enjoy their work and making all of their own decisions. These people can also be comfortable with jobs in the health or service industry because of their need to help others.

If the Aries/Virgo combination of energy gets out of balance, these two energy patterns can struggle internally. The fiery Moon pushes to move forward and take action, while the flexible earthy side resists confining commitments. She is slow to connect with others in relationships and does not want to feel trapped without choices or flexibility. They may also become quite critical when put into a decision-making role. Therefore, even when an action seems like a good idea, they need to wait and think it through before committing. Virgo has a changeable nature, and is ultimately searching for practical solutions. Virgo's lack of confidence can cause her to worry, so she needs to be careful not to be pushed into action by people with more fixed, decisive energy.

The soul lesson of the Moon in Aries and Sun in Virgo is to corral the impatient, hasty soul into holding back, and processing all of the possibilities before any decisions are made. Once she harnesses the high-powered fire energy, this critical-thinking Earth sign can handle great quantities of detail work and still have time to take care of her family. Efficiency is part of the Virgo gift.

Keep moving, Aries Moon and Virgo Sun, in a smooth steady flow of divine energy directing your strong personal need for freedom into an organized, controlled work routine.

Sun in Libra (Air) with the Moon in Aries (Fire)

"From a fiery, free-spirited child
to a quick-thinking, socially skilled negotiator."

When the Moon is in Aries and the Sun is in Libra, the soul is born at the time of the Full Moon. This opposing pattern for the two lights creates a full view of the personal issues around relationships. The lit up face of the Moon accentuates all of the emotional energy the Aries can muster. As Aries contributes the Fire, Libra adds enough air to fuel it. This Fire and Air combination has great power for good or evil. Although the fiery energy makes the person appear daring, aggressive, and independent, the Libra spirit wants to live in harmony and peaceful surroundings.

Since both of these signs are great initiators, new relationships feel more exciting and challenging than old ones to this high-energy soul. The little Aries child within may think up new adventures and challenge old ways that make the Libra peacekeeper very uncomfortable. One of the greatest tests for this Full Moon phase soul is finding balance in personal relationships. Fiery emotions stirred to the maximum can bring on extreme mood swings and emotional upheaval. Aries wants their own way while Libra wants everyone to be happy. These social interactions always seem to be out of balance. There is a need for much freedom with this combination, both during childhood and in the adult years.

The Libra-Venus nature appears to be more pleasant and gracious in the adult than in the child, when the Aries Mars aggressiveness was more visible. Both energies are still present in the adult, but as the child matures, Venus always brings more charm and poise to any situation. There is a gift of mental refinement that can be used to become a successful negotiator and mediator as long as this combination includes change. With that said, the strong need for new adventure will always be part of the base personality in this combination. Their bravery needs to lead them into situations where they can be entrepreneurial as well as compromising.

If the Aries/Libra combination of initiating full Moon energy gets out of balance, the Aries Moon will fight for independence and freedom, while the Libra Sun will yield to the will of others to avoid conflict and disharmony. So just when it appears that there is resolution in a conflict with this dualistic person, they will switch or come up with a new argument. The Aries Moon never wants to give up their personal freedom unless there is no other choice, because deep down they will always believe that their way is the right one. Sometimes it comes down to choosing independence or relationship before the warrior will yield to the ultimate need of Libra to be in partnership.

The soul lesson of the Moon in Aries and Sun in Libra is to blend and bond the already compatible Fire and Air elements into a dynamic, forward-moving, risk-taking lifetime. Libra's lesson is to interact harmoniously with others without losing one's identity or without taking over by insisting the whole plan go their own Aries way. Overall balance—give and take—is the needed ingredient to help this soul create and maintain loving, trusting relationships with all of the people in their world.

Keep moving, Aries Moon and Libra Sun, in a smooth steady flow of divine energy toward controlling personal ambitions through integration with others in harmonious, balanced relationships.

Sun in Scorpio (Water) with Moon in Aries (Fire)

"From a fiery, free-spirited child to a warm, determined, focused, project manager."

When the Moon is in Aries and the Sun is in Scorpio, there is a strong fiery Mars nature that drives all actions in this lifetime. In this unconscious Moon phase, the soul pattern has not yet reached the point of fullness, so it is still unaware of its need to relate and blend. This relationship between the two lights again creates a struggle between inner and outer focus. The masculine Fire energy resists the more receptive Water senses.

The Aries Moon tends to rush out into life to challenge all new experiences, while the Scorpio Sun holds back and observes situations with caution and hesitation. You will find this young person quite often playing in the corner by themselves very happily. In the young years, they appear more reckless, while the Scorpio part of the self holds out for restraint and deliberation.

The ambitious drive is held in check by a strong realistic view of life. Because Mars holds rulership over both signs (Aries/Scorpio) in traditional astrology, this person feels all emotions intensely, and must guard against extreme anger and overly assertive tendencies. When stirred up, the Fire and Water elements again can build up powerful steam or explosive eruptions. The power in this combination can bring great drive and determination to any career choice. They will champion and fight for whatever cause or goal they commit to.

If the Aries/Scorpio combination of Martian energy gets out of balance, the risk is that the passion for whatever this soul desires may overshadow rational thought. Aggressive, tyrannical behavior can result from too much drive and ambition. Also, Mars energy must always guard against being volatile. In this combination, any sexual attraction will bring out intense passion and has the potential to express extreme jealousy or possessiveness. There is no worry here of disinterest or apathy about life's purpose: This combination feels passionate about its interests or it has no interest at all.

The soul lesson of the Moon in Aries and Sun in Scorpio combination is to direct the strong assertive Mars energy in a controlled and structured manner. Because of the intensity of the steamy Fire/Water combination, all of Scorpio's fixed tenacity will be needed. There is incredible power here, if it can be channeled correctly, and deep devotion in relationships when their profound loyalty is placed with discernment. The goal here is to slow down and pace the Aries warrior so that the more intense Mars energy can penetrate and control the outcome to a very high result. Once Aries impatience is calmed, the cautious, perceptive critical thinking of Scorpio will carry any project to victory.

Keep moving, Aries Moon and Scorpio Sun, in a smooth steady flow of divine energy toward control over impulsive emotional responses while developing a much deeper understanding of personal spiritual power.

Sun in Sagittarius (Fire) with Moon in Aries (Fire)

"From a fiery, free-spirited child
to an adventuresome, risk-taking traveler."

When the Moon is in Aries and the Sun is in Sagittarius, both signs are vibrating to the positive, masculine fire element. Because the Moon phase is in a waxing unconscious state, there is a strong outflow of action energy. This Fire-Fire combination creates great energy for the subconscious to draw from.

Particularly in the early years, the urge is to rush out impulsively and then become discontented very quickly and change directions. Aries Fire energy moves instantly and it also tends to keep going. Sagittarius Fire energy acts differently in that it keeps switching gears as well as projects. There is always a lot of enthusiasm and restlessness even for the young child. Much like Gemini, these youngsters talk early and openly. If you want the truth, ask a Sagittarian. There is great curiosity all through life, but particularly in the early years.

Jupiter is the planet that rules Sagittarius, and he is known for his grand and generous spirit. When we combine Mars, ruler of Aries, with Jupiter, we see fast movement with a broad vision and a strong drive to excel beyond the competition. Risk and adventure, which may include travel. This one needs action and flexibility to succeed. Church, religion, and the bigger questions of life are always of interest to this high-spirited seeker. Because of their intense sense of honor and integrity, they can be very successful in government, the clergy, legal fields, or in fields of reform.

If the Aries/Sagittarius combination of Fire energy gets out of balance, the world perceives this person as flighty, unstable, and changeable. Staying on track or remaining committed could become a problem if there is no fixity in the rest of the chart. Sagittarius always has the challenge of being too honest and too open, but when combined with Mars their opinions could be out of their mouths before they have even had time to think about it. Tolerating slow, repetitive projects could be one of this soul's most difficult tasks. The development of patience is definitely listed as one of their assignments.

The soul lesson of the Moon in Aries and Sun in Sagittarius is to stay on track and complete all of the projects that they start. When all of this high-spirited Fire energy is directed toward a task, there is nothing this one can't accomplish. As long as this soul feels a sense of freedom in the everyday world, their high tolerance level for change allows them to handle many challenging tasks at once. Their motto: Take action, get it done, and move on.

Keep moving, Aries Moon and Sagittarius Sun, in a smooth steady flow of divine energy toward independent leadership while striving to be a living example of sound spiritual principles based on Divine Order.

Sun in Capricorn (Earth) with Moon in Aries (Fire)

*"From a fiery, free-spirited child
to a responsible, initiating, entrepreneur."*

When the Moon is in Aries and the Sun is in Capricorn, the blending of Fire and Earth energies take a slightly different twist. The major theme of both of these signs is to initiate action. The goal is to continue grounding the active, moving warrior energy of Mars while developing leadership and take charge attitudes. Since the Moon is still in the waxing, unconscious phase, this soul is not really aware of their constant urge to push forward and take control, but they are aware of their incredible mental power.

The early restless Aries drive pushes them to begin over-achieving in school, even at an early age. Their buried determination to rule quickens and strengthens with age. Executive ability becomes apparent before most other young people have figured out what they want to do. Leading, accepting responsibility, and acting as an authority figure come naturally to the Aries Capricorn person. This one may even parent their parents and their siblings.

The symbol of the Goat reflects mature Capricorn's tenacity and determination to climb the mountain at all costs. There is a strong need to be first in both their personal and professional life. This combination is meant to be an entrepreneur or the head of the company. Capricorn wants to sit at top of mountain.

If the Aries/Capricorn combination of forward-moving action energy gets out of balance, the person may be too bossy or blunt. With the Moon in Aries, the person can be totally convinced that they are right about everything. Then when the Capricorn perfectionist piece is strengthened, the authoritarian ruler could overpower all other combinations. Always assuming the head leadership position can become overbearing if the Aries Capricorn is not careful. Between the

Aries Ram power and the Capricorn Goat control, there can be quite a bit of head butting and stomping of hoofs when this one does not get their own way.

Both of these signs' greatest talents are to be able to stay calm, cool, and collected while they initiate, take charge, organize, and then delegate the details to someone else while they move on to the next new project. They function best in the boss's seat.

The soul lesson of the Moon in Aries and Sun in Capricorn is to apply the quick, mental energy wisely to stay organized and follow the initial plan, which will allow Capricorn's strong management skills to shine.

Keep moving, Aries Moon and Capricorn Sun, in a smooth steady flow of divine energy toward tempering the entrepreneurial spirit to fit into an organized, controlled leadership position at the top of any organization.

Sun in Aquarius (Air) with Moon in Aries (Fire)

"From a fiery, free-spirited child
to a strong, social group leader."

When the Moon is in Aries and the Sun is in Aquarius, the two elements of Fire and Air again join together but this time there is an emphasis on intellectual stability. With the Moon phase waxing and struggling to express itself, these two mentally active energies find it hard to relate to others in a conscious fashion. Fire and Air elements are both masculine and positive which shows up as rather abruptly direct.

As a little person, they don't meet many strangers and make friends easily. There won't be much warm and fuzzy affection in this combination. However, they will always be willing to go on a new adventure either alone or with a friend. This quick witty energy keeps things fun, light and exciting.

The Mars Fire energy comes on strong in this combination and tends to take charge quickly, asking few questions. Because their love of learning appears to be a rather detached style, they consider themselves to be intellectually superior on many subjects. The erratic energy of Aquarius needs social interaction, so friends rank high on their priority list. However, cuddling is not very important to them because too much emotional involvement slows them down. This combination cannot endure being controlled or limited in any way, and they will go to any lengths to be in charge of their own lives. This one will be successful in owning their own business or in being the leader of the group. No one will not control their thoughts or actions.

If the Aries/Aquarius combination of energy gets out of balance, this extremely positive soul will appear selfish and cool. Their detached, aloof attitude can become very chilly when someone else comes between this person and their planned activity. They can exhibit a strong superiority complex when their authority is challenged. This is another combination that believes they are usually right. Friends are near and dear to these people, unless they get in the way of the bigger plan and then all social politeness may go right out the window. Be cautious in handling this highly individualistic fireball, who definitely has their own way of doing things.

Part of their own personal growth is tapping into the kind and open manner of the positive social Air element whether it is in a group setting or in a personal relationship. Their broad sympathies and humane compassion, when awakened, drive them to fight for the highest and best outcome possible. However, Aquarius finds personal encounters to be more difficult.

The soul lesson of the Moon in Aries and Sun in Aquarius is to blend their fast thinking mind with their humanitarian attitudes for the higher good of the group. They may take up the cause of the family group, the tribal group, the community group, or a corporate business group, but this soul loves to fight for the higher cause. There is no stronger advocate for a needy cause than the Fire Air combo.

Keep moving, Aries Moon and Aquarius Sun, in a smooth steady flow of divine energy toward directing that highly freedom-oriented spirit into a position to maintain individuality while leading groups for the higher good of all.

Sun in Pisces (Water) with Moon in Aries (Fire)

"From a fiery, free-spirited child
to a compassionate, independent server to mankind."

When the Moon is in Aries and the Sun is in Pisces, the natural flow from the Fire element to the Water element should occur easily. The New Moon phase is still in effect which allows the energy to rush out in a rather impetuous fast flow.

Since the direction is from Fire to Water, the child exudes a rather restless, unsettled attitude. Many fears overshadow this young anxious Mars warrior, which makes it much easier to lead them than to force them in any direction. The impulsive Aries Moon finds itself in all kinds of victim/martyr roles because of the gullibility of the watery idealistic nature. If there is no spiritual guidance in the early life, this child can wander through some dark and frightening experiences before they find their Higher Self. When the early family does provide a backdrop of spiritual awareness, then this soul develops their deep intuitive inclinations at an early age. Dreams can create a great spiritual teaching ground for the open-minded Aries under the right family conditions.

As they mature, this Aries fiery energy will follow them throughout life. Some confusion reigns here until the spiritual side takes charge and focuses on the Higher Good for all. A strong compassion for those less fortunate should always bring this Pisces back to empathy and service where they feel most satisfied. They are at their best when they are leading the charge in a service mission. Creativity and artistic talent will emerge. This combination will find success in using creative expression in the arts, design or even architecture. As a sensitive adult, intuition and vision may drive their artistic creations. Dreams may serve them well for inspiration.

If the Pisces/Aries combination of energy gets out of balance, imagination and fantasy may go to a lower level and manifest as avoidance and escape. Fire signs tend to deal with stress by taking action, so when the going gets tough, this Fire Water energy might just take off. Running too fast and burning out is a common pattern, since Pisces does not have the long-term staying power of some of the other signs. Even when the Pisces side is hurt and hiding, the Aries remains self-sufficient in its own world and can take care of itself. The victim role does not last long here because Mars' willful instinct is to fight instead of cry when their feelings are hurt. If they quit fighting and curl up in a ball, it will take some time before they work through their victim role.

The soul lesson of the Moon in Aries and Sun in Pisces is to learn to pause long enough before taking action to allow the intuition to speak. The Mars warrior jumps to be busy and move briskly while Pisces has trouble making up their mind which way they want to move.

Keep moving, Aries Moon and Pisces Sun, in a smooth steady flow of divine energy toward initiating action that will support your higher need to serve and sacrifice for the spiritual good of the group.

Moon in Taurus

Moon in Taurus (with all signs)

Each chapter begins with a description of the Moon's purpose for those readers who will want to go straight to a specific Moon/Sun combination.

Imagine a giant mirror reflecting past actions and experiences. According to mythology, the sign that the Moon was in at the time of your birth explains your soul response's in this lifetime. Understanding how the Moon's energy impacts your behavior and emotional reactions is key to understanding your hidden soul pattern and personal timing. You are the center of your own universe and the creator of your own destiny, so you need to understand your gifts and future goals. The eternal questions of the soul are: "Where have I come from?" and "Where am I going?" The most important eternal question, of course, is "Why am I here?"

Moon in Taurus (Earth)

The energy of Taurus comes from the Earth element. In the sign of the Bull, the Moon is considered to work at its highest, most positive level. Here the responsive Moon acts in a grounded, calm, gentle, and consistent manner. Security and material comfort represent a primary need for this soul.

Being ruled by the sign of Venus, as a child the Taurus Moon's cuddly good nature ensures that she will avoid conflict. She will quietly pursue her dreams with an unyielding determination. This child thrives in a calm, stable environment and responds very well to reasonable, common sense explanations.

A cautious nature will save them in risky situations. Parents should be prepared to warn their Earthy slow-mover of any major changes long before it occurs.

Her intense stubbornness may not be visible on the surface until the little Taurus Bull digs in her heels. Feeding the Taurus Moon child, for example, is usually a joy because she loves what she loves. However, if the child refuses to eat a particular food, the parent may decide it's not worth the fight. This same philosophy holds true in other areas of life: You must pick your battles carefully with Taurus, because the struggle may be drawn out.

Colors and sounds are an important part of the Taurus development, so she should have a large selection of crayons and paints to work with. These tools will encourage her artistic talents. Paint her room with soft, warm colors to make her feel secure and safe.

The music around them needs to be calm but fun; in fact, they may want their own collection of children's music, so they can play it themselves. This child probably has a natural musical talent and should begin music or voice lessons early.

As this Venus-ruled sign begins to grow up, her warm, charming disposition will help her maintain the consistency and calm that she craves in her life. This child will do best in a fixed classroom setting with one teacher and a set daily routine. Most Taurus Moon students do well in school because they are willing to follow the rules, even if they may turn in their homework papers late. She responds well to praise and lots of positive touch, like hugs and love pats; she is also quick to show affection in return. After school, let this little Venus person cuddle up in her favorite chair with her favorite snack and her favorite TV show just long enough for them to rest and relax.

The goal is for the Taurus Moon to maintain their easy disposition as they get older, and she will be called to grow through the differing energies expressed in the birth chart. As she begins to blend the Moon with the Sun sign energy, her charming Venus style will continue to provide stability and be a calming, smoothing influence. Hopefully, this fixed earth person can avoid stubbornness and draw spiritual growth through the strong vibrant leading energy of their Sun sign.

Sun in Aries (Fire) with Moon in Taurus (Earth)

"From a slow, cautious, pondering child to a strong, independent warrior."

When the Moon is in Taurus and the Sun is in Aries, both lights are considered to be exalted or in a high state of harmony. The Moon remains in the New Moon phase rushing out before the Sun to meet life in a rather impetuous manner. However, the Moon in a fixed sign will always provide stability even when paired with fiery Aries Sun energy. The soul movement should flow from Earth to Fire in this lifetime. This requires taking the grounded, practical feminine Moon instinct and infusing it with the masculine will and vitality to take charge.

In the early years, this Taurus is cautious and slow to move. As they mature, that early caution seems to be buried as they become more and more independent and direct. Their Venus/Moon training makes them appear gracious and willing to please, but the reality is that Aries always manages to get what they want. It is important for this soul to maintain a level of charm and tact because Aries can become very direct and sharp in their delivery when pushed.

As the Aries energy gets stronger with age, their independence will far overshadow any of the cautiousness from their youth. This combination should form the pattern to create a very determined leader. The Aries Sun energy leads toward an executive career positions where Mars', the Aries ruler, acts as an asset with its quick thinking and reactions. The Earth/Fire combination usually knows how to accumulate the comforts of life and toys of the adult variety because Taurus knows how to handle money.

If the Taurus/Aries combination of energy gets out of balance, stubbornness can become the number one problem. One of the great lessons here is to learn to rule without becoming dominating or controlling. The plodding Taurus-Bull syndrome should fall away as the Sun brings an energy that is called to action and to move forward. Hopefully, the action will not be too fiery and aggressive as only Aries can do. This one needs to avoid a dogmatic position of authority while they are busily taking charge.

The soul lesson of the Moon in Taurus and Sun in Aries is to keep moving in a consistent path while allowing the fast-moving Fire energy to rush forward with enthusiasm and spontaneity. Embrace the new without throwing out the old. The Bull can be appeased by taking care of business first. The older you get the more of a risk-taker you should become. Go, be, do, and throw some of that Taurus caution to the wind. This is a lifetime to learn to take action and risk at all costs. The lesson of Mars is to learn to take care of the self first and foremost. Survival is the name of the game for the Aries Sun.

Keep moving, Taurus Moon and Aries Sun, in a smooth steady flow of divine energy toward being self-reliant while maintaining a steady pace of forward movement.

Sun in Taurus (Earth) with Moon in Taurus (Earth)

*"From a slow, cautious pondering child
to a steady, methodical decisive adult."*

When both luminaries (Sun and Moon) fall in the same sign, the Moon phase may be either New or Balsamic in phase, and both of these call for much self reflection and self-motivation with the keyword being "Self". With the Sun and Moon in Taurus together, the task must be to harness this intense determination for the purposes of greater manifestation. The lesson is the refinement of the essence of that energy, in this case, fixed Earth energy. The lunar phases calls for the soul to focus on self-growth whether it is internal or external.

The test here is to stay on task without becoming obstinate and set in one pattern. Especially when they are young, affection, touching, stroking, and cuddling continue to be very important to this Venus-ruled soul and continue throughout their life. Routine and consistency will be the recipe for early education success. As this Taurus begins to mature, pleasant surroundings make all the difference to Venus people. The ability to combine colors and create harmonious surroundings comes naturally here.

Being quite fixed in nature, this Bull always needs a long-range plan to manifest a strong sense of stability. Once Taurus is in motion they have incredible staying power and endurance for the long haul. This person needs to be working on a job that rewards patience and tenacity. No one should expect this one to do well in situations that are constantly fluctuating and requiring quick change. The Bull needs time to react and shift directions slowly. Certainly this soul is here to manifest things in the earthly realm and to learn to handle money and to accumulate possessions.

If the Taurus/Taurus combination of energy gets out of balance, there can be incredible stubbornness and self-centeredness. When determination becomes fixed thinking, no amount of reason can change their minds. Self-indulgence and a love of sweets can also become a compulsive downfall for Taurus which can become a dangerous situation when sugars and starches affect their physical bodies. There may be weaknesses in the area of the throat and neck. It is said that symptoms of a stiff neck come from an unwillingness to turn the head to see another perspective; in other words a stiff neck could come from fixed thinking. They should guard against letting their bullheadedness limit their ability to embrace new experiences.

The soul lesson of the Moon and Sun in Taurus is to maintain a steady course without becoming entrenched into a deep rut that is boring and rigid. Tenacity and accomplishment are considered to be good things but if everything needs to be their way they might find themselves alone with no one to hug. It is only fun to have money and beautiful houses if there is someone to share them with. They need to be responsible but also be giving. The lesson of the fixed earth sign is to remain constant.

Keep moving, Taurus Moon and Sun, in a smooth steady flow of divine energy toward being a long-distance runner who can sustain their pace for the long haul.

Sun in Gemini (Air) with Moon in Taurus (Earth)

*"From a slow, cautious pondering child
to a quick-witted, busy student."*

With the Moon in Taurus and the Sun in Gemini, the higher purpose is to blend the Earth and Air elements. The shift from being grounded to social, requires some effort on the part of the instinctual Earth being. The Moon phase has moved back to the phase called Balsamic and requires the soul to finish up old connections and lessons.

When the emotions are based in feminine Earth energy, this young soul starts out with a deliberate determination and strong emotional desires. Coming from a gentle, persistent, family dynamic this young bull will thrive. The Sun's masculine vitality flowing through the Air element strengthens this combination by introducing more social skills and initiative. These new energies can manifest as an easy ability to make good friends as well as developing many acquaintances.

This maturing adult needs to become more flexible and mentally stimulated. Friendships and social outings will be important to this one This grounded energy is also good at planning, organizing, and managing. This combination would thrive in a career of city planning, event organizer or middle management at a stable company. The Venus/Moon combination may be willing to give up harmony and status quo in return for Mercury's high level of intellectual stimulation. The Gemini Sun becomes bored and restless much more quickly than the Taurus side of this person. When these two energies are working harmoniously together, there is great loyalty in their relationships along with a wonderful talent for being flexible and understanding with those they love. This should be a great combination for business success because the Earth energy brings sound financial judgment while the Air element adds good negotiating skills and lots of common sense. Social leadership is a natural ability here. Add strong people skills to the ability to make money and this dynamic personality becomes successful. This grounded energy is also good at planning, organizing, and managing. This combination would thrive in a career of city planning, event organizer or middle management at a stable company.

If the Taurus/Gemini combination of energy gets out of balance, it may be hard to settle down to accomplish the goals that the Taurus has planned. Gemini is known to scatter their energies by starting too many projects. When Taurus the Bull becomes overwhelmed, he may just dig in his heels and do nothing. One way to lighten the heavy Earthy load is to sit down and prioritize the "To Do" list. The mutable energy of Gemini tries to do too much and eventually needs to use their great mental planning talents to get back on track. Once the slow-moving Bull sits down, it is hard to get things going again.

The soul lesson of the Moon in Taurus and Sun in Gemini is to keep on task long enough to complete all the projects they begin and still be open to new ideas and new ways of doing things. Because of their great ability to make friends, people are always willing to help them and support them.

Keep moving, Taurus Moon and Gemini Sun, in a smooth steady flow of divine energy toward creating a solid, comfortable, prosperous earth life this time around.

Sun in Cancer (Water) with Moon in Taurus (Earth)

*"From a slow, cautious pondering child
to a sensitive, nurturing caretaker."*

When the Moon is in Taurus and the Sun is in Cancer, the transition in this lifetime is from the Earth element to the Water element. Both of these signs are feminine and receptive, so it is a less challenging combination. The waning Moon's purpose is to integrate in relationships consciously and deliberately in this Last Quarter phase of emotional shedding. Stable earthy Taurus likes to take their time and make cautious decisions as does Watery Cancer.

High emotional sensitivity presents itself at birth and will reign throughout the lifetime. Venus-ruled Taurus, when combined with the emotional ebb and flow of the Moon who rules Cancer, always gives a gracious manner, but they struggle with speaking up about their true feelings, especially when they are young. This soul can be overly receptive to the wishes of others which causes them to lose their own identity.

Their psychic intuition can be a blessing or a curse depending upon whether this person can be strong enough to stand their own ground and guard their own space. When the Bullish Moon finally decides to make a move, it acts swiftly and definitely. Since both Taurus and Cancer love home and family, life changes usually do not include them going to far away. Because of the stable nature of the Taurus Moon, this soul is not afraid to go after or work for what they want. The challenge here is timing. Since the Bull may not move too quickly and the emotional Cancer Crab does not push, it usually takes an outside force to move this even-tempered, passive personality forward. When they need to be strong, their Earthy practicality kicks in and they can take charge and make those hard practical decisions. If they can stay on stable ground, life will be comfortable and safe most of the time, for this combination will not go out there and force the world to make changes for them. This combination would do well working for the government, hospital or any stable organization. Stability and creativity is the name of the game to success for the sensitive Taurus Moon.

If the Taurus/Cancer combination of energy gets out of balance, there will be a lot of sensitive feelings flowing. The stubborn Bull can become very unreasonable when they feel that they have been wrongly treated. It usually takes more than an apology to heal their wounds. The Cancer energy retreats into their shell and locks the shutters behind them. There will be no answer on the telephone and no answering the door, and it will take lots of pleading and begging to get forgiveness here. The only other area where this soul may suffer shows up in the department of self-discipline. Both of these energies enjoy comfort and relaxation. Finally, when the action-oriented Cancer Crab begins to move, results will show up quickly. It just may take a little coaxing to get them up and on their feet.

The soul lesson of the Moon in Taurus and Sun in Cancer is to keep emotions in check while the enthusiasm flows. It is important for them to maintain their realistic attitude while they keep their feelings in check. Moodiness and an ever changing mind are both common behaviors for the Cancer. But when a compassionate friend is needed the Taurus Cancer can be pulled into service and they will listen and empathize all evening long.

Keep moving, Taurus Moon and Cancer Sun, in a steady flow of divine energy toward going with the flow and being "steady as she goes", just like the great ships on the rolling seas.

Sun in Leo (Fire) with Moon in Taurus (Earth)

*"From a slow, cautious pondering child
to powerful, confident leader."*

When the Moon is in Taurus and the Sun is in Leo, there exists a challenge between the elements which can create a blockage. Taurus belongs to the feminine, receptive Earth element while Leo belongs to the masculine, positive Fire element. Earth and Fire in this position tend to square off and become too fixed for their own good. The Moon is in its waning phase where the soul tries to peel off old behaviors and work on integration through relationship.

This Venus-ruled child starts out as a pleaser who has a very warm disposition. Then as they grow into Sun-ruled Leo lions, their pride and leadership qualities become much more obvious. Both Venus and the Sun energies love to look good, so a stylish appearance and a quality wardrobe will always be important to this person. This young person has tremendous stamina and physical vitality because both the Bull and the Lion are known for their strength and muscle power.

As they begin to develop their courage and diplomacy in school, it may at first come across as hard-headedness and appear as an unyielding position. During these transition years, the Lion can come out with strong opinions and a strong will, but when the same criticism comes back at them, their sensitive Venus-ruled Moon becomes defensive and wounded. Sustained foresight and courage certainly give them executive career goals and ability when their dramatic power is used wisely. This one will shine in corporate America where a stable company and stage to shine on will both be important. Financial success will be the driving factor for long term career success.

If the Taurus/Leo combination of energy gets out of balance, stubbornness and obstinacy reign supreme. Both the Bull and the Lion are known for their fixed opinions. This combination may have originally created the "great standoff" idea. There can be an over abundance of pride and vanity if these fixed energies feel like they are being pushed around. Never embarrass a young Leo in public because they will be forced to create a scene that makes them look like they are right. The Taurus/Leo combination does not like to admit that they might be in the wrong. It takes a long time to get past their pouting spells. If Venus gets out of balance, there can be a little too much relaxation and pleasure-seeking in the instinct. When the Sun's playful childish piece is also considered, this soul could be too attracted to the fun and easy life.

The soul lesson of the Moon in Taurus and Sun in Leo is to maintain stability without constantly needing to have a concrete plan. Staying on course is honorable, but fighting an unyielding battle, just to be right, becomes overkill. For these fixed signs, one of the greatest lessons points to learning when to compromise and when to make a stand.

Keep moving, Taurus Moon and Leo Sun, in a smooth steady flow of divine energy by using your gifts of great determination for major accomplishments when all their Earth and Fire energies are flowing in a positive direction.

Sun in Virgo (Earth) with Moon in Taurus (Earth)

"From a slow, cautious pondering child to an efficient, precise processor."

When the Moon is in Taurus and the Sun is in Virgo, the Earth element creates a realistic, grounded foundation for the soul for using both the signs energies. The waning phase of the Moon purpose, for the two signs, calls for the soul to consciously integrate communication in relationships. The practical Earth elements are both feminine and receptive therefore, the theme for the entire lifetime includes elements of polite and reserved behavior.

There is no real challenging pattern between the Moon and the Sun; therefore, it is not an ambitious lifetime. Ease and comfort seem to set the pace, minimizing the need for competition. In the early years, the Taurus love of comfort may allow for some over-indulgence but when the conscientious nature of Virgo kicks in, this soul will become more health-conscious and diligent with their exercise. Family support and reinforcement are common with this combination.

Mercury, the planet that rules Virgo, will contribute a strong scientific, practical side to the thinking process as this soul matures. These sharp mental attributes bring solid business success to this solid Earth pattern. These skills support this conservative worker both as an employee and as a boss. Since there is strong harmony flowing between the Moon and the Sun in this lifetime, good luck and prosperity seem to follow this soul in their development. Strong Venus and Mercury abilities combine to give the great gift of smooth communication and strong writing skills. This soul can publish, speak, and lead in the business community without much limitation.

If the Taurus/Virgo combination of Earth energy gets out of balance, there could be very little forward movement. This practical energy can get pretty basic and dry if it is not careful. Too much worry and too much caution could keep this soul from taking the necessary risks that are naturally required for spiritual growth in a lifetime. There could be a real tendency to take life for granted and not appreciate the great gifts and surprises that life can deliver to us if we are willing to go out there and be open. Work and security are certainly important, but there needs to be passion and laughter also. The biggest danger for this lifetime is not pushing the envelope to experience new things.

The soul lesson of the Moon in Taurus and Sun in Virgo is to use the comfortable flow of spiritual energy to expand their life experiences without being forced and challenged. Taurus brings with it the ability to make money, so there should be enough prosperity and success to allow for the easy life that the soul planned for this time around.

Keep moving, Taurus Moon and Virgo Sun, in a smooth steady flow of divine energy toward success you enjoy that includes the detailed processes where you excel.

Sun in Libra (Air) with Moon in Taurus (Earth)

*"From a slow, cautious pondering child
to a social, outgoing gatherer of people."*

When the Moon is in Taurus and the Sun is in Libra, the Moon cycle is waning as it comes out of its emotional Full Moon phase. The flow of elemental energy goes from Earth to Air, from practical grounded energy to thinking and initiating energy.

From childhood to adulthood, the smooth, sweet behavior of the Venus goddess blesses the temperament of this soul. Relationships, love, comfort, harmony and balance remain major themes for this whole lifetime. Both of these signs are Venus-ruled which leads to a strong need for comfort, serenity and beautiful surroundings all through life. This young Taurus will think long and hard about making changes but will try to make everyone happy as they do it.

The soul struggles with situations that are not harmonious, such as loud music and loud voices, and so the Venus keeps searching for that perfect partner relationship which is hard to find. Because this energy is attractive and charming, there are many opportunities for partnership; however, they may come and go. Because Taurus brings perseverance and persistence to the personality, a strong relationship could be the perfect one in this lifetime. Taurus and Venus also brings the ability to make money and the ability to manage it. Libra brings the gift of knowing how to enjoy it and will share the rewards of financial benefit. In fact, too much comfort could get this Venus energy into trouble if they get hooked on the "good life". When these two are combined harmoniously as only Lady Venus can do, the soul is capable of great success and comfort in their later years.

If the Taurus/Libra combination of energy gets out of balance, rich foods and rich living could cause problems. Too much of any good thing ceases to be good. Even too much romance can become addictive, and then obsessive relationships can spoil the balance of one's focus. Venus-ruled people need to be cautious with starches and sweets because it appears that the body does not process them well but tends to store them. So this soul must guard against storing away both calories and money in preparation for "a rainy day". Because this soul is so easily hooked on any situation that brings peace and harmony, they must guard diligently against telling people what they want to hear. This can be the sign of the appeaser.

The soul lesson of the Moon in Taurus and Sun in Libra is to use the strong, dynamic power of the Venus energy wisely. This soul can smooth rough waters, negotiate tough deals, charm desirable partners, and be the delight of any social gathering. While they are spreading their charm, they must maintain their integrity and their need for solid, loyal relationships. It will not be hard to attract new friends and partners, but it is necessary to maintain the discernment that the fixed Taurus energy understands. The Earth element brings stability and consistency; the Air element brings strong social and mental attributes.

Keep moving, Taurus Moon and Libra Sun, in a smooth steady flow of divine energy toward ease and comfort in your happy social circle.

Sun in Scorpio (Water) with Moon in Taurus (Earth)

"From a slow, cautious pondering child
to an intense, perceptive observer."

When the Moon is in Taurus and the Sun is in Scorpio, the Moon phase is Full Moon which brings an emotional need to seek balance through relationship challenges. The flow of elemental energy goes from Earth to Water, from practical, grounded energy to emotional, inspirational energy. Fixity and determination remain throughout the lifetime because both of these signs remain in stable fixed signs. While staying focused and determined to succeed, the instinct of this soul is to maintain a high quality of life by staying the course.

As a child, this soul is loving and kind and as an adult they are still loving but in a much more intense and grand manner. The Taurus soul energy leads with the planet Venus which is a smooth and easy flow and then the shift is to a Mars growth position which conveys a much more intense, aggressive approach.

Venus and Mars together create a highly passionate, charismatic magnetism which draws in people easily. The attraction principle builds as this soul matures. Not only does the physical magnetism grow, but also the mystical magnetism. These souls have a natural ability to tap into deeper levels of consciousness and are drawn to deeper studies. People who are interested in the deeper meaning of life seem to be drawn to these metaphysical souls. A career track must be focused and with long term goals. This one thrives on a 10 year plan. Research and finance are natural interests for them.

If the Taurus/Scorpio combination of energy gets out of balance, there can be incredible obstinacy and deviousness. There is no greater scorn than that of an angry scorpion that will attempt to sting and kill its betrayer with malice and forethought. When this intensely focused soul feels justified in defending itself, the object of that anger is in great danger. Having pointed out the severity of the danger, it would be incredibly rare for any energy coming out of the Taurus sign to be totally deadly. However, if the Taurus Bull is pushed too far, then the lower side of Scorpio will respond. There is a true danger of severing long-term relationships when there are hurt feelings because when this soul draws a line or shuts a door they seldom go back. When they are done, they are done.

The soul lesson of the Moon in Taurus and Sun in Scorpio is to maintain and control their great power as they accomplish whatever highest goal they have set. The flying eagle symbolizes the highest expression of the Water energy. Its courage and calmness mark it as one of the most spiritual symbols in the metaphysical world. The eagle flies high, sees clearly, and moves quietly to complete its mission.

Keep moving, Taurus Moon and Scorpio Sun, in a smooth steady flow of divine energy toward using the strength of Taurus to combine with the Scorpio intensity; then there is nothing that you cannot accomplish.

Sun in Sagittarius (Fire) with Moon in Taurus (Earth)

"From a slow, cautious pondering child
to an adventuresome, open seeker."

When the Moon is in Taurus and the Sun is in Sagittarius, the soul movement should flow from Earth to Fire. This shift requires that the feminine, receptive Earth energy become infused with a lighter, freer, masculine, positive life force. The waxing Moon phase keeps the awareness at the unconscious level, but the hidden goal is to be the student or the disciple of life.

Everyone embraces the open-minded, fast-thinking energy of the young Sag Archer. Even though Earth stabilizes Fire, there is still a warm, generous, sympathetic disposition that flows out to the world. Everyone loves Sagittarius because of their great optimism, and when this is blended with the Bull's stamina, this Jupiter spirit blesses any groups they encounter. The grounded Taurus stability can never be burned up by the flighty Fire energy; however, the mood will certainly become lighter as this soul grows beyond their youth. More fun and laughter occur as the free spirit of Jupiter-ruled Sagittarius arises on the scene.

As this one matures, there should be a good balance of reasonable caution to go with the fast changing moods of the Fire spirit. An artistic talent dominates this soul as they are drawn to creative projects such as painting and weaving. There is a natural musical talent here also; they only need access to the instruments and they can probably play by ear without any formal training. Since the Venus-ruled sign knows how to be frugal with money, the Jupiter spender will be toned down. These talents will most naturally be success full in positions that have a structured base but all a level of much needed flexibility. Careers in sales or traveling engineer where no two days are the same.

If the Taurus/Sagittarius combination of energy gets out of balance, major adjustments in attitude may be required. The Sagittarian energy can flare out and try to overspend its base by giving in to its wanderlust nature. Then the Taurus need for security and stability kick in to dampen the spirits of the Fire. Depression can end up being a real danger with this combination. Too much or too little is the seesaw motion of these two signs as this soul tries to go from a solid beginning to an adventuresome life.

The soul lesson of the Moon in Taurus and Sun in Sagittarius is to move out of a grounded, stable pattern and into a spontaneous, willing-to-risk pattern without tilting the scales out of balance. This is not an easy shift for the soul and requires several adjustments in the thinking pattern. On the positive side, the Fiery Sagittarian loves to learn and study new subjects, so they will probably be quite willing to look at old behaviors with a willingness to change them.

Keep moving, Taurus Moon and Sagittarius Sun, in a smooth steady flow of divine energy toward becoming the joyful idealist who hangs onto a small portion of realism to stay grounded as you are the curious one.

Sun in Capricorn (Earth) with Moon in Taurus (Earth)

"From a slow, cautious pondering child to a mature, practical controller."

When the Moon is in Taurus and the Sun is in Capricorn, the element of Earth remains strong in this soul's purpose. Because of the waxing cycle of the Moon, some of the innate drive is unconscious. The tenacity of the Bull remains intact throughout this lifetime because the grounded Earth energy will be supported by the growing influence of the Sun's Earth focus.

A "whatever-it-takes" attitude is already anchored in the soul upon arrival. The Taurus Moon child will methodically go forward with an inborn drive to overcome any obstacles to get what they want and achieve their goal, to make their life comfortable. Blending within the Earth field usually comes with ease as it is not the destiny of this soul to struggle during this life journey.

The goal is toward worldly accomplishments and forward movement. A persistent mind added to very strong self-control feeds a need to elevate their status above the common man. Earth energy requires a grounded, stable, take charge attitude that encourages the personality to acquire fame and fortune. This is the mark of a strong business person who is driven toward success. Because this is the most practical of the Earth combinations, once wealth is established there should be wisdom to do worthy projects with it. The family will definitely benefit from the worldly success of this clever business person.

If the Taurus/Capricorn combination of "double" Earth energy gets out of balance, the old Bull can dig in their heels and refuse to budge an inch. Too much caution and too much practicality can stifle any spontaneous creativity that other planets in the chart might conjure up. It is a real challenge not to get ground into practical outcomes with this combination. Destiny may have a real struggle here to bring forth magic and gaiety if these two reality-based Earth signs sense that their security might be threatened. The Capricorn Goat must avoid using intimidation and a disapproving attitude when it feels out of control. In this scenario, no action might be a safer/better option for this earth based soul than taking the risk of making the wrong decision.

The soul lesson of the Moon in Taurus and Sun in Capricorn is to stay the course and make the money but do it with some grace and ease. Maintaining a kind and gentle approach will bring favor to this serious pairing. Taking care of one's own family is a primary characteristic of the successful Goat. This devoted spouse and parent will direct their charges with firm conviction and must guard against the tendency to be seen as a strict disciplinarian.

Keep moving, Taurus Moon and Capricorn Sun, in a smooth steady flow of divine energy toward becoming a well-grounded provider who remembers to keep a light side in their daily routine, so you remain secure, pleasant and very comfortable.

Sun in Aquarius (Air) with Moon in Taurus (Earth)

*"From a slow, cautious pondering child
to an objective, intellectual observer."*

When the Moon is in Taurus and the Sun is in Aquarius, the energy flow should go from the Earth element to the Air element. This soul is moving from a grounded, slow pace to a light, airy demeanor. Since the waxing phase of the Moon is a struggling phase, this transition provides some rather strenuous challenges for the cautious Bull. Both of these signs have a fixed approach to life, so the shift from practical routine to intellectual logic strains the inner-structure of this soul.

Education should play a role in their development since the Aquarian reveres successful people with several academic degrees. One of the young Water Bearer's greatest challenges is to break old family patterns to make way for a much more unique and individualistic lifestyle. School may be just the place to allow this transformation to occur. Even the Taurus Moon's family training cannot resist the unorthodox characteristics that are fermented in an academic setting.

As they mature, strong emotional and intellectual natures begin to blend, a surprising "live and let live" persona comes alive. This combination expresses a faithful, firm, and reliable personality that does well in either political or business life. Whatever career they ultimately choose, they seldom alter their course because of a deep need for long-range planning.

If the Taurus/Aquarius combination of energy gets out of balance, a nagging reluctance to change can hold back any urge for the mental stimulation that a strong Air sign seeks. Getting into a rut and being unwilling to yield can create severe gridlocks for these two fixed signs. When the Taurus Bull has had enough of any aggravation, he will dig in and close his mind to any new solutions. The Aquarian Water Bearer is also capable of some of the same rigid thinking. So, when this combination shuts down, they may become their own worst enemy. The Uranus-ruled Aquarius can become cool, aloof and detached quicker than any other sign in the zodiac.

The soul lesson of the Moon in Taurus and Sun in Aquarius includes handling the permanent need for security and consistency conservatively. This combination definitely needs people in their life as long as this person has a plan that allows them their own space. Everyone around them can be free to do whatever they need to do. The Air element brings a strong set of social skills, so this soul has the gift of planning, organizing and blending all the different personality patterns together.

Keep moving, Taurus Moon and Aquarius Sun, in a smooth steady flow of divine energy toward leadership in the professional area where you will be seen as confident and sure-minded.

Sun in Pisces (Water) with Moon in Taurus (Earth)

"From a slow, cautious pondering child to a creative, insightful senser."

When the Moon is in Taurus and the Sun is in Pisces, the energy movement is from Earth to Water. Because both of these elements are feminine and responsive, the transition is generally smooth and easy. Since Taurus has an Earthy stable sense about it, it likes to take its time in making decisions. Sensitive Pisces also feels cautious about commitments, so these two energies are in a natural agreement. The waxing New Moon phase causes a natural unconscious flow of energy to go out into life without pre-meditation.

When gentle childlike Venus-ruled Taurus nature combines with the psychic, emotional energy of Neptune-ruled Pisces, there is plenty of sensing and telepathic persuasion going on with this youth. Shyness continues to stay with this little soul because of their gentle nature. This small child is not prone to make waves or take daring risks.

They have a strong sense of responsibility when it comes to finances but most Pisces are not driven by a need for lots of possessions. The drive for this combination is for security. The Fish has a mystical side to their personality which attracts them to music and the arts as well as all the hidden studies. This soul would rather spend their free time retreating near water than being on the move unless some other planetary pattern is prominent in the chart. The need for politeness and proper speech goes along with their Venusian need for good manners. They see everyone in their best light as they typically wear the "Rose-colored glasses" seeing none of the human bawdy traits in those around them. Because of their kind and sympathetic nature, they will do well in careers where they are in service to others and middle-managers.

If the Taurus/Pisces combination of energy gets out of balance, there can be great fear and confusion that erupts around change. These souls can become overly cautious and concerned about matters of the unknown because the Neptune energy tends to fog over and mask the real situation. Since Taurus would prefer not to make fast changes, the personality goes into a holding pattern where it may stagnate if some outside force does not intervene. Decision making is not a strength for them.

The soul lesson of the Moon in Taurus and Sun in Pisces is to use the high sensitivity and artistic talents to their advantage in this lifetime. Being able to tune into the essence of a beautiful flower or the calming rhythmic pattern of a flowing mountain stream is a rare gift that this Venus/Neptune energy is blessed with. This understanding of universal flow can be used to handle people or it can be used in artistic pursuits but it definitely needs to be integrated into the career and expression of life. An intuitive psychic sensitivity goes with this combination also. The messages from the unconscious should not be ignored as these talents have probably taken lifetimes to develop.

Keep moving, Taurus Moon and Pisces Sun, in a smooth steady flow of divine energy toward experiencing a mellow, sensitive, calm, and stable lifestyle this time as a reward for great effort in the past.

Moon in Gemini

Moon in Gemini (with all signs)

Each chapter begins with a description of the Moon's purpose for those readers who will want to go straight to a specific Moon/Sun combination.

Imagine a giant mirror reflecting past actions and experiences. According to mythology, the sign that the Moon was in at the time of your birth explains your soul response's in this lifetime. Understanding how the Moon's energy impacts your behavior and emotional reactions is key to understanding your hidden soul pattern and personal timing. You are the center of your own universe and the creator of your own destiny, so you need to understand your gifts and future goals. The eternal questions of the soul are: "Where have I come from?" and "Where am I going?" The most important eternal question, of course, is "Why am I here?"

Moon in Gemini (Air)

The energy of Gemini comes from the Air element. People born with this Moon are very busy thinkers and communicators. A soul that chooses this Moon placement comes from a very mental and lighthearted past experience. Even in the nursery, this infant will be cooing and making lots of noise. His early urge is to talk and communicate, using his voice, eyes, and hands.

The twin personality has two very different sides: One twin does not want to do anything alone, while the other twin is very impatient and can't wait for other people to catch up. It takes time for you to tune into which half of your personality you are dealing with at any given moment.

Mental stimulation represents one of the most important aspects of raising this Mercury-ruled little person. He will miss nothing as his eyes will track every activity. Provide a great variety of toys and books to look at because he won't focus on any one object for very long. He gets bored very quickly, so he needs to be in the center of whatever is going on. If he is upset or hungry, he is easily distracted. Constant motion will keep him happy.

Once this airy Gemini figures out how to walk—usually early—there will be no peace. Playpens are not usually a good idea for this Moon energy because they can feel confined or restricted. If you want this little one to be happy, throw a blanket on the floor and let them explore, move around, and touch as many different textures as possible.

When you take Gemini Moon child out in public, expect him to talk to everyone he meets. People are always attracted to these children because they are often laughing and curious, grabbing everything in sight. As a teenager, he can run his mouth when he thinks he's right.

One of the major lessons for the Mercury-ruled Moon is staying focused enough to complete a task before starting two more. Gemini Moon is most happy with lots of activities, friends, and options. As this Gemini begins to grow up, attention span can become a problem. They are known to scatter their belongings as well as their thoughts even in their older years.

For fun, the Gemini ruler, Mercury, loves to travel, whether to a new store on the far side of town or to a new outlet mall. When all else fails, give this Gemini Moon a good movie to watch to calm their busy mind.

The Gemini Moon should hold on to their social and curious nature. They have the ability to make anyone feel at ease because they have never met a stranger, and can get along with anyone for a short time. It's never hard to strike up a conversation with this master communicator unless their Sun sign energy dampens their airy spirit.

Sun in Aries (Fire) with Moon in Gemini (Air)

"From a busy, curious child
to a fiery, independent pioneer."

When the Moon is in Gemini and the Sun is in Aries, the soul growth flows from the Air element to the Fire element. There is little resistance here because both elements are positive and masculine in nature, both reaching out to express individuality in this lifetime. The relationship between the two signs falls within the waxing phase of the Moon that unconsciously pushes the soul forward with a need to express itself independently.

This talkative Moon energy stays in a state of change and curiosity throughout the early life and loves to learn new information all the time. The Mercury-ruled child will have trouble maintaining their own opinion and can be easily swayed by the opinions of others. However, their quick wit and clever use of words gives them creative writing and speaking skills early in the educational process. The challenge with these two active signs is to stay on course and follow through on all of their creative, exciting ideas.

The Aries Ram loves to jump out front and be the initiator. He is a great starter but dislikes routine work. As they mature, the planets Mercury and Mars are combined, a very quick mind can become very quick tongued. This gift of presenting logic, reason, and insight makes the Gemini Moon appear to be very well informed and educated whether they have endured the process for academic degrees or not. This one is very entrepreneurial and loves to think of new ideas first. Owning a bookstore or working in one's own sales territory would suit this soul quite well. Working in the educational environment feels attractive to the Gemini soul if there is a lot of freedom inside this setting.

If the Gemini/Aries combination of energy gets out of balance, mental activity can overrun consciousness. An overactive mind can aggravate the nervous system and cause anxiety and nervousness. The Mercury ruled Gemini can scatter their thoughts as well as their energies among many activities and projects. When the Fire element flashes out of control, the soul tends to jump up, run too fast, and burn out quickly. When these two signs are not working together, quick action can make for a fast start with great ideas, but there are no end results. In relationships, superficiality may occur since both Gemini and Aries are more interested in the excitement and early exchange than in the long-term interaction. They require another person with a similar need for new exchange and new adventure for a permanent marriage to work.

The soul lesson of the Moon in Gemini and Sun in Aries is to use the high curiosity of this combination to further one's education and create an independent work environment. Nothing pleases Aries more than to be in charge of their own time and their own space.

Keep moving, Gemini Moon and Aries Sun, in a smooth steady flow of divine energy toward stabilizing your mental activity, so you can enjoy career freedom that will provide plenty of extra income for travel adventures.

Sun in Taurus (Earth) with Moon in Gemini (Air)

"From a busy, curious child
to a determined, consistent stabilizer."

When the Moon is in Gemini and the Sun is in Taurus, the soul pattern should move from an emphasis in the Air element of mental activity to a focus in the Earth element of manifestation and success. Since Air energy is masculine and positive, and Earth energy is feminine and receptive, the young Taurus Sun needs to shift into a gentler, more passive response to life's challenges. However, the Moon phase for this combination is still New Moon which continues to push the individual thoughts out into the world in an unconscious manner.

With the Moon in Gemini, the tendency of this child is to start out with great enthusiasm and big plans. A youth in the Air energy of learning and socializing must apply discipline in their educational pursuits and then use this discipline in the business world. The goal of this student is to stay on track.

Without a long-range reward in the program, the career probably won't sustain itself into the adult years. The mature Taurus must develop their tenacity and organizational skills to achieve their goals. Security and financial success will be important to the professional image of this Bull.

If the Gemini/Taurus combination of energy gets out of balance, there definitely could be some selfishness in money matters. If this soul does not acquire the proper education to provide financial security, they may become despondent and lose their career motivation. Hidden fears of poverty can plague them, so they may jump from job to job looking for the perfect security situation. If the Bull locks into one of its unmovable postures, she could miss out on the opportunity to receive financial rewards through divine order.

The soul lesson of the Moon in Gemini and Sun in Taurus points toward using their quick mind to their advantage while learning to discipline themselves to "keep on keeping on." The Venus-ruled Earth energy must gain appreciation for the beauty in life instead of skipping blindly through Earth's meadows without stopping to smell the flowers. Being able to stop, appreciate, look around, and enjoy the perfection of God's world is a real gift that most souls coming from Air energy do not understand.

Keep moving, Gemini Moon and Taurus Sun, in a smooth steady flow of divine energy that allows you to use all of your strong communication skills in a way that brings steady prosperity flowing into your life.

Sun in Gemini (Air) with Moon in Gemini (Air)

*"From a busy, curious child
to a multi-tasking, quick moving communicator."*

When both luminaries (Sun and Moon) fall in the same sign, the Moon phase may be either New or Balsamic in phase and both of these call for much self reflection and self-motivation with the keyword being "Self". With the Sun and Moon in Gemini together, the soul's emphasis stays in the element of Air and continues to be ruled by the planet Mercury. Mercury is known as the Winged Messenger and a master communicator throughout the universe. He gathers and disseminates knowledge. Gemini is depicted by the symbol of the Twins who represent the concrete and practical as well as the intellectual and the ideal. Because of the two-sided nature of this energy, others refer to them as fickle and restless.

This double Gemini Air child is quite chatty and busy. They are extremely creative and fun, never turn your back on this active little person. Teach them to read and speak at an early age.

Because of the high need for self-focus and a strong emphasis on the positive, masculine outward flow of Gemini, relationships may tend towards superficial in this lifetime. In either case, the individual moves toward the same pattern they came from in a past incarnation. This means the essence of Airy Gemini needs perfecting and refining by developing stronger control between thoughts and speech. They need to be associated with education, teaching, and speaking.

If the Gemini/Gemini combination of energy gets out of balance, the soul can turn into a ball of restless chatter. They may have trouble staying on track with their thoughts. Their memory may become a problem if they do not make every effort to pay attention when people speak. Because these Mercury-ruled people get bored very quickly, once they complete an educational degree they may never use it.

Having the ability to adapt to change quickly can be a great asset but when change is a more attractive solution than solving a problem or finishing a project, the restless Gemini may be in trouble.

The soul lesson of the Moon and Sun in Gemini is to harness their fast-moving minds, so they can take advantage of all of the knowledge and information they collect. An old axiom says that "knowledge without application is useless." The Winged Messenger can be guilty of not sticking around long enough to teach the information he has gathered.

Keep moving, Gemini Moon and Sun, in a smooth steady flow of divine energy toward applying all of your knowledge to make your own life a more stable and interesting experience by staying in the rhythm of life.

Sun in Cancer (Water) with Moon in Gemini (Air)

*"From a busy, curious child
to an emotional, sensitive caretaker."*

With the Moon in Gemini and the Sun in Cancer, positive masculine Air energy moves towards the feminine, receptive energy of the Water element. To combine the young Gemini communicator and socializer with the emotional and feeling nature of Cancer, this soul needs to use their quick mental agility to handle emotional situations that continually arise. With the New Moon phase expressed, the unconscious instinct pushes to rush out spontaneously without thinking first.

Since this child struggles with emotional instability, they need a consistent, nurturing home environment to flourish. This one may be slower to mature because of the need for family and security. Gemini Moon will thrive in a positive learning environment.

They constantly need to keep their facts and figures straight because logic and reason can be their saving trait. When the behaviors of Mercury and the Moon are combined, the instinctual emotional response can fluctuate drastically. It can bring a heightened intuitive awareness of the real motivation underlying any situation. This one could be a great motivational speaker, counselor, or coach. Working with the public in a service position or selling real estate will use the best talents of this caretaker.

If the Gemini/Cancer combination of energy gets out of balance, overly-emotional thinking takes charge of a situation. An out-of-control Mercury blurts out thoughts that have not been processed. Then the sensitive, feeling Cancer becomes defensive and unwilling to listen to the other side of the story. The restless side of Gemini prefers not to stay home and do domestic chores, so this combination can become irritable when trapped in a caretaking job only. When confined to home, Gemini Cancer may become depressed and not answer the phone.

The soul lesson of the Moon in Gemini and Sun in Cancer points toward using the adaptability and flexibility that this soul was born with to cultivate a nurturing, caring home life. A flexible job that taps into the sympathetic, maternal traits of this Moon-ruled soul will foster the highest qualities of this combination.

Keep moving, Gemini Moon and Cancer Sun, in a smooth steady flow of divine energy toward initiating logical and practical solutions in a caring, sensitive manner to create the success and comforts of the world that you wish for your family.

Sun in Leo (Fire) with Moon in Gemini (Air)

"From a busy, curious child
to an energetic, strong willed-leader."

When the Moon is in Gemini and the Sun is in Leo, the goal of the soul is to blend the Air and Fire elements. This shift occurs easily since both elements function in a masculine, positive manner. The Last Quarter Moon phase demands that the soul consciously work at integrating positive responses in relationships.

With Mercury-ruled Gemini establishing the Moon's instinctive response pattern, this little one operates from a logical, rational method of dealing with its feelings. One of the dangers of the Gemini Moon is to exert too much emotional instability early in life which keeps the Leo Lion from feeling secure. When the young, proud Leo does not feel important, he can become quite bossy and demanding.

As Leo matures, he collects facts and details before he decides what the appropriate response to an emotional crisis ought to be. The Sun-ruled Leo performs at his highest when receiving strong praise and appreciation as a reward for relentless loyalty. The instinct for both Gemini/Leo signs is to reach out and take action in a dominant fashion. Any career that calls upon this soul's dynamic creativity and leadership abilities will allow them to excel and achieve the top slot.

If the Gemini/Leo combination of energy gets out of balance, too much verbal arrogance can boil up to protect this very sensitive ego. Mercury-ruled Gemini quite often talks a better game than they are prepared to uphold. Leo can roar and threaten but their bark is usually much stronger than their bite. This combination acts as their own worst enemy in a conflict because they appear so fearsome when all they really want is love and appreciation. Gemini energy always needs to think before speaking.

The soul lesson of the Moon in Gemini and Sun in Leo is to direct their quick mental perception into a controlled leadership environment. This combination holds an incredible amount of positive, out-flowing force that functions best when it has a place to rule. If this soul is fortunate enough to come from a strong family, their enthusiastic outgoingness will bloom very early and their recognition could begin while they are still in school.

Keep moving, Gemini Moon and Leo Sun, in a smooth steady flow of divine energy toward integrating strong social skills you were born with to build a powerful leadership position where your creative problem solving abilities can shine.

Sun in Virgo (Earth) to Moon in Gemini (Air)

"From a curious, busy child
to a grounded, analytical problem-solver."

When the Moon is in Gemini and the Sun is in Virgo, the flow of energy goes from the Air element to the Earth element. This requires the taming of some scattered mental processes into an analytical, grounded pattern. Both of these signs are ruled by Mercury, the Winged Messenger, who calls for more clarity of thought in grasping details as the mental energy becomes more grounded in this lifetime. The Moon phase relationship between the Moon and Sun is waning which calls for conscious action around integrating in partnerships.

Even when young, this Virgo will not want their hands dirty. They will thrive on change because boredom is their enemy. As they begin to mature, the process of organizing and being neat comes into focus. This one will always have manual dexterity as a talent.

Refinement of physical dexterity improves along with a mental acumen that is geared more toward a scientific or professional career. Other areas where this Mercury person can excel include an editor, journalist, clerk, or educational professional. Clerks and business administrators fare well using their analytical Mercury processes also. This soul may have more than one career throughout her working years.

If the Gemini/Virgo combination of energy gets out of balance, it will be hard for the Gemini energy to settle down to allow Earth Virgo to establish enough stability to follow through on planned tasks. Gemini has been known to scatter its energies by starting too many projects. Then when the Mercury-ruled Virgo energy tries to take over and also lacks the tenacity to complete, Virgo can become very critical and picky about details and never manage to complete the project. This soul does better when actually doing the work than when they try to manage other people. Easily overloaded, they may totally shut down emotionally when there is too much stress. In these times, the tendency will be to over-analyze the problem.

The soul lesson of the Moon in Gemini and Sun in Virgo is to use your mental powers in an intellectual educational career where detail and precision are rewarded. Because of Gemini's natural ability to make friends and meet new people, this individual will attract people to help them as long as their Virgo reserved energy does not hold the willing stranger at arms length. The Virgo energy must resist giving off an aura of judgment because their Earthy seriousness appears to be aloof.

Keep moving, Gemini Moon and Virgo Sun, in a smooth steady flow of divine energy toward manifesting a solid career plan in this lifetime where you can use your strong mental capabilities in a precise manner while you retain your outgoing social personality.

Sun in Libra (Air) with Moon in Gemini (Air)

"From a busy, curious child
to a social, peace-keeping negotiator."

When the Moon is in Gemini and the Sun is in Libra, both lights remain in the Air element where social communication skills are revered. The Moon phase for this combination is still waning which calls for more social integration through relationships. The focus on the Air element makes people skills develop easily.

While the Moon in Gemini child operates with a great deal of flexibility in the mental arena, growth and maturity includes interaction in one-to-one relationships with love and sharing. Venus-ruled Libra adds refinement and artistic talents to the expressive behavior pattern. This young student's thirst for knowledge intensifies into intellectual aspirations which can be used in professional leadership.

With maturity comes a strong need for harmony which could end up looking like indecision because these signs deplore confrontation and aggression. A strong need to be in relationship as well as mobile gives this soul a love of travel with a wide range of social groups. They are usually charming with a great gift of conversation that makes any party more fun. To express the need for balance and leadership, professions focused on mediation and negotiation allow this soul to shine.

If the Gemini/Libra combination of energy gets out of balance, a mental block can occur about making final decisions that include other people. A need to be the peacemaker may override a practical choice and cause the person to yield to peer pressure. If they become embarrassed or unsure, they may chatter and tell more than they should. However, when good reasoning is needed, this Mercury and Venus-ruled person can use very influential powers of speech to settle arguments and debates. The most difficult task for the Gemini Libra remains staying grounded instead of creating the solution in their head and never being able to execute the plan.

The soul lesson of the Moon in Gemini and Sun in Libra is to direct their quick, expressive thoughts into real situations where their negotiating abilities will manifest positive results. It is important for them to remain engaged long enough to sustain deeper commitments. Friends may come and go in relationship to current interests.

Keep moving, Gemini Moon and Libra Sun, in a smooth steady flow of divine energy toward applying your strong mental skills in areas that allow your social abilities of leadership to shine.

Sun in Scorpio (Water) with Moon in Gemini (Air)

"From a busy, curious child
to a determined, focused project manager."

When the Moon is in Gemini and the Sun is in Scorpio, the transition from the Air element to the Water does not come easily. The Moon phase pattern falls into a Full Moon that brings forth a conscious need to integrate into relationships.

During the younger years, Mercury-ruled Gemini can be inclined to vacillate in their friendships and have trouble staying in commitments. Their great sense of humor and sensual charm makes them attractive to the opposite sex. A quick wit can turn into biting sarcasm when this soul feels threatened or betrayed. Even though Gemini is social and outgoing, Scorpio needs their privacy, so they have a unique knack of disappearing when life gets too chaotic.

As the Mars-Pluto energy awakens, this soul energy develops incredible focus and control over their will. Their hidden need to feel in control is usually masked by a friendly open demeanor. Career options for this clear-minded individual include physician, surgeon, and researcher because any of these professions take advantage of the strong perception and focus embodied here.

If the Gemini/Scorpio combination of energy gets out of balance, stinging verbal battles can occur. Mercury-ruled signs are normally easy going; however, when the Scorpio warrior is awakened, poison arrows can fly straight into the heart of the issue and the sarcasm can burn. Scorpio has an ability to wait patiently until the battle lines are drawn and then this Mars energy can wage a lethal attack. There may be no reasoning with a wounded, sensitive Scorpio soul. Water signs feel very deeply and seldom forget any injury. Even if the battle appears to be over, Scorpio never forgets. Much conversation serves as the only antidote.

The soul lesson of the Moon in Gemini and Sun in Scorpio aims at keeping their light, airy nature leading in social situations. If the heavy Water energy gets too withdrawn, a new hobby or a little trip can re-inspire the creative side of Gemini. This Mars-Pluto person will find it hard in early life to identify with their feelings and then in later life it will be hard not to get absorbed by them.

Keep moving, Gemini Moon and Scorpio Sun, in a smooth steady flow of divine energy toward using all that creative mental cleverness in writing and speech because you have the focus to accomplish anything that you set as a goal.

Sun in Sagittarius (Fire) with Moon in Gemini (Air)

*"From a busy, curious child
to an adventuresome, risk-taking traveler."*

When the Moon is in Gemini and the Sun is in Sagittarius, the flow goes from the Air element which is focused on communication, to the Fire element which is focused on action and movement. These two signs relate in the Full Moon phase that calls for integration through conscious awareness. Because both Air and Fire elements act in a positive and masculine out-flowing fashion, this soul responds to life in an impulsive manner.

The instinctive nature of this young Gemini is to speak their truth without any thought to the consequences of their words. There is no maliciousness in their hearts, nor is there any deliberate bluntness delivered with their opinions. With this personality, "what you see is what you get".

When Mercury-ruled Gemini and Jupiter-ruled Sagittarius join forces, significant communication talents are present. Mercury brings a quick, creative writing ability and Jupiter brings the gift of expansion, expression of vision and the "Big Picture". Teaching and writing are strong career options for this mentally focused individual. People who might benefit by this combination include a church group, a neighbor, or even a family member. The danger here is an urge to over-expand or get carried away by enthusiasm.

If the Gemini/Sagittarius combination of energy gets out of balance, it is easy to over-extend one's capabilities. Too much activity and too much excitement create a nervous anxiety that can lock up the Air flow. Jupiter's natural desire strives to be the biggest and the best, but its philosophical nature does not lend itself to staying on task. Therefore, there may be many great ideas but little follow through. Because of the restless nature of both of these signs, variety needs to be part of the lifestyle.

The soul lesson of the Moon in Gemini and Sun in Sagittarius is to be able to keep all of their intellectual interests active. When Air Fire energy feels confined or unfocused, it can behave in an irrational and irritable manner. The gift here lies with the ability to read, study, and comprehend a variety of different subjects. The goal calls for being able to use the information to write, speak, or share in a counseling setting in a way that will help others.

Keep moving, Gemini Moon and Sagittarius Sun, in a smooth steady flow of divine energy toward staying in the now and continuing to study and learn throughout this lifetime.

Sun in Capricorn (Earth) with Moon in Gemini (Air)

"From a busy, curious child
to a responsible, initiating entrepreneur."

When the Moon is in Gemini and the Sun is in Capricorn, the energy flow goes from the Air element to the Earth element. Since the Moon phase for this combination is waxing and still unconscious, there is an instinctive need to study about soul growth to gain information on the laws of divine order.

With Mercury's natural attraction to education and knowledge, this young Gemini excels in the academic environment. Particularly in youth, there exists a strong tendency to scatter one's thoughts while this one struggles with follow through on tasks. Saturn-ruled Capricorn provides a strong sense of responsibility, so that there is plenty of guilt when the job or homework does not get done.

Gemini seeks variety and invention while Capricorn needs a place to be in charge. There is resistance between these two signs with one saying "go, be free" while the other says "be studious; be successful." This soul has the talent to succeed in government or other forms of public life. She could also do well as a professional traveler or public speaker.

If the Gemini/Capricorn combination of energy gets out of balance, they could make professional commitments and then never follow through. A natural restlessness and boredom could keep the success-driven Capricorn from ever receiving the recognition they so desperately crave. When The Goat feels ignored, she can become determined to be first at the top of the mountain. Capricorn will come out of its hidden isolation and take charge when "winning" is at stake. This combination struggles from within about whether to stand back and keep their freedom, or to step forward and be the perfect boss.

The soul lesson of the Moon in Gemini and Sun in Capricorn is to keep an open mind to new learning and information while they continue to work in the real world at a job that rewards routine and discipline. There could be a risk of Capricorn believing that they can do things better than anyone else. A pompous attitude could destroy the image that Capricorn has worked so hard to build.

Keep moving, Gemini Moon and Capricorn Sun, in a smooth steady flow of divine energy toward the adjustment between a very airy disposition and a strong need to be seen as successful and competent in the professional arena.

Sun in Aquarius (Air) with Moon in Gemini (Air)

*"From a busy, curious child
to a big picture, social group leader."*

When the Moon is in Gemini and the Sun is in Aquarius, both signs vibrate to the same Air element. Mental stimulation and intellectual pursuits always measure high on the altruistic priority list of any Air person. Since the Moon phase falls to the waxing side of the cycle, there is an unconscious urge to break out and become self motivated. Because Mercury-ruled Gemini always speaks out with a strong need to express personal opinions, a blending with Uranus-ruled Aquarius only establishes a leaning toward intellectual superiority even more prevalent.

This airy, social child loves to be busy. Curiosity and a love of learning make this young person fun to teach. Friendships are very important even in early childhood. Start them in pre-school as soon as possible. Teach them to read early.

Combining the energies of Mercury and Uranus in a complementary element enhances the intuitive knowing process. This gift can bring auric vision and precognitive messages that arrive long before the actual event occurs. High spiritual expectations can cause blocks and disappointments in love when potential partners do not live up to the romantic fantasy of a totally open relationship. However, in social situations, an open, detached attitude allows this soul to become a strong group leader or corporate player. With a good educational background, this objective speaker can excel in the educational arena or on the public speaking platform. They should use their creative mental energy long term in a career where originality and uniqueness can be rewarded.

If the Gemini/Aquarius combination of Air energy gets out of balance, too much mental confusion can cloud the thought processes.

Too many facts, too much information, too many options – all of these jam up the nervous system so that no decisions can occur. An Aquarian response can be to detach, become cool, and appear aloof when this Air sign feels threatened. When the Gemini tendency to speak whatever comes into their head is also activated, an atmosphere of discontent settles around this dual energy and they go off into their own safe world. Unstable Air energy may bounce off in any direction causing whirlwinds.

The soul lesson of the Moon in Gemini and Sun in Aquarius is to use their broad social skills to lead in any group setting. If they are lucky enough to find a partner who can also be their best friend, they stand a chance of having an open, easy love relationship.

Keep moving, Gemini Moon and Aquarius Sun, in a smooth steady flow of divine energy toward applying your quick mental communication skills with a strong need for a higher purpose that can be used in the right "New Age" humanitarian group.

Sun in Pisces (Water) with Moon in Gemini (Air)

"From a busy, curious child
to a compassionate, sensitive server of mankind."

When the Moon is in Gemini and the Sun is in Pisces, the energy flow needs to go from the Air element to the Water element. Emotional sensitivity needs to be infused into the soul's strong reasoning, logical approach to life. As the Moon phase moves away from New Moon toward First Quarter Moon, it remains waxing and unconscious in behavior.

This child struggles to create a structured environment where it feels safe and secure. Mercury-ruled Gemini has a natural conversational gift. When young, this combination may entertain imaginary friends. They love to meet people. These people can talk to anyone and even in a new place they operate as if they were in their own personal space. They have the ability to chat with a total stranger and discuss almost any topic comfortably.

Because both planets Jupiter and Neptune have rulership over the sign of Pisces, there is highly sensitive psychic energy exposed that automatically picks up the vibes surrounding any situation. The Pisces Water energy tunes into the real thought patterns and the Mercury Gemini energy sorts through these messages and frames them into logical, reasoning mental messages. There is a real talent for writing and acting with this creative soul. Because of the indirect changing nature of the thoughts, these people lack confidence in their own impressions, as well as their choice of love partners. A strong idealism allows these souls to put loved ones on a pedestal.

If the Gemini/Pisces combination of energy gets out of balance, there is not much natural stability to support them. Because of the changeable essence of both signs, unsure feelings wash over these souls at every difficult juncture. Worry can engulf the Gemini Pisces combination whenever their decisions are questioned. They can become frozen in fear when they meet criticism from people they respect. Jumping from solution to solution only makes Pisces' situation worse. The least desired response for these flexible signs is to panic and make un-thought out choices.

The soul lesson of the Moon in Gemini and Sun in Pisces encourages well thought out decisions. There is an intellectual knowing that can combine with the Pisces strong sense of feeling to allow this soul to function from a strong gut level. No matter how much information has been gathered on any situation, this Water sign should trust their deeper feelings in the end. Living near the sea can heal the buried wounds of the soul as Pisces needs to be comfortable, surrounded by art, music and water.

Keep moving, Gemini Moon and Pisces Sun, in a smooth steady flow of divine energy toward blending your mental and sensing receivers to keep you tuned into the harmonious vibrations of Earth where you can find peace.

Moon in Cancer

Moon in Cancer (with all signs)

Each chapter begins with a description of the Moon's purpose for those readers who will want to go straight to a specific Moon/Sun combination.

Imagine a giant mirror reflecting past actions and experiences. According to mythology, the sign that the Moon was in at the time of your birth explains your soul response's in this lifetime. Understanding how the Moon's energy impacts your behavior and emotional reactions is key to understanding your hidden soul pattern and personal timing. You are the center of your own universe and the creator of your own destiny, so you need to understand your gifts and future goals. The eternal questions of the soul are: "Where have I come from?" and "Where am I going?" The most important eternal question, of course, is "Why am I here?"

Moon in Cancer (Water)

The energy of Cancer comes from the Water element, known for its extreme emotional responses to life. This feminine sensitivity reacts to all that surrounds it since this sign is where the Moon is at its most powerful. An infant with a Water Moon requires a lot of extra comfort and nurturing.

The most important things to a Watery Crab baby are home and mother; these are the strongest bonds for this infant. They are emotionally attached to their family even at this age, and will feel the highs and lows around them. Because Cancer is an action-oriented sign, this Moon child's attention is easily redirected. Hugs and kisses or a special treat can help make her feel supported and secure.

If the sensitive Crab feels slighted, tears will flow easily and she may overreact by pouting. Take special care to convince this Cancer Moon that she is precious, smart, and appreciated, or she may feel rejected and hold on to that feeling. This Moon child needs lots of nurturing and cuddling, so she does not lock away her emotions and become less responsive as an adult.

If you cannot find the Cancer Moon child when they are feeling overly sensitive, try looking for them hiding in their room where the energy is quiet and safe. During these vulnerable times they may not respond; the Crab pulls their protective "home" shell up around them and disappears inside. These moody spells never last too long because Cancer needs lots of action.

As this Cancer Moon child grows up, their need for family support remains. They will always make family a priority. Nurture and protect this Cancer Moon child and you will reap the benefits as you get older.

The goal of the adult with a Cancer Moon is to manage their emotions without pushing and pulling at the people they love. Just like the ocean tides ebb and flow so does their emotional body flow with the currents of the Moon—sometimes gentle, sensitive, and caring, and at other times sulky, moody, and clingy. Consider yourself fortunate if you are chosen to receive this warm, patient, care-giving energy.

Sun in Aries (Fire) with the Moon in Cancer (Water)

"From a sensitive, emotional child to a fiery, brave warrior."

When the Moon is in Cancer and the Sun is in Aries, the flow of energy travels from the feminine, emotional Water element to the masculine, high-spirited Fire element. The Moon phase is waxing at the First Quarter point of the cycle where energy flows unconsciously out into experience.

Since this young child is coming from a protected, nurturing environment and is moving into an action-oriented and independent space; it feels vulnerable and sometimes out of control. They may resort to drama during these times because they have a natural talent for the stage. The sensitive Cancer youth may struggle with being on their own and leaving the protection of the family home. Even though this soul knows what makes the loved ones in their environment happy, the Aries part of them may not be willing to sacrifice their own dreams for the comfort of others.

One part of this soul loves home, family and sentimental moments while the other part loves bold action, independence, and lots of freedom. they overcome their fear of failure, worldly success can definitely be theirs. When the Cancer/Aries energy is working together, they create a strong, determination to live up to the very best executive effort that this soul can produce. The Moon's intuitive understanding enhances the quick mental perception making this soul a visionary entrepreneur. Once they overcome their underlying fear of failure, worldly success can definitely be theirs.

If the Cancer/Aries combination of energy gets out of balance, a lot of highly reactive, emotional energy floats around. When the two energy patterns square off against each other, the drive of the self-focused Mars warrior wins out over the sensitive Moon. Once this soul feels safe in their surroundings, they usually become bored, restless, and easily irritated. The Moon-Mars combination can become very aggressive in their speech when they feel provoked. The mood swings become very confusing to their loved ones who cannot figure out what will make this action-oriented soul happy at any given moment.

The soul lesson of the Moon in Cancer and Sun in Aries is to strengthen their sensitive, deep feeling nature using the fiery warrior initiative of the Aries. It is difficult to remain kind and sensitive to the feelings of others while being called to charge forward to break new ground in an effort to do things their own way. The danger here is that the soul will become self-centered and worry only about creating their own nest without consideration for anyone else.

Keep moving, Cancer Moon and Aries Sun, in a smooth steady flow of divine energy toward fitting the nurturing protective part of you into the person who becomes a strong initiating leader.

Sun in Taurus (Earth) with Moon in Cancer (Water)

*"From a sensitive, emotional child
to a practical, purposeful leader."*

When the Moon is in Cancer and the Sun is in Taurus, the energy flow is from the Water element to the Earth element. The Cancer Moon is known to express in sentimental emotional language while the Taurus Earth sign seeks practical, realistic descriptions for life scenarios. Taurus and Cancer are both feminine and receptive, so this is not a challenging combination. Since the Moon phase is waxing in an unconscious flow, the soul may not be aware that it struggles with making people understand their emotional point of view.

As a child, their over-reactive nature become very apparent when they feel threatened about their home life or their security. Anxiety can result from feeling out of touch with the family support system. In the early years, this little one should be encouraged to have a savings bank and manage their own allowance. This will allow them to feel safe and comfortable.

Even though the Taurus energy contributes a deep understanding of financial affairs, the Cancer need to hoard may always keep this combination feeling like there is never enough money and security to last a lifetime.Actually, this Moon and Venus combination usually attracts gain through property and perhaps some family inheritance. Once the Cancer Moon has created a comfortable home and the Taurus Sun has saved enough money for a few exotic trips and a solid retirement, this soul can sit back and enjoy the fruits of their labor.

If the Cancer/Taurus combination of energy gets out of balance, a stubborn unwillingness to listen can become dominant. One of the greatest cautions with any combination of Moon Venus energy is an inability to speak up to defend one's self. Diplomacy can be a virtue but it can also be a crutch when it keeps the person from being truthful and forthright. When a strong Venus need for harmony overrides all other traits, the soul may need a partner that will teach them how to fight and defend their personal position. They must learn the art of graciously defending their own feelings. Both Cancer and Taurus love their comfort, so this soul must guard against becoming too sedentary in their favorite comfortable armchair.

The soul lesson of the Moon in Cancer and Sun in Taurus is to stabilize the emotional waves that follow the flow of the Moon. Taurus needs stability and consistency in their everyday lives at all cost. Friends will always create a pleasant entertainment, but security is based in the family for this soul.

Keep moving, Cancer Moon and Taurus Sun, in a smooth steady flow of divine energy toward developing your own stable family with a dedicated partner who also wants to live happily ever after.

Sun in Gemini (Air) with Moon in Cancer (Water)

*"From a sensitive, emotional child
to a fast-paced, mentally quick, achiever."*

When the Moon is in Cancer and the Sun is in Gemini, the Moon phase is still waxing but it is very close to the Sun which makes it respond as a New Moon. The New Moon unconsciously rushes out to meet life without being aware of where it is going.

This emotionally sensitive child becomes more outgoing as they get older. Because of their highly intuitive sympathetic radar, they feel vulnerable in stressful family situations. Their fears can produce anxious moments and nervous habits in their youth when they feel they have no control over their own security. Most Mercury-ruled people love school which includes the whole learning process.

The Moon and Mercury rule very different personal energies. While the Moon activates the emotions, Mercury activates the mind, so there is a seesaw effect here between the heart and the mind. The child responds through their senses and the adult responds through their logic and reason. As soon as they have completed their education, which Gemini considers to be very important, they need to establish their own home where they can experience calm and serenity. This soul has a natural ability to draw pictures or write stories that express sensitivity. In fact, this combination has multiple talents that could be developed. The problem with Gemini is that they do not want to be tied down to one vocation or career.

If the Cancer/Gemini combination of energy gets out of balance, overly-emotional reactions take charge of the situation and logic goes away. An angry wounded Crab will strike out without thinking and is prepared to defend itself to the death. The Mercury-ruled Gemini might say anything when they feel wounded. One of their base instincts is to pack up their belongings and move away. Unfortunately for the child, there is usually nowhere for them to go except to their own bedroom, and that is exactly where they run to hide. This soul needs a place to go when stress gets high, so they can regroup and focus in a new direction.

The soul lesson of the Moon in Cancer and Sun in Gemini is to harness their high emotional energy and use it in a creative manner. These people love the adventure of travel but the Cancer Moon loves to come home, so they never go too far or stay too long.

Keep moving, Cancer Moon and Gemini Sun, in a steady flow of divine energy toward keeping an open trusting heart while you expand your communication skills and learn to speak your true convictions.

Sun in Cancer (Water) with Moon in Cancer (Water)

*"From a sensitive, emotional child
to a nurturing, kind, decision-maker."*

When both luminaries (Sun and Moon) fall in the same sign, the Moon phase may be either New or Balsamic in phase and both of these call for much self reflection and self-motivation with the keyword being "Self". There is a strong unconscious rushing out of instinctual energy with this soul. With the Moon and Sun together in Cancer, the element that the soul needs to refine would be the Water element. The expression of the Water energy focuses on emotions, feeling, and sensitivity while it relates to the world as feminine and receptive.

The Sun does not stand strong in its individuality in the sign of Cancer because the Moon rules here and dampens the fire of the Sun's rays. This emotional Moon child definitely carries its Crab shell around all the time with this combination as a constant protection from hurtful attachments and painful criticisms. Their reactions in youth tend to be irrational and extreme at times, so they tend to keep a small circle of friends and family. The mother always plays a significant role in the life of this person, for good or for bad.

The sympathetic receptiveness of Cancer makes these souls sensitive to the unspoken emotional feelings of people around them. When emotional waves get too high, this Cancer heads for home where they feel safe. Because of the Moon's high intuition, it brings a shrewd business sense to the negotiating table. They have a natural leadership ability in groups which may be a family business, a community organization, or a national corporation. Land and real estate are good investments for this combination because they seem to have a sense about what has worth and what will sell. They make good salespeople for things that have an emotional attachment such as houses, cars, and vacation packages.

If the Cancer/Cancer combination of double water element energy gets out of balance, overly emotional responses can make them feel wounded at both real and imaginary offenses. Part of their extreme reaction may be to become suspicious or overly cautious. When this soul pulls into their shell, they may become a recluse who has no physical activity. If this Cancer Moon did not receive lots of nurturing and cuddling during childhood, no amount of reassurance may be able to heal that wound. An out-of-control Cancer may become defensive and unwilling to listen to any explanations.

The soul lesson of the Moon and Sun in Cancer is to use the strong take charge ability this soul was born with to become a perceptive leader in a group situation. Good listening skills are part of its defense and Cancer is better at defense than offense. Being the tribal protector is the goal.

Keep moving, Cancer Moon and Sun, in a smooth steady flow of divine energy toward developing the highest level of intuition to help with becoming a kind, stabilizing force in the family and the community.

Sun in Leo (Fire) with Moon in Cancer (Water)

"From a sensitive, emotional child
to a fast-paced, outgoing leader."

When the Moon is in Cancer and the Sun is in Leo, the soul energy takes a natural flow from the Water element to the Fire element. Each of these planets remains very strong in their characteristics because each is in the sign that they naturally rule. The Moon phase is Balsamic which means the cycle is waning and is almost at a completion point where the soul finishes up several life cycles. This is called the "Dark Moon" energy where the soul pulls back into itself.

The Cancer Moon child responses are typically emotional and extremely reactive. They are dependent upon the approval of their family and always attached to the mother, even as an adult. As the youth takes on their own individual persona, they become incredibly strong in their leadership abilities.

Love relationships may suffer in the early years because of a false pride or fear of making a fool of themselves. Leo always has a quick sense of humor which includes a dramatic flare that people find very entertaining. Their exciting, playful manner can lighten up any crowd. They must strive to excel in corporations and sales organizations where their management skills can be rewarded. As self-esteem grows, this soul may achieve public recognition or the ability to speak in public forums.

If the Cancer/Leo combination of energy gets out of balance, emotional fits and an egotistical attitude can rise up to make this person difficult to handle. In public, this soul dresses well and appears outgoing and confident; but in private, they actually can be insecure and emotionally needy. They may create dramatic scenes when they feel that they are not getting enough attention or appreciation. A wounded Lion strikes out at anyone who tries to get close when he feels threatened, and this Lion is no exception. At its worst, this Watery Moon can whine and pout and act like a spoiled child.

The soul lesson of the Moon in Cancer and Sun in Leo is to capture all of the emotionally sensitive and intuitive awareness that Cancer can muster and direct it into making the Leo leader more compassionate and aware. They must avoid wallowing in self-pity and allow their Leo courage to shine. Leaving home may be the hardest challenge that is soul conquers in this life.

Keep moving, Cancer Moon and Leo Sun, in a smooth steady flow of divine energy toward becoming a caring family leader who stands strong in a leadership role in your professional life.

Sun in Virgo (Earth) with Moon in Cancer (Water)

"From a sensitive, emotional child to a grounded, analytical, problem-solver."

When the Moon is in Cancer and the Sun is in Virgo, the energy flow goes from the Water element to the Earth element. This is an easy transition because both elements are feminine and receptive, allowing for an easy inflow of universal energy. The Moon phase for this combination falls in the waning cycle where the focus is on consciously learning to integrate with others while stripping away old illusions or beliefs of the soul.

This sensitive Moon child has an underlying sweetness and shyness that endears them to the world. However, their fluctuating moodiness makes it difficult for closer family members to deal with their unpredictable behavior. When the Moon and Mercury join forces, this soul has access to a fast-thinking, intuitive thought process. They excel in academics as long as there are no major emotional traumas occurring within their family unit. Once this person feels comfortable in a group, their dry wit can be hilarious.

In the work environment, this combination produces their best creative analysis in a private, non-competitive support setting. Because of their quick, clever mind, they can handle more than one assignment at a time. They love multiple, simultaneous projects, so they don't get bored. Their critical thinking abilities make them an asset to any management team as long as they are not given the head position. Research, architecture and engineering all use the best assets from both of these signs.

Even though this combination is rather conservative in their dress and their behavior, they love all kinds of unusual people. Animals and pets may also be a big part of this Virgo's attention. They are dedicated to home and family and make good parents and adult role-models.

If the Cancer/Virgo combination of energy gets out of balance, emotional stress can shut down the analytical side of Virgo. Nervous tensions bring out the retiring, shy instincts, so the soul retires to a safe position behind the scenes. If the Virgo becomes over-critical and picky, their defenses flare and logic can go right out the window. It is very difficult to try to reason with a sulky, negative over-analytical Cancer Virgo when they get overwhelmed. The only hope is to wait for the phase of the Moon to change and then the Cancer's mood will shift and they will get interested in a new idea.

The soul lesson of the Moon in Cancer and Sun in Virgo is to use their high intuitive sensitivity as an asset while developing the left-brain processing mental skills. These souls work well from home because they flourish in a protected environment. Unless there are other leadership indicators in the birth chart, this person prefers to be allowed to do their work quietly behind the scenes.

Keep moving, Cancer Moon and Virgo Sun, in a smooth steady flow of divine energy toward building a harmonious connection between a warm, supportive home environment and a consistent, mentally-challenging work career where you are fulfilling a deep soul need to serve.

Sun in Libra (Air) with Moon in Cancer (Water)

*"From a sensitive, emotional child
to quick-thinking, social negotiator."*

When the Moon is in Cancer and the Sun is in Libra, the energy flow is from the Water element to the Air element. These two patterns challenge each other as the soul must shift from a receptive, feminine sensitive focus to a positive, masculine aggressive approach. The Moon phase is in the waning cycle calling for a conscious integration of balance in relationships.

This child's emotional Cancer shyness can create blockage as the Libra reaches out for constant social interaction. The early childhood sensitivity may slow down Libra's social curiosity and keep this little Crab at home. However, both of these signs are initiators and love to rush out into new adventures and challenges. Their nurturing side can become buried.

Since the child within reveres the security of home and family, they need to create a stable home environment in their adult relationships. It is important for this Venus person to create a comfortable, well-decorated home. The soul instinct guides toward following the lead of the parents. If rapport with the parents was a positive experience, then instinctively following their same pattern is good. But if the early parent experience was difficult, there may be karmic lessons to be learned from the problems of the parents to consciously avoid repeating them. Because they can see both sides of any issue and want to be fair, they do well in most sales arenas as well as in their own business. Middle management positions are also a natural for this cardinal energy.

If the Cancer/Libra combination of energy gets out of balance, there can be serious extremes in emotional responses that surround personal relationships. Their moodiness can make them difficult life partners. When the Venus-ruled Libra energy is feeling social, they will invite everyone into their home and make everyone feel welcome. But when the Moon-ruler Cancer becomes overly-sensitive and defensive, they need to be allowed to head for their hiding place in the basement where they can sulk and process their deeper feelings alone. These dark moods never last long because of the changing nature of these signs.

The soul lesson of the Moon in Cancer and Sun in Libra is to learn to balance their strong initiating urges to experience new activities in business and friendships, while having a need to maintain stability in the family life. This Moon Venus combination has difficulty saying what they really want, so their tendency is to just "do it" and then explain later. They tend to jump from social activity to social activity always making new friends along the way. The problem with the constant action is that it does not allow time for deeper commitments and relationships.

Keep moving, Cancer Moon and Libra Sun, in a smooth steady flow of divine energy toward holding onto your intuitive sensitivity and dedication to family as you move out into the bigger social world which needs to include a strong love partner by your side.

Sun in Scorpio (Water) with Moon in Cancer (Water)

"From a sensitive, emotional child to a determined, focused, project manager."

When the Moon is in Cancer and the Sun is in Scorpio, the natural flow of energy stays within the Water element where the refining process focuses on establishing deeper emotional commitments and developing a deeper understanding of the universal laws. This Moon phase falls in the waning cycle that consciously reaches out to integrate with others in a crusader, teacher mode.

The urge of this passionate Water energy is to share their experiences on a very deep level with other harmonious souls who cross their path. In their younger years, this one may feel insecure and cling to home. As a child and as an adult this water combination acts intensely. These souls have a sensual magnetism that attracts sexual relationships, sometimes before they are emotionally prepared to handle them. If this soul marries or commits early in life, there may be an unfinished karmic contract that needs to be completed.

As they mature, the receptive Moon combines with the intense Mars-Pluto combination of Scorpio, an incredibly focused laser beam highlights a sensitivity to all of the healing arts. Their acute perceptions pierce the facade of those who come into their personal space. Not much can be hidden from these caretakers, particularly in the family circle. Their ferocious drive to create the biggest and the best has the power to carry another less directed soul along with them in their passion. It is not unusual for these souls to practice ancient healing energy techniques to pave their path to success. In the workplace, they do well in careers that deal with the medical field. They are dedicated to understanding the complexities of the human body and the human psyche. It would be rare to find this person involved in any group or personal relationship that did not have depth and strong cause.

If the Cancer/Scorpio combination of energy gets out of balance, there is potential involvement in the underworld or dark side of society. Mars-Pluto energy can manifest as the sexual seducer for a career or just for fun. The energy of the feminine Cancer Moon can become very needy for attention and if they do not get it from their partner they may find their emotional salve somewhere else. Moon-Mars-Pluto energy can build into quite an explosion if the hidden emotions stay buried for a long time. It is important for this combination to find someone they feel they can trust to talk out their deepest fears, so that they do not have an emotional eruption. An eruption of this sort can appear as intense anger and violence or it can take the shape of a silent black cloud that shuts out all communication. Whether Cancer Scorpio shuts down or explodes, the result can be the same. There can be permanent devastation.

The soul lesson of the Moon in Cancer and Sun in Scorpio is to use their emotional compassion to help others understand that sensitivity can be an asset. The natural self-confidence displayed in this pattern can act as a role model for souls who lack the tenacity to complete with determination whatever they start. They have an instinctual understanding of universal law but they may struggle with making it work for them.

Keep moving, Cancer Moon and Scorpio Sun, in a smooth steady flow of divine energy toward expanding your spiritual awareness by staying focused on your own life commitments that lead to your higher purpose.

Sun in Sagittarius (Fire) with Moon in Cancer (Water)

*"From a sensitive, emotional child
to an adventuresome, risk-taking traveler."*

When the Moon is in Cancer and the Sun is in Sagittarius, the energy flow is from the Water element to the Fire element. The expression makes a tough transition from feminine, emotional Cancer which acts instinctually to masculine, free-spirited Sagittarius which acts out in a direct obvious manner. With the Moon phase being in the waning cycle the soul's urge is to integrate consciously with other people. Blending the soft with the sharp requires some adjustment within one's behavior pattern.

A Cancer Moon child feels everything in their surroundings, and the Sagittarian Archer openly says whatever they perceive as the truth about the happenings. The two approaches are drastically different in their delivery, so people have trouble understanding this combination. When the highly intuitive, sensitive energies are showing, poetry and artistic talents are flowing. Cancer Moon usually has trouble leaving home, but Sagittarius Jupiter considers the world to be their home and cannot wait for the next adventure.

Another paradox shows up for this struggling soul. When they are at home, they love being at home. When they are on the road, they love the excitement of being out in the world. Both the Moon and Jupiter have a sense of naivety and openness that can lead to being easily fooled. When Jupiter's broad, seeking, philosophical attitudes are the ruling behavior, the educated, quick mind provides a clear business sense. Because education is so important to the Sagittarian, this soul will always aspire to higher learning, and as they get older the learning will turn toward the higher-consciousness levels of spiritual understanding. Once they develop their own clear philosophy, they can make inspiring counselors and ministers.

If the Cancer/Sagittarius combination of energy gets out of balance, they have real problems trying to decide what they really want in life. The Cancer side wants to have a beautiful home and a loving family; the Sagittarius side wants to be free to travel, wander the world, and answer to no one. Because of the open and direct honesty of the Fire element, Sagittarius can be brutally truthful about their feelings. Since their emotions change with the phases of the Moon, their perceptions do not remain stable for long. Loved ones trying to juggle these mixed messages may never know what will really make this person happy. Unfortunately, this Moon Jupiter person may not know what makes them happy either.

The soul lesson of the Moon in Cancer and Sun in Sagittarius is to keep the fluctuating emotional tides of Cancer under control, so that the restless, impulsive Sagittarius will continue to seek high wisdom and understanding without abandoning the home front. This Jupiter-ruled soul grows through adventure and a willingness to take risks. They need to guard against experiencing their high excitement at the gambling tables at the risk of threatening their stable Earth.

Keep moving, Cancer Moon and Sagittarius Sun, in a smooth steady flow of divine energy toward nurturing your intuitive feminine side while you allow the Archer in you to reach for the universal classroom where you can gain spiritual wisdom.

Sun in Capricorn (Earth)
with Moon in Cancer (Water)

"From a sensitive, emotional child
to a responsible, initiating entrepreneur."

When the Moon is in Cancer and the Sun is in Capricorn, the flow of energy goes from the feminine, receptive Cancer in the Water element to the feminine, receptive Capricorn Earth element. Water and Earth blend naturally in a harmonious fashion to ground the feelings into a nurturing environment. These two signs represent the Full Moon cycle of the Moon-Sun relationship. The Full Moon highlights the emotional needs of the soul, so when it falls in the sign of Cancer it reaches its peak intensity.

These little people need family stability in their lives because their emotional reactions can swell out of control when they have no grounding purpose. Their parents are usually honorable, solid people. Emotional reactiveness is the challenge at hand for these kids. Because of a need to take charge, these action-oriented souls like to initiate projects and organize the program and then turn it over to the fixed energies to manage.

When the mature Capricorn Goat decides to take charge, she could climb up over the top of others to be in authority. This ones deeper purpose of life is to accept family responsibility. Success is the motivating push because this soul wants quality and will do whatever it takes to get it. If she uses her insight and sensitivity, the Goat will find herself in management or supervision without trying.

If the Cancer/Capricorn combination of energy gets out of balance, rare eruptions can occur that are hard to settle down. However, unpredictable mood swings don't usually show themselves unless the Full Moon triggers them. The controlled Capricorn normally has a thoughtful, self-contained disposition that feels distant and a little cool. The Goat is a master of intimidation when situations get out of control. It becomes very difficult to settle a disagreement with this energy combination because they will remove themselves if they feel threatened.

The soul lesson of the Moon in Cancer and Sun in Capricorn is to remain emotionally available while stepping forward to take the head position. It is not easy for the Cancer Moon to expose their vulnerable side when the energy is connected to the practical Saturn-ruled Capricorn. When the solid Earth sign makes a commitment, there is not much question that it will be done.

Keep moving, Cancer Moon and Capricorn Sun, in a smooth steady flow of divine energy to lead family and business relationships with a warmth and sympathetic kindness that only the Water and Earth elements can produce.

Sun in Aquarius (Air) with Moon in Cancer (Water)

*"From a sensitive, emotional child
to a strong, social group leader."*

When the Moon is in Cancer and the Sun is in Aquarius, the energy flow goes from the feminine, receptive Water element to the masculine, positive Air element. This pattern falls within the waxing cycle of the Moon, holding the instinctual sensitivity at an unconscious level. Even though Aquarius is Air, which establishes it with a strong mental interest, their emotions are capable of running away with the intellect. It is not easy to transition from an intensely emotional reactive Moon soul to an objective, detached social leader.

This young child starts out very sensitive, shy and clingy as the strong Cancer Moon energy feels a compulsive need for the mother's protection. Once the family ties are secure, this very social Air sign begins to reach out to build group alliances in school and outside school.

As they mature, this energy combination needs companionship and challenging mental stimulation, when they do not get it from their family they will reach out for new relationships to fill the gap. There is an adventuresome spirit tucked inside this nurturer that pushes them to seek excitement outside the traditional structure. They have a natural attraction for the creative and unique situations or people. In fact, these people befriend the characters of the world who come from very different backgrounds. In their career, they have a strong need to stand out and be recognized for their own talents, intellect and accomplishments. They are attracted to professions where their instinctual intuitive nature can be used. For this reason, these souls end up in counseling situations or in the arts where their unconscious senses can flow.

If the Cancer/Aquarius combination of energy gets out of balance, then the emotions may take over and push all of Aquarius' common sense aside. The planet Uranus, ruler of Aquarius, is known for its electrical shocking outflow of energy. When this current flies out of control, shocking results can be expected. If they feel that someone else is trying to control them, they can shut down and become totally unavailable to any outside reasoning. The only way to break through their icy barrier is to appeal to their caring nurturing side or make them think about how their actions are impacting their family. Under that defensive casual armor, there is a very big heart that cares deeply about the people the love.

The soul lesson of the Moon in Cancer and Sun in Aquarius is to attempt to integrate the two very different sides of their personality. It is important for them to continue to support the domestic home front by acting as the protector or role model of the group. It also is very necessary for them to step beyond the traditional family model and to develop a unique identity out in the world. This soul does not want to be known only as a member of their original birth group.

Keep moving, Cancer Moon and Aquarius Sun, in a smooth steady flow of divine energy that combines all of your caring, loving attributes with your incredible flare for unique, individualistic leadership.

Sun in Pisces (Water) with Moon in Cancer (Water)

"From a sensitive, emotional child
to a compassionate, sacrificing server."

When the Moon is in Cancer and the Sun is in Pisces, the feminine, receptive Water Element maintains rulership over the lifetime. The refinement of Water energy calls for a focus on emotions, responsiveness, feelings, and the intuitive flow between souls. An intense sensitivity should be nurtured to help the soul become more receptive to the emotional needs of those around them. The Moon relates to the Sun in a waxing phase which keeps the naturally out-flowing energy unconscious.

This young soul is not aware that they are picking up all of the vibrations around them like a sponge. Vivid dreams may haunt them. This child must learn to seal their energy field against too much psychic input. Because this soul is so receptive to outside stimuli, they are extremely compassionate and will always reach out to defend the "under-dog".

This combination can excel on the stage because they totally relate to the part they are playing, and they know just what the audience wants to hear. However, if they need to stand up and speak before an audience, they may not be able to because of the shy, self-consciousness of the Pisces energy. Neptune-ruled Pisces is known for struggling with aggressive energy. Since the Moon and Neptune are both recognized as receiving, responsive energies, this soul will retain their hesitant, imaginative quality even as an adult. These souls who are dominantly Water are always drawn to the service industry where their awareness of the emotional and mental workings of others is considered to be an asset. They make good doctors, nurses, ministers, and parents.

If the Cancer/Pisces combination of energy gets out of balance, there can be an intense overload of emotion flowing out. Reason and logic do no good if this person will not listen. They can appear spacey under stress and will overreact defensively to perceived criticism. Sometimes hysteria sets in and then the only salvation is for them to go to bed. Neptune-ruled Pisces needs lots of sleep, or they can crumble. This very sensitive energy needs to be careful with any drugs or alcohol because they do not have a high tolerance for anything that can put them farther into their own dream world.

The soul lesson of the Moon in Cancer and Sun in Pisces is to apply the highly intuitive sensory radar that is built into the soul pattern in this lifetime. The Moon energy needs to extend out into the world and then flow back into the soul without swelling up into a storm. The Neptune energy needs be willing to sacrifice and melt away old karmic blockages without the soul retreating into the victim/martyr syndrome. Both of these gentle, giving patterns must join forces to serve whoever crosses the path of this soul.

Keep moving, Cancer Moon and Pisces Sun, in a smooth steady flow of divine energy toward balancing the unfinished business of many lifetimes by using all the spiritual gifts hidden in your subconscious, so you can meet the challenges of this journey without running away.

Moon in Leo

Moon in Leo (with all signs)

Each chapter begins with a description of the Moon's purpose for those readers who will want to go straight to a specific Moon/Sun combination.

Imagine a giant mirror reflecting past actions and experiences. According to mythology, the sign that the Moon was in at the time of your birth explains your soul response's in this lifetime. Understanding how the Moon's energy impacts your behavior and emotional reactions is key to understanding your hidden soul pattern and personal timing. You are the center of your own universe and the creator of your own destiny, so you need to understand your gifts and future goals. The eternal questions of the soul are: "Where have I come from?" and "Where am I going?" The most important eternal question, of course, is "Why am I here?"

Moon in Leo (Fire)

The energy of Leo comes from the Fire element, known for its vitality, leadership, and spirited passion. This soul instinctively feels like he from comes from royalty or a position of power. An infant with a fiery Moon has a strong sense of entitlement and pride.

As long as this little Lion Moon is the center of attention, they will smile, pose for pictures, entertain guests, and show lots of affection. Leo Moon children need to feel special. However, if they are ignored or put to bed before they are ready, there will be a steep price to pay: The dramatic young lion can roar louder and longer than any other sign. It's very important to know not to correct this child in public because their pride does not recover quickly.

The young Leo Moon energy has a very strong-willed character and always insists on having the very best. Parents need to be prepared to let him choose his own clothes because anyone else's choices will not be good enough. It is important not to overly pamper him when he is young because he could become too accustomed to it. Be warned that a spoiled Lion child may become lazy and can expect others to cater to him. When there is fun to be had, this Leo cub has plenty of energy; when it is time for work, they can become extremely tired and need to rest or be taken care of.

One of the Leo child's biggest life lessons is to learn to take turns, so that others will like them. The instinctual need to lead gives the child an unconscious urge to take charge of all situations and give directions to all of their "followers". In school, the Lion loves to be at the head of the class, so he usually excels academically, but his teachers may struggle with his need to take over the classroom. Others may consider this little Lion to be a bit bossy.

Leadership is a natural asset for the Fire element. As this Sun-ruled Moon sign begins to mature, he will want to lead all his teenage friends. During the adolescent years, his hair and dress become critically important, so he may need to have an extra mirror or two. Since he needs lots of attention, romance is always a crisis for the youthful Leo Moon. He will want to have more than one love interest at a time until he grows into his Sun sign energy.

The goal of the Leo Moon is to shine, and to lead gracefully without always needing to be right. He will always need lots of praise and affection and in return he will give back incredible loyalty and joy. They need to understand that their greatest goal is to keep their sense of humor and to excel with humility.

Sun in Aries (Fire) with Moon in Leo (Fire)

*"From a strong-willed, creative child
to a fiery, brave warrior."*

When the Moon is in Leo and the Sun is in Aries, both signs are vibrating to the positive, masculine Fire element. Fire energy provides high vitality, determination, and a desire to take action. As the Moon is separating from the Sun in the waxing phase, the out flowing energy is in an unconscious state encouraging the soul to find its own pathway.

This high energy child has an impulsive nature and a love of new adventure that can get them into trouble; however, the little Leo Moon wants approval more than freedom. It is important to set boundaries for this high-spirited cub, or they will be running the show before the parents know what happened.

Their leadership qualities surface early and when blended with their natural ability to make friends, people surround this confident Fire energy all the time. Because of their confidence and good-humor, this soul makes an excellent presenter and salesperson. The fact that they dress well and always have a smile also makes them a magnet for love relationships. In spite of all the charisma that this combination generates, as the Aries Sun gains strength it becomes self-motivated all the time. Mars-ruled Aries wants and needs the independence and freedom to do it all their way. If life becomes too easy for this combination, they may procrastinate and never break loose to build their own empire. If the Mars-ruled Aries Ram will take the lead and take charge, great success can be achieved.

If the Leo/Aries combination of energy gets out of balance, there may be more play than accomplishment. The young Leo Moon has been given rulership over children and the little Lion remains childlike much longer than most signs. If they become embarrassed or get ignored, they can fire up and throw a pretty good fit. The Aries temper flares up fast but it burns out quickly, so the drama is usually over quickly unless the little Leo decides to create a dramatic scene. When this occurs, it may take some time for the temper-tantrum to burn out. When Fire signs get too worked up, they can create quite a blast but when that energy burns out so does the body. They need to be aware that they can burn, crash, and then go into depression while they regroup.

The soul lesson of the Moon in Leo and Sun in Aries is to direct and control their fiery high energy. Because there is some procrastination here, this native starts out with great plans and enthusiasm but may wear down before the project is done. The more they stay on course, the more successful they become, and the more successful they become the more toys they can buy. This makes the Leo Aries combination very happy.

Keep moving, Leo Moon and Aries Sun, in a smooth steady flow of divine energy toward directing your incredibly high vibration into the success of your own business where you can have as much freedom as you need.

Sun in Taurus (Earth) with Moon in Leo (Fire)

*"From a strong-willed, creative child
to a practical, purposeful leader."*

When the Moon is in Leo and the Sun is in Taurus, the energy is flowing from the Fire element to the Earth element. Since Fire energy is masculine and positive, and Earth is feminine and receptive, there is a major shift in direction requiring some grounding this lifetime. The Moon phase is still in the waxing cycle, so the flow is unconscious and struggling to express itself. It appears difficult for growth to spring up easily.

Since this young Taurus Bull does not respond well to sudden shifts in direction or to unscheduled surprises, stubbornness can become a real issue. As they grow up, they have a creative, executive aptitude that supports them as they develop their leadership skills. The tendency here is for them to take charge in any social group and rise quickly to a position of social executive.

There is much fixity in this pattern, so the Sun-ruled Leo energy may get caught up in their own identity and not want to change or do things differently. Venus-ruled Taurus loves comfort and so does the pampered Leo Lion, so this soul may opt for a life of luxury and ease. They definitely know exactly what they like and what they do not like. Their outgoing personality makes any sales arena a natural success. This powerful Leo Taurus combination may also have a strong appetite for rich foods and other excesses that the "good life" brings. However, they also have a strong constitution and a strong heart, so they can withstand a little extra weight. When these energies are harmonizing, success can come from the financial industry or big business. Because of the Venus input from the Taurus energy, they become better looking and more charming the older they get.

If the Leo/Taurus combination of energy gets out of balance, excess may be their downfall. Whether the abundance is in the social life, food, or just strong opinions, this soul struggles with the urge to overdo. There is a tendency here to dominate relationships instead of being a strong participant. The Leo Moon child may sit down and sulk if they cannot be in charge. However, if the adult Taurus Bull gets their pride hurt, they may pull back and establish an aloof attitude that holds people at a distance.

The soul lesson of the Moon in Leo and Sun in Taurus is to stay on a steady course without becoming ground into a rut pattern where there is no deviation from the plan. Leo brings excitement and drama to the lifestyle while Taurus insists on continuity and graciousness.

Keep moving, Leo Moon and Taurus Sun, in a smooth steady flow of divine energy toward the eventual success and comfort that you desire by using your creative mental processes to develop a better plan.

Sun in Gemini (Air) with Moon in Leo (Fire)

*"From a strong-willed, creative child
to a fast-paced, mentally quick achiever."*

When the Moon is in Leo and the Sun is in Gemini, the energy flow goes from the Leo Fire element to the Gemini Air element. Since both of these elements are positive and masculine, a natural harmony exists in the shift of emphasis. The Moon phase still remains within the waxing unconscious pattern meaning that the soul instinctively reacts to situations in life.

The young Leo Moon always brings lively drama to any situation, so when the talkative Mercury-ruled Gemini energy is added to the mix, a creative communicator is in the development stages. Much of their dramatic energy is played out in the use of their Mercury-ruled hands which are usually flying around demonstrating a point. In the early years, this playful Leo focuses much more on friends and socializing than on studies. However, as they get older, learning becomes a high priority, so educational degrees and advanced certifications are the goal.

Most Gemini people remain students for their entire lives. The older this soul grows the more ardent and demonstrative they become about subjects that capture their passion. This soul needs to understand that being recognized for their talents is important to them. Surrounding themselves with high vitality, curious business associates, partners, and friends is crucial because they tend to get bored very quickly. In the business world, this dynamic energy takes charge in any setting but they have a wonderful ability to promote and convince, so they belong in the sales arena.

If the Leo/Gemini combination of energy gets out of balance, they may become an overly dramatic chatterer who does not know when to give up center stage. They have the ability to embellish a story beyond any believable level. When they become angry, the Lion's roar can be very loud and their opinions can become unyielding. However, the intensity of this soul mellows with age as their Gemini energy is much more flexible than the Leo Moon pattern. In their love life, they have a secret need to hold the attention of the partner, so they feel special but as they get older that hidden jealousy mellows also.

The soul lesson of the Moon in Leo and Sun in Gemini is to control the powerful dramatic desire to be first and blend it with their naturally friendly, outgoing ability to talk to anyone. If this perpetual student can build up their self-confidence in their own mental abilities, they have the power to challenge or debate in any forum. It is also very important for them to pick a mate who will adore them as well as be a mental challenge on a variety of different subjects.

Keep moving, Leo Moon and Gemini Sun, in a smooth steady flow of divine energy toward the application of your strong leadership skills in a mentally-stimulating group where your quick intellectual awareness can be shared and appreciated.

Sun in Cancer (Water) with Moon in Leo (Fire)

*"From a strong-willed, creative child
to a nurturing, kind decision maker."*

When the Moon is in Leo and the Sun is in Cancer, a shift in energy is required to go from the Leo Fire element to the Cancer Water element. Since Fire energy flows in a positive, masculine form and Water energy flows in a feminine, receptive form, these two patterns complement one another but differ in expression. The Moon phase causes the New Moon energy to rush out unconsciously in an unbalanced nature.

This soul is not aware of how forcefully they project their ideas and an insistence on being right. This playful Leo cub can be dramatic and want lots of attention. Don't ever reprimand this one in public and give them lots of praise. This one is highly motivated by rewards.

As the soul matures, it is necessary to calm the dynamic, dramatic force of the Leo Moon. Soul growth requires that the emotionally receptive nature of the Cancer Sun contribute its softness to create a more accommodating and sympathetic manner. The goal at an instinctual level is to tame the Leo Lion's pride and allow the world to see the soft, nurturing side of the Cancer caretaker. This soul's aim is to lead in a group where they can protect and nurture. In the career world, this energy excels in positions of leadership where management or parenting is considered to be an asset.

If the Leo/Cancer combination of energy gets out of balance, a strong need to control and be the prince or princess can expose a very demanding side of the personality. Emotions may escalate beyond acceptable bounds and the defenses may rise to protect the high sensitivity that Leo Moon has trouble displaying. Family and close loved ones usually feel the burden of these uproars. Yelling and screaming may be the mask that is used to keep this very vulnerable one from weeping and wailing. Whatever the reactions, they are always intense with this energy combination.

The soul lesson of the Moon in Leo and Sun in Cancer is to learn to harness the strong determined Fire energy of Leo while establishing a softer, gentler approach to loved ones. Cancer's Water energy needs to get attention without making others feel less important or that Cancer's needs take precedence over anyone else's. Great determination in this soul keeps them going even when the urge is to retreat and hide in their shell.

Keep moving, Leo Moon and Cancer Sun, in a steady flow of divine energy toward dynamically creating exciting activities for yourself and others while applying your gifts of shrewdness and sensitivity to make people feel safer and useful.

Sun in Leo (Fire) with Moon in Leo (Fire)

*"From a strong-willed, creative child
to a fast-paced, outgoing leader."*

When both luminaries (Sun and Moon) fall in the same sign, the Moon phase may be either New or Balsamic in phase, and both of these call for much self-reflection and self-motivation with the keyword being "Self". With the Moon and Sun together in Leo, there is a strong emphasis in the positive, masculine Fire element which brings high vitality and fierce determination. There is a real challenge here to keep centered on being responsible for one's own behavior first.

Even as a child, this outgoing soul loves adventure and will attack any challenge with ferocious courage and seldom ever backs down from a fight. They fear very little and if they are afraid, the pride of the Leo Moon would not allow them to admit it. Since these dramatic little ones love the limelight, they usually become over-achievers in the academic environment. There is no shortage of ambition in work or enthusiasm in play here.

In the career arena, they can succeed anywhere they want because they have charismatic leadership abilities supported by their strong physical endurance. They usually have quite a few mirrors around the house, so they can keep checking to see how they look, particularly their hair. It is always important to the Leo lion that they are "looking good". Being in charge—looking the part—contributes to Leo's classic charm. Leadership flows naturally for this powerhouse, so they need to find a group to lead.

If the Leo/Leo combination of "double" fire energy gets out of balance, self-centered, stubborn, demanding behavior can result. When the Fire element flares, lots of heat and lots of anger flash. Out-of-control pride is Leo's greatest enemy. Since this combination tends to take any slight personally, they assume any conflict or unhappiness is all about them. In reality, the situation may have nothing to do with this Leo but they find themselves on the defensive when it is not necessary. When the lion's feelings are hurt, it takes a long time for them to get over it because they have a strong stubborn streak and don't yield easily. Even though this fixed energy can be slow to move, the lion can strike out with the speed of a wounded cat when they feel cornered. It is best not to push their Sunny disposition too far.

The soul lesson of the Moon and Sun in Leo is applying their incredible strength, determination, and will-power to positive goals. Gold stars, award ribbons, and strong pats-on-the-back motivate them. If this soul who actually lacks self-confidence is ignored or criticized, they can become uncooperative and extremely bossy. To encourage the double Leo to maximize their creative talents, the parent, lover, or boss needs to give them lots of praise and stroking. If they do not feel appropriately motivated, they can become incredible procrastinators.

Keep moving, Leo Moon and Sun, in a smooth steady flow of divine energy toward directing your dramatic leadership talents into a positive program, so that you can achieve the high success you have prepared for in this lifetime.

Sun in Virgo (Earth) with Moon in Leo (Fire)

"From a strong-willed, creative child
to a grounded, analytical problem solver."

When the Moon is in Leo and the Sun is in Virgo, the energy flow is going from the positive, masculine Fire element to the feminine, receptive Earth element. The Moon phase places the Moon behind the Sun in a waning Balsamic position which calls for the soul to pull back into the self by completing many relationships that come and go in this lifetime.

The young child part of this soul appears much more outgoing, friendly, and precocious than the reserved, shy adult. In school, this combination can do extremely well in school plays and group leadership positions because they still have a strong need to be seen, appreciated, and applauded.

But as they mature, most Virgo Earth energy prefers to work behind the scenes being only responsible for their own work. Mercury-ruled Virgo operates from a strong analytical perspective with a critical eye for detail. Because the Leo Moon takes great pride in their work and the Virgo Sun can be too much of a perfectionist with any project, this soul does not do well in management positions unless other planets in the birth chart soften their "need to be perfect" attitude. The Sun-ruled Leo energy constantly feeds their naturally Sunny disposition. This playful spirit attracts love relationships quite easily, but picky earthy Virgo usually isn't interested unless the suitor is bright, humorous, and dresses well. Neat clothing plus a sophisticated vocabulary are required to impress the Leo Virgo combination. They need to learn to apply their warm-hearted, generous nature out in the world and in their career where they will receive recognition and rewards for their hard work. Hopefully, their work includes a need for detailed, perfectionist finishing.

If the Leo/Virgo combination of energy gets out of balance, it can come across as being too proud with a quiet snobbery. Usually when Leo energy expresses snobbishly, the fiery Lion is feeling insecure and off-balance. There is a deep lack of confidence in this energy combination that probably could be traced back to a past life experience. They may feel more comfortable with children than adults because of this inhibition. When this soul does not feel appreciated, they become defensive and may turn into an irritating nit-picker who will not listen. This stubborn attitude will not last long with Virgo's changeable nature, so they should sleep on decisions overnight before giving final answers.

The soul lesson for Moon in Leo and Sun in Virgo is to be able to maintain the confidence and determination of youth when life gets harder in the adult years. There may be some health challenges that show up to force the soul into taking better care of themselves. An innocent naivety may have to be sacrificed if this soul is going to find the success they so deeply want.

Keep moving, Leo Moon and Virgo Sun, in a smooth steady flow of divine energy toward using your strong personal pride constructively to become a creative, detailed worker who finds satisfaction in the service industry.

Sun in Libra (Air) with Moon in Leo (Fire)

"From a strong-willed, creative child to a quick-thinking, social negotiator."

When the Moon is in Leo and the Sun is in Libra, there is a natural easy energy flow between both positive, masculine Fire and Air elements. The Moon phase remains in the waning cycle that requires conscious effort toward integrating with others in relationship.

The Sun-ruled Leo Moon child was born with a high creative ability and a strong sense of color. He excels in any kind of art class from paper-mache to watercolor painting. The little Leo Moon loves to play, laugh, and be social. Friends are always important to this soul as the combination of the Fire and Air elements both smoothly reach out to the world in a harmonious way.

The planetary rulers, the Sun and Venus, create a refined, spiritual soul that instinctively tries to keep the peace in their personal circle. Since there is not a major energy struggle within this individual, their spiritual consciousness seems to vibrate to a high idealistic frequency. These souls excel out in the business world because they intuitively know how to negotiate compromise and still be pleasant and fair-minded. However, unless there are other planetary patterns that would indicate strong ambition, this combination does not feel the overpowering need to drive the self just to achieve success. Romance and love rank much higher on the priority list for this Leo Libra than corporate business executive status.

If the Leo/Libra combination of energy gets out of balance, an idealistic naiveté surfaces that could lead this soul into dangerous territory. Venus-ruled Libra is known for falling in love with love. This soul can become obsessed with the dream of the potential relationship and ignores the reality of what is really happening in the now. The Leo side of the personality loves the drama of romance and will create exciting fantasies that cannot be sustained in a real give-and-take partnership. When the planet Venus goes into its over-generous and overly-social mode, the real work world becomes a second priority which can cause a financial problem.

The soul lesson of the Moon in Leo and Sun in Libra is to keep playfulness and joy in life without being overtaken by the romantic dream that when the prince or princess arrives everyone will love happily ever after. By allowing the positive beliefs that "All is Good" in the universe to become a way of thinking, the Leo Moon has the determination to move forward with spiritual conviction. As long as this soul stays focused on fulfilling their life work as well as finding that perfect mate, balance can be maintained, so Libra can express its essence. The greatest test of the Libra Sun energy is to keep one's own identity while learning to integrate into a deep relationship.

Keep moving, Leo Moon and Libra Sun, in a smooth steady flow of divine energy toward the integration of your soul's ego with the soul ego of an intimate partner. The goal is to remain objective enough to use your personal creative challenges.

Sun in Scorpio (Water) with Moon in Leo (Fire)

"From a strong-willed, creative child
to a determined, focused project manager."

When the Moon is in Leo and the Sun is in Scorpio, the energy is flowing from the Fire element to the Water element. Since Fire energy is masculine and positive, and Water is feminine and receptive, a major shift in direction requires some emotional sensing in this lifetime. Since the Moon is in the waning phase of its cycle, the soul feels the need to consciously strip away all illusion and look honestly at relationships in this life.

There is a fixed quality in both of these signs making change feel like a struggle. The proud, fiery Leo Moon resists becoming stealthy and quietly perceptive in true Scorpio fashion. This soul was born with incredible determination to control and rule, but the method needs to be adjusted. The young Leo loves grandeur and the dramatic show and is trying to subdue the drama into a more influential sedate posture where they can organize and direct situations from behind the scenes.

A high quality of passion and desire runs through any relationship or project that this soul becomes involved in. Because of their high standards and intense focus, it is almost impossible to side track this soul once they have a strong understanding of the goal. Most other souls cannot measure up when it comes to strong leadership and a focused drive to succeed. Great success can be achieved in careers that reward tenacity and an unyielding drive to overcome. Doctors, surgeons, scientists, investigators, researchers, and sales/investment executives can all benefit from this determined pattern.

If the Leo/Scorpio Combination of energy gets out of balance, romantic passion can take over and shut out any other aspirations in life. The emotional influence can become quite obsessive and overpower the Moon in Leo's bright positive outlook. If these intense passionate feelings are not managed and become displaced, there is a danger that seduction and sensationalism will take tremendous hold and derail the main focus of this life. This fixed energy can also become severely obstinate and demanding if there are no other planetary patterns to soften this unyielding nature. Unfortunately Leo can make some bad choices out of stubborn pride, and Scorpio will not allow this soul to admit they may be wrong. It is better to give this soul an alternative solution or behavior option rather than to expect them to admit outright that they are wrong.

The soul lesson of the Moon in Leo and Sun in Scorpio is to manage the powerful focus and determination that this soul has from the time of birth. Staying on track without digging into a deep rut is the mission. Once this soul becomes clear about their destiny and career path they will dig in and press onward without any need for supervision.

Keep moving, Leo Moon and Scorpio Sun, in a smooth steady flow of divine energy toward combining your Fire and Water energies in a creative fashion to become a regal, focused, capable, perceptive leader who has control of their personal ego-need to take over and take charge.

Sun in Sagittarius (Fire) with Moon in Leo (Fire)

"From a strong-willed, creative child
to an adventuresome, risk-taking traveler."

When the Moon is in Leo and the Sun is in Sagittarius, the high-spirited Fire element creates the major focus for the soul growth in the lifetime. Since the Fire element represents positive, masculine energy reaching out in a spiritual spontaneity to create movement and action, there will be a whole life journey of excitement for the soul. In the Full Moon phase, relationship is the focus for this combination.

This child carries a passion for life that is contagious when it is activated by honorable ambitions that carry it toward a spiritual, intuitive awareness of the people who come into their life path. These souls deliver a contagious joy and excitement for life that is priceless to other souls who act as receivers. Their open, honest demeanor can warm people's hearts or shock them if there is too much direct honesty. However, when the Leo Moon child gets rooted in their pride and a fear of growing up, they can become withdrawn and defensive. Dramatic creativity can take several channels of manifestation when young and continue as they mature.

The natural flow of Fire energy rushes out to take action. When it has strong direction, this soul develops relationships that bring high admiration, respect, and dignity. When the Jupiter-ruled Sagittarius energy is added to the Leo Moon, easy growth occurs along with a sense of being the master of one's own fate. The Leo/Sagittarius combination loves to play and be creative with their expanded imagination. These gifts allow them to become successful in careers that involve charming people. Because of a dynamic charisma, these souls have the natural ability to woo the public with their insightful perceptions. They are incredibly astute, quick, and alert. Any profession that involves leadership will be attractive to their fiery nature.

If the Leo/Sagittarius combination of energy gets out of balance, this feisty Fire element can burn those who get too close. They can become too blunt, too direct, and too brutally honest for their own good. Their dramatic nature can cause problems if the imagination gets carried away. The youthful Leo Moon energy can procrastinate but when they commit they usually follow through. Sagittarius, on the other hand, vacillates in their interests, so they may get bored and go in a different direction. The "going" may be figurative or literal because this Jupiter-ruled energy loves adventure and travel. If the Sagittarius wonder-lust activates however, this soul could take off on an adventure that keeps them in a childlike state to avoid the responsibilities of adulthood.

The soul lesson of the Moon in Leo and Sun in Sagittarius is to direct their high physical and intellectual forces into becoming successful in society's eyes. Love relations may come and go in their life until they decide that they are willing to commit and settle down. It is a reality that Sagittarius is slow to give up their sense of freedom. Once committed, there is no more loyal combination than this fun-loving soul.

Keep moving, Leo Moon and Sagittarius Sun, in a smooth steady flow of divine energy toward the finer attunement of the highly spiritual Fire element to become recognized as a powerful visionary leader in our society.

Sun in Capricorn (Earth) with Moon in Leo (Fire)

"From a strong-willed, creative child to a responsible initiating entrepreneur."

When the Moon is in Leo and the Sun is in Capricorn, the energy flow needs to go from the spiritual, energetic Fire element toward the practical, grounded Earth element. The waning phase of the Moon to the Sun calls for the soul to make a conscious effort to integrate the personality within relationships.

In youth, the movement by Leo is consistent and deliberate while the Capricorn energy takes on an aggressive, initiating force. The early years bring a love of romance, fun, and excitement until that Earth energy begins to override with an ambitious drive to be the achiever. There is a strong ability for this soul to make friends among powerful and influential individuals even in the younger years.

As the Saturn-ruled Capricorn energy develops, this soul has the potential to occupy a prominent position that has the rewards of dignity and authority. Because both Leo and Capricorn energies enjoy the very best quality in all things, these souls are drawn to situations that will benefit them financially in marriage and business partnerships. Their generosity and warm-heartedness may allow them to share their monetary victories with people less fortunate. Children's charities hold a special place in the heart of this philanthropist. The incredible drive to succeed always pushes this soul to accumulate money, so it is best for all when they are recognized for their generosity.

If the Leo/Capricorn combination of energy gets out of balance, there can be major conflicts that include bossiness and power struggles. The childish Leo Moon can roar and become very demanding. Then when the earthy determination of Capricorn is added to the soul mix, a master intimidator can develop. The Saturn-ruled Capricorn can go to their cold, practical thinking process that creates an aloof attitude that can chill the challengers' bones. Materialism can take over if their need to help humanity gets pushed aside.

The soul lesson of the Moon in Leo and Sun in Capricorn is to channel their need for control into positive arenas. Timing remains a major test for this soul as Leo has a natural urge to procrastinate while Capricorn must learn to use time wisely. This energy combination must learn to focus so that they work when they work and play when they play. Relaxation, sleep, and rest are lessons that do not come easily to this one. In the well-developed soul, there can be a machine-like precision that people consider to be a mark of heart-warming dedication.

Keep moving, Leo Moon and Capricorn Sun, in a smooth steady flow of divine energy toward a refinement of the human ego in relationships as it becomes tested in the world arena of business and material success.

Sun in Aquarius (Air) with Moon in Leo (Fire)

*"From a strong-willed, creative child
to a strong, social group leader."*

When the Moon is in Leo and the Sun is in Aquarius, the Leo Fire element blends easily with the Aquarius Air element to direct a strong feisty energy flow into a witty intellectual pattern. This combination appears extremely outgoing because of the positive, masculine nature of these elements. The Moon phase is Full in relation to the Sun which calls for a new conscious awareness of self, relative to other people. The Full Moon phase always makes relationship the main learning field.

There is an integration of energy through interaction required for soul growth here. This means that the soul must learn how to participate and share in partnerships of all kinds. The Sun-ruled Moon brings animated, creative talents into the growing up period making the childhood active and dramatic. As the mental need for challenge expands, this Uranus-ruled Aquarian becomes even more social with an attraction to people who are unique and very individualistic.

Both Leo and Aquarius love a stage where they can entertain and show their witty leadership style. Warmth, charm, and a lively imagination make this soul able to achieve great things if they can settle down and focus on the goal. Even though there is substantial fixed thinking and stubbornness here, a progressive attitude allows them to stay open to new ideas and ways of being. They can use their talents in careers such as organizational management and sales leadership. Their strong people skills make them good in any group.

If the Leo/Aquarius combination of energy gets out of balance, an unyielding stubbornness can block any new thinking. When the pride of the Leo Moon feels challenged there can be an incredible fiery drama that is difficult to calm down. The other side of this determined combination brings an aloof, detached attitude of disinterest when wounded. Aquarius can drop back and do their own thing quicker than any other sign. An intellectual superiority complex can rise up when their authority is questioned. It is safer to be a friend than a family member with this person because friends and social life come first.

The soul lesson of the Moon in Leo and Sun in Aquarius is to maintain a stable life plan while allowing new ideas and creative visions to flourish. There is a gift in allowing this Sunny disposition and generous nature to shine. The goal is to find a place in high leadership where strong confidence will be appreciated and rewarded.

Keep moving, Leo Moon and Aquarius Sun, in a smooth steady flow of divine energy toward expanding a highly developed creativity in humanitarian ways to serve the greater population through small and large groups.

Sun in Pisces (Water) with Moon in Leo (Fire)

*"From a strong-willed, creative child
to a compassionate, visionary server."*

When the Moon is in Leo and the Sun is in Pisces, the energy flows from the Fire to the Water element in an urge to calm the soul. This highly energetic nature needs spiritual training and focus, so the sensitivity can emerge. The inner and outer forces of the soul are pulling against each other because of the nature of Leo and Pisces. Masculine outgoing Fire energy struggles with the receptive flow of feminine Water patterns. The Moon's soul energy is still functioning from an instinctual, unconscious Gibbous Moon phase, placing their behavior in the pattern of the student or disciple.

Since the soul arrives into this life with the power of Leo energy, growth demands a tempering by the nature of Sun which is now placed in an emotional water sign. When these Fire and Water elements work in harmony, powerful steam can be generated which can create an incredible moving force. Leo Moon exudes a strong, determined will in youth while the Pisces Sun strives to become more sensitive to the needs and wants of others.

Throughout the lifetime, the soul's ambitious drive feels suffocated by its own highly sensitive emotional reactions to others. This combination may experience life as "I can dish it out, but I can't take it". The subtle visionary creative forces of Pisces express most often through music and art. When these two expansive energies combine, there is a natural foundation for writing movies, plays, poetry and music. Many successful Hollywood and Broadway stars and authors have these qualities to access in their soul toolbox.

If the Leo/Pisces combination of energy gets out balance, defensiveness and victimization can occur. The Sun's nature is to shine and be seen. However, if the heat of the solar focus becomes too intense, it has a tendency to scorch or burn anything or anybody that is too close. The difficult side of this combination occurs when the person's watery Neptune Pisces overreacts to any fiery response from other people. The confident, outgoing Sunny child loves to perform but does not like to be critiqued or challenged. This particular growth pattern requires that the soul make adjustments in its confident, outward expression to allow for the spiritual, intuitive powers to develop and manifest. If this shift does not occur, the soul may appear overbearing and unwilling to face the fire "in the kitchen" which they created.

The soul lesson of the Moon in Leo and Sun in Pisces is to learn to step back and tune into their intuitive senses to understand a situation before jumping in and taking charge. A highly developed expressive, creative ability lies within the Leo soul that can be built upon when the Pisces Sun is vibrating at its highest pitch. At the core of the Pisces Sun sign is the need to serve and sacrifice for the higher good of all. Showing compassion for the less fortunate will continue to come up as a test for the ego of the Leo Moon throughout the life. These souls are vibrating at their highest when they are using their dynamic strength to defend or support a universal cause that benefits the masses.

Keep moving, Leo Moon and Pisces Sun, in a smooth steady flow of divine energy toward using those leadership qualities to organize and lead the charge in activities that will help others who are struggling or unable to advocate for themselves.

Moon in Virgo

Moon in Virgo (with all signs)

Each chapter begins with a description of the Moon's purpose for those readers who will want to go straight to a specific Moon/Sun combination.

Imagine a giant mirror reflecting past actions and experiences. According to mythology, the sign that the Moon was in at the time of your birth explains your soul response's in this lifetime. Understanding how the Moon's energy impacts your behavior and emotional reactions is key to understanding your hidden soul pattern and personal timing. You are the center of your own universe and the creator of your own destiny, so you need to understand your gifts and future goals. The eternal questions of the soul are: "Where have I come from?" and "Where am I going?" The most important eternal question, of course, is "Why am I here?"

Moon in Virgo (Earth)

The energy of Virgo comes from the Earth element, known for methodically grounding emotional responses. Virgo it can act shy and reserved. When this infant enters our world, she will usually choose a family that is analytical and unemotional.

The Virgo infant Moon will not be a demanding child who needs constant attention. This child is cautious and hesitant. The only time this little one becomes visibly cranky and irritated is when a diaper change is needed; this child does not enjoy being dirty.

Educational achievement is important to this self-conscious young person, because they doubt their own abilities. In school, this shy Virgo Moon child may not speak up even when she knows the correct answer. If encouraged, her diligence, attention to detail, and honesty can help her become the best student in the class.

Give this Virgo Moon projects to organize in her own methodical way to build self-confidence. For fun, let Virgo Moon assemble and disassemble toys, radios, and games. The exercise will help develop her manual dexterity.

Virgo always appears proper in public until they become comfortable in their surroundings. In the family setting, they can be quite a chatterbox, but are usually not outgoing around strangers. Once she becomes more familiar with you, her Mercury need to talk will draw her out.

As the Virgo Moon young adult begins to mature, it will become clear that she is gifted at analytical tasks; she will naturally excel at accounting, engineering, or drafting. She never wants to give up her neat and tidy appearance because her earthy colors will always need to match. She will never lose that critical eye for detail.

Even though this precise Virgo can be critical and nit-picky with others, she cannot handle the same criticism herself, so be careful how you approach any flaws in her armor. She will shut down and become defensive very quickly. Hopefully, they become less critical as they mature.

The goal of Virgo Moon is to use their natural analytical ability to organize and structure groups of people and information. They have a natural talent for understanding the characters in a situation. Once they understand what they are supposed to do, they are quite gifted workers.

Sun in Aries (Fire) with Moon in Virgo (Earth)

"From a shy, hesitant child
to a fiery, brave warrior."

When the Moon is in Virgo and the Sun is in Aries, a need to blend the Earth and Fire elements calls for a focus on initiating. The flexible Virgo Moon energy gets caught up in multiple projects and doesn't finish any of them. One of their greatest lessons here is to take action and get it done. The Moon phase is not yet full, so the soul's unconscious instinct is to be the student, still in a position of learning and self-evaluation.

Young earthy, grounded Virgo acts from instinct and waits to respond to stimuli instead of reaching out like the Fire signs do. A natural need to do good for society begins to grow as they begin to mature. Their awareness begins to extend outward beyond self. The symbol of the puritan virgin describes a natural shyness in this youth that grows into strong discrimination with soul maturity. With the planet Mercury, ruler of Virgo, strong in the early life, this youth may over-think, over-process, and over-analyze.

Maturity brings out a strong need for self-direction. The Aries urge for action creates a tug-of-war within this fiery rebel who also has an incessant need to review every detail. As this impulsive Mars-ruled Aries soul gains freedom, a deep conflict develops between definitive action and the need to process slowly. This conflicting energetic dilemma continues to haunt the Virgo/Aries combination throughout their life.

If the Virgo/Aries combination of very different energy gets out of balance, an internal struggle occurs. Virgo's need for critical analysis resists the push of Mars to take action. This person feels torn between doing the project "right" and just "getting it done". The naturally practical, scientific mind becomes stuck in detail when forced to respond. Mars aggressiveness comes flying forward when this person feels questioned. They pride themselves on doing things right the first time and can be critical of those who do not do the same. Because this soul has a quick-response system and a scientific mind that works more efficiently than most, they must guard against a "holier than thou" attitude which makes them sound judgmental. They must also guard against becoming impatient with others who do not mentally process quickly. This person may become their own boss or create a situation where they are in charge of their projects and time. They function well in a subordinate position as long as they have freedom to operate independently.

The soul lesson of the Moon in Virgo and Sun in Aries is to use their fine critical, scientific thinking skills in a way that allows them to work independently. Strong educational and intellectual training is needed to harness all of this knowledge and put it to use.

Keep moving, Virgo Moon and Aries Sun, in a smooth steady flow of divine energy toward developing that strong personal drive by applying those sharp mental, critical thinking skills that were brought forward from past experience.

Sun in Taurus (Earth) with Moon in Virgo (Earth)

"From a shy, hesitant child
to a practical, purposeful leader."

When the Moon in Virgo and the Sun in Taurus, strong emphasis is on the Earth element which is feminine and receptive by nature. This element calls for grounding and practical application of the intellectual processes. Since security ranks high on the personal needs list, there is a strong soul push to work hard and make money. The waxing Moon phase between the Sun and Moon makes the need for consistency unconscious. This instinct pushes the soul out into the work world early.

The Virgo Moon energy will always push this soul to continue to learn in a very analytical fashion. An uncanny instinctual knowledge of how things work seems embedded in their memory. As this little shy child begins to grow up, an easy Taurus charm and grace help them in social situations, so they naturally know how to handle themselves. A conscientious and health-conscious attitude from early childhood helps to keep the Taurus Bull from becoming too lazy and over-indulgent.

Money and possessions should come easily because of a natural work ethic. Since this is not a competitive energy, maintaining the status quo and not challenging people seems to work best. The combination of the planets Mercury and Venus, as ruling planets, gives this person a natural ability to communicate and write smoothly as well as having a well-developed speaking voice. These talents make it easy to have a career where speaking and writing well will be rewarded. Security and financial freedom become more important with maturity, so this soul needs to prepare for the future and invest as they go. If Taurus has not prepared for their own retirement then they will usually attach to someone who has had this foresight.

If the Virgo/Taurus combination of energy gets out of balance, inertia may set in. It is always dangerous for the Virgo Moon to get caught up in details and perfection which keeps them from finishing anything. Since Taurus is also Earth energy, it too can get into a pattern of plodding along in slow motion without a drive to complete the task in a timely manner. Taurus definitely has the tenacity to finish what it starts but not quickly. The Taurus Bull moves methodically through the process and can become quite literal in analysis. The Earth element has a need for everything to work perfectly, and life does not always work that way. This combination really needs to avoid getting into a rut or becoming too comfortable with the status quo.

The soul lesson of the Moon in Virgo and Sun in Taurus is to use their strong mental processing skills to allow this Venus ruled Taurus to find a comfortable niche to express harmoniously. Being non-combative by nature, this soul's urge is to expand its spiritual energy without being forced or challenged.

Keep moving, Virgo Moon and Taurus Sun, in a smooth steady flow of divine energy toward using Mercury's quick summation of each situation to easily allow yourself to blend comfortably into any lifestyle that provides beauty, quality, and comfort in your adult years.

Sun in Gemini (Air) with Moon in Virgo (Earth)

"From a shy, hesitant child
to a fast-paced, mentally quick achiever."

When the Moon in Virgo and the Sun in Gemini, the Earth element and the Air Element tend to challenge each other. There is an underlying unconscious Moon phase drive to break loose but this flexible energy struggles with decisions. With the Moon in a waxing phase of growth, the urge to pull away instinctually nudges the soul out into the world.

The young cautious Virgo soul over thinks its position and hesitates to make any moves. The shift from being analytical to being more social requires some deliberate control on the part of this Mercury-ruled thinker. One thing this Mercury child is not short on is ideas because they never stop asking questions and being curious. They are naturally particular about their own toys and belongings and take good care of anything that is theirs. One of the strongest messages to this soul is to stay flexible.

They must not become set on just one path in life because their intellectual probing will call them to jump from one learning experience to the next topic all the way through life. Romanticism might be colored here by the worship of the mind and a constant search for a mental affinity. This can be dangerous because this Mercury-ruled person may secretly consider themselves intellectually above their circle or their partner. Growing up creates an inner struggle because blockage builds up around being airily intellectually open and being Earthly conservative and cautious. Conflicting signals for Virgo/ Gemini around communications continue to follow this combination through the lifetime. When stimulated by good conversation, this sign becomes the world's most charismatic convincing sales person whose use of the language can mesmerize their listeners.

If the Virgo/Gemini combination of energy gets out of balance, the instinctive Virgo shyness will shut down any tendencies to over expose personal feelings and fears. Task energy can become very scattered and the urge is to over commit to projects which makes it even more difficult to bring planned action to completion. Too much focus on detail and critical analysis can derail the thought process. This soul does better with an organized plan and specific time line under stress conditions. Worry and anxiety are the worst enemies for this combination. They can totally withdraw when stress and complexity overwhelm them. The tendency here can be to become frustrated with too much activity and then to shut down all projects without completing any of them.

The soul lesson of the Moon in Virgo and Sun in Gemini is to contain the flexible mental energies of these two signs in an organized pattern so that the focus is aimed at a clear communication and training style. Since the Virgo Moon tends to hesitate and stand back when surrounded by a large group of people, Gemini needs to push forward into intellectual circles where their creative thinking skills will be applauded. Hiding in the shadows may make Gemini quite nervous which can cause the flexible Air sign to chatter busily without bringing their thoughts to any conclusion. It can become quite difficult to follow their thoughts which can jump from one topic to another.

Keep moving, Virgo Moon and Gemini Sun, in a flexible fashion so that new learning and new experiences can keep you excited and engaged in life's activities while you dazzle your intellectual friends with your smooth talk and winning smile.

Sun in Cancer (Water) with Moon in Virgo (Earth)

"From a shy, hesitant child to a nurturing, kind decision maker."

When the Moon is in Virgo and the Sun is in Cancer, the movement by element in this lifetime is from the Earth element to the Water element. Because both of these elements are feminine and receptive in nature, there is no internal conflict between feelings and purpose. The growth flow is experienced as easy and natural. The Moon phase is waxing, so the focus is on instinctive experiential learning by struggling with the fear of going out into the world alone.

This timid, cautious Moon child seldom reacts quickly or outwardly even though their restless nature nudges them to retreat and run in fear. There is a deep-seated worry that this child will not be accepted no matter how much others try to reassure them. When Mercury and the Moon work together, this soul is very receptive to psychic influences. However, the inborn analytical nature instinctively questions and often blocks the psychic flow.

The learning style is conscientious with a strong need for approval. This soul seeks a supportive, non-competitive environment in which to grow and work on confidence. Their conservative gentle behavior allows others to be soft and encouraging which usually insures their popularity. The Virgo's attention to detail and tidiness helps to make them great homemakers, parents, and career role models. When they are young, these people make great support staff for businesses who deal with the public. As they mature, business, management and leadership become natural pathways for their career. The strong critical thinking skills usually push this person into management out in the public eye in later years.

If the Virgo/Cancer combination of energy gets out of balance, Earthy, practical thinking can block the sensitive flowing side of Cancer.

Virgo's over-analyzing can hold this person in a state of worry where they struggle to move forward to complete any task. Their naturally cautious shadowy responses keep movement from occurring and that is when logic goes right out the window. Cancer must be careful not to overreact, sulk, and then retreat to their home base where they will begin to nervously clean. On the rare occasions when these negative defenses flare, just wait a couple of days until the powerful Moon changes signs. Then the mood will shift, so reason and sensitivity can return to this normally peaceful personality.

The soul lesson of the Moon in Virgo and Sun in Cancer is to use the detailed, analytical thought processes to support the strong leadership qualities of Cancer. There is a psychic sense of what people think, need and want which gives this person the power to use their authority wisely.

Keep moving, Virgo Moon and Cancer Sun, in a steady flow of divine energy toward building harmonious connection between a methodical, consistent work pattern and a warm, security-based home life where everyone feels welcome and comfortable.

Sun in Leo (Fire) with Moon in Virgo (Earth)

*"From a shy, hesitant child
to an outgoing, fast-paced leader."*

When the Moon is in Virgo and the Sun is in Leo, the energy flow is going from the feminine, receptive Earth element to the masculine, positive Fire element. The Moon phase places the Moon just in front of the Sun in an unconscious growth-oriented position, known as the waxing Moon.

The early childhood hesitation and shyness of Virgo does not last long under the strong presence of the Leo Sun sign. Since this Fire sign craves praise and attention, this combination should utilize their critical mental and analytical capabilities in an intellectual or business setting where there is recognition for every accomplishment.

The natural flow for this energy pattern is from the shadows of the worker to the front of the performer's stage. This individual grows from being a quiet critical thinker to a place of strong opinions. This internally insecure soul may appear confident and in command, but underneath there lies a hidden pride that could hold this energy back. This one belongs in a leadership position where their detailed organizational skills are an asset. Careers in management, politics or in sales is where they may thrive.

If the Virgo/Leo combination of energy gets out of balance, the analytical Earthy criticalness of the Moon could appear distant, aloof, or disinterested. There can be a restlessness and anxiousness that causes this person to retreat in an effort to hide their inferiority complex which may be rooted deep in the past life pattern of the Virgo Moon. There may also be a hidden Puritanical side to this charming romantic lover who only appears available. The Leo energy can become aggressive to hide their vulnerability and lack of confidence. In any stressful situation, this individual needs time to withdraw, regroup, and then present themselves anew within their own time frame. There is an old saying that warns never to corner a wounded Lion/Leo.

The soul lesson of the Moon in Virgo and Sun in Leo is to be able to grow from the clear thinking, methodical analyzer into a full-blown creative presenter who can use their mental tools to succeed. There will be a need to learn to excel, to shine, and to lead gracefully. It will be important to observe the dress of the most successful, so there can be a shift from tailored conservative colors to bright, bold colors and styles which better fit the Leo style. The Virgo Moon will always be concerned about the detail and the organization while the Sunny Leo will be much more concerned about the show and the final product.

Keep moving, Virgo Moon and Leo Sun, in a smooth steady flow of divine energy toward applying your practical, organizational sense to a growing artistic, dramatic capability to command and direct people in a responsible leadership role.

Sun in Virgo (Earth) with Moon in Virgo (Earth)

"From a shy, hesitant child to a grounded, analytical problem solver."

When both luminaries (Sun and Moon) fall in the same sign, the Moon phase may be either New or Balsamic in phase, and both of these call for much self-reflection and self-motivation with the keyword being "Self". With the Moon and Sun in Virgo together, the focus for the soul is to refine the element of Earth. The soul during this life journey is going toward the same energy that they came from which is to refine the practical mundane mental focus.

The Earth energy strives to ground the life activities in a structured, detailed process for the purpose of accomplishing accurate results. Being able to complete tasks is a challenge for this young child. As they mature, service projects allow this soul to experience success through their life work. Because this is a New Moon or Balsamic phase for the soul, they will experience life as an instinctual rushing out to meet the world with independence and self-reliance.

The planet Mercury dominates the person's priorities by stressing intellectual interests and people. When both luminaries reside within the same mutable sign, there is a tendency to be too methodical, too precise, and too self-contained. This hard worker continues to be one who is usually frugal and persevering throughout the life. She also maintains a strong sense of moral values based on tradition with a great respect for law and order. The nature is polite and well-bred which usually indicates good breeding from a strong family. They have the great gift of perceptive writing skills and smooth communication. This Virgo can publish, speak, and handle the budgets for the business community without any struggle.

If the Virgo/Virgo combination of double Earth energy gets out of balance, communications usually become defensive, critical, and often melancholy. They may experience difficulty expressing their clear thoughts because the mind becomes scattered. When their refined taste for people, food, dress, and proper etiquette is offended, they can become snobbish and critical of others' behavior. People who are boring or uneducated can really set off their sense of wanting to move on. This combination needs to avoid positions of top authority where there is a need for fast final decisions. Reasonableness and thoroughness act as a detriment in these positions. Mercury's indecisiveness could become blatantly obvious when out front, so be content to be the power behind the throne.

The soul lesson of the Moon and Sun in Virgo is to learn to harness the practical, efficient, accurate thinking process of Mercury. It is important to remain in a support role because Virgo energy thrives on change and variety. When this mutable sign gets stuck in a lead position, all of the flexibility disappears and so does the joy.

Keep moving, Virgo Moon and Sun, in a smooth steady flow of divine energy toward using your grounding talents to support those flamboyant leaders who come and go while the Virgo continues to serve and analyze from behind the scenes.

Sun in Libra (Air) with Moon in Virgo (Earth)

*"From a shy, hesitant child
to a quick-thinking, social mediator."*

When the Moon is in Virgo and the Sun is in Libra, the energy flow is going from the feminine Earth element to the positive, masculine Air element. The Moon phase places the Moon behind the Sun in a waning Balsamic position which calls for the soul to complete relationships and experiences throughout life.

Because the young child energy in this combination behaves in a shy and conservative manner, relationships are difficult and strained. In early school, this Virgo excels at problem-solving and analytical processes with a strong emphasis on critical thinking. However, on the playground, this cautious soul tends to hold back and remain on the sidelines or in the shadows of activity.

Social graces show up as this soul begins to mature. Then Libra's charm flows out at all of the appropriate times even though the inner child is still hesitant and lacking in confidence. Venus, the ruler of Libra, attracts money while Mercury, the ruler of Virgo, adds a practical sense to manage it conservatively, so success is promised. This Mercury-Venus blend provides a natural talent for an eloquent communication style. There is a natural abundance of artistic mental energies that can be developed into creative writing skills and dramatic speech talents. These gifts should be used and expanded into strong negotiation skills in the business world.

If the Virgo/Libra combination of energy gets out of balance, this soul can be critical and detached. A shift occurs because Libra naturally falls in love with the idea of love. Then since there is little emotion attached to their relationships, it is easy for this one to become analytical over love difficulties and retreat into work projects. Health issues can manifest if the emotional tension builds too high because

Virgos are known for having hypochondriac tendencies. These Venus people do not like to be alone, so they will eventually compromise and talk the problems through to maintain the partnership. The hidden insecurities may push this combination into being too much of a people pleaser.

The soul lesson of the Moon in Virgo and Sun in Libra is to sustain a positive expression without becoming over compliant to others. It is important for the shy Virgo to persevere long enough in relationship to build a deep, long lasting commitment.

Keep moving, Virgo Moon and Libra Sun, in a smooth steady flow of divine energy toward using all of your creative mental cleverness in the gift of smooth convincing speech with an analytical twist.

Sun in Scorpio (Water) with Moon in Virgo (Earth)

"From a shy, hesitant child
to a determined, focused researcher."

When the Moon is in Virgo and the Sun is in Scorpio, the movement from the feminine Earth element to the feminine Water element flows gently without resistance. The yin feminine force has a grounded energy with a soft receptive feeling. The Moon phase pattern is also a waning completing energy, so the overall theme for this combination expresses deep mental and emotional perception.

During the youthful years, Mercury-ruled Virgo creates a shy, cautious, serious little person who appears older than her years. This child may be found during recess periods in the science room instead of out on the playground with the other children. Virgo's flexibility begins to stabilize during the teenage years as Scorpio's fixity begins to take action.

As the soul gets older, determination and focus harness the scattered mental energy, so the young adult sees the path to success clearly. The instinct of this soul is to gather information, analyze it, and then apply the knowledge using organized and aggressive research methods. The planets Mercury and Mars working together create a strong quick-response mental ability and communication style. If the water element of Scorpio is properly developed, this soul can tap deeper levels of consciousness. A strong mental aptitude combined with an intense drive to succeed can bring success or destruction in their career. The developed critical thinking skills can lead to great success in the literary arts or they can be directed toward medicine and science. Whether the energy supports a doctor or a chemist, there is a natural talent around scientific discovery.

If the Virgo/Scorpio combination of energy gets out of balance, an over-critical, compulsive attitude can develop that holds people at a distance. The inner feminine quality here can make this person a recluse who hides in the privacy of their own mind. This can be the most critical of all of the Virgo Moon combinations, so the soul must guard against becoming sarcastic and bitter in speech. The Mercury Mars blend may turn on itself and become severely self-critical due to an innate desire for an unattainable perfection. Knowing oneself is helpful with this combination, so they can guard against the urge to sever long-term relationships when they experience hurt feelings.

The soul lesson of the Moon in Virgo and Sun in Scorpio is to direct the powerful force and determination of Scorpio by using the practical, literal, processing mind of Virgo to analyze data and focus on high goals. Staying on track and not getting caught in the details will stress the Virgo need for thoroughness.

Keep moving, Virgo Moon and Scorpio Sun, in a smooth steady flow of divine energy toward combining your Earth and Water energies into a grounded and receptive approach to the people and experiences in your life. Use your depth and perception wisely.

Sun in Sagittarius (Fire) with Moon in Virgo (Earth)

"From a shy, hesitant child
to an adventuresome, risk-taking seeker."

When the Moon is in Virgo and the Sun is in Sagittarius, the energy movement goes from the receptive feminine Earth element to the outgoing masculine Fire element. It requires a shift from a grounded realistic attitude to a much lighter, freer, positive approach. The waning Moon phase brings forth a conscious awareness of the need to strip away old limiting patterns and move forward into higher philosophies and expansive thinking.

The Virgo child begins life as a shy hesitant soul who prefers to stand behind their parents in the shadows. As Jupiter, the ruling planet of Sagittarius, arrives on the scene, the personality becomes much more direct and merry. Everyone loves the open-minded, fast-thinking energy of the Archer.

As they mature, hopefully, Earth will stabilize Fire, so the Sagittarian's warm, open, generous disposition can freely flow out into the world. Virgo's analytical process should help ground the fast changing moods of the Fire spirit. However, both or these signs are flexible, so it may be difficult to stay on track. Using the intuition with a strong power of language gives a clear intellectual ability that can be applied to literature, law, the ministry, and higher education. It would be a natural flow to hold a position of public appointment sometime during life.

If the Virgo/Sagittarius combination of energy gets out of balance, major stabilizing forces are needed. The inhibited emotional responses of the Moon block the outgoing frivolity of the Sun creating a waffling effect between caution and sullenness to giddiness and direct speech. There can be great difficulty staying on track or completing one's commitments. If Mars and Mercury are acting at odds, there can be a sharp tongue with critical attacks as well as some bitter honesty. The need for tolerance and patience are definitely on the list of assignments for this lifetime.

The soul lesson of the Moon in Virgo and Sun in Sagittarius is to stay on track to complete all of the projects they begin. There is a shift in thinking that is required from grounded, factual to spontaneous, risk taking. On the growth side, the fiery energy loves to learn and study new subjects, so they will be quite willing to give up old behaviors.

Keep moving, Virgo Moon and Sagittarius Sun, in a smooth steady flow of divine energy by allowing the changeable nature of the Sun and Moon to focus on multi-tasking styles that encourage growth and openness.

Sun in Capricorn (Earth) with Moon in Virgo (Earth)

"From a shy, hesitant child
to a responsible, initiating engineer."

When the Moon is in Virgo and the Sun is in Capricorn, the Earth element maintains its powerful position in the life purpose. The critical and analytical capabilities of Virgo are softened by the contemplative seriousness of Capricorn. Because of the waning phase of the Moon, the innate drive to share knowledge is very conscious and deliberate.

Even within the reticent tendencies of Virgo, there is a blending with the Earth element that feels easy because it is not the destiny of this young child to experience internal struggle during this lifetime. This combination can be known for being old when they are young and young when they are old.

The goal is to manifest success, worldly accomplishments and visible results. Since this Virgo is the most critical thinker of the zodiac, business acts as the most natural medium for growth. Earth energy provides a grounded, solid, take charge attitude that leads the soul to acquire fame and control. This is the sign combination of "the Boss".

If the Virgo/Capricorn combination of double Earth energy gets out of balance, there can be narrow-minded thinking and an obsession with detail. A strong exterior presence may be hiding a high level of timidity. Under stress, this grounded Earth person may become too literal in their analytical reasoning when their security is being threatened. The temptation is to become grounded in practical outcomes which holds back feelings of happiness and gaiety. The Capricorn goat must resist using intimidation and a disapproving attitude to maintain control in personal interactions. Even though Earth can become dry and hard, it can also become muddy and unclear when too much emotion is thrown into the mix.

The soul lesson of the Moon in Virgo and Sun in Capricorn is use their practical mental faculties to stay on track and then take charge of completing major projects with a critical eye to detail and an appearance of authority. Being organized and following through with plans will utilize Capricorn's great managerial skills. There is a natural talent here for staying calm, cool, and collected while the person takes charge and learns to delegate the details to others.

Keep moving, Virgo Moon and Capricorn Sun, in a smooth steady flow of divine energy that will take advantage of all of the orderly, reliable, and responsible traits that are part of this soul pattern.

Sun in Aquarius (Air) with Moon in Virgo (Earth)

"From a shy, hesitant child
to a strong, confident, social group leader."

When the Moon is in Virgo and the Sun is in Aquarius, the energy flow struggles to go from the receptive slow-moving Earth element to the light, social Air element. It is not easy for the Virgo energy to transition from a flexible multi-tasking style to a fixed, structured long-range plan. In a waning Moon phase, the soul is consciously working on balancing out of balance relationship energy in a very practical manner.

The Virgo child often appears shy and serious in social settings but while young they already have the ability to detach and observe the surroundings. They are careful, reserved, and slow to warm up to new situations. This young one will be slow to make friends.

There is a natural ability for this native to reason problems out by using their strong mind power and ability to remove themselves from personal considerations. The love life may suffer from an instinctive urge to be cautious and undemonstrative with affections. Too much analysis and reason can get in the way of the rare moments of spontaneous affection. If there is an opportunity for good education, a natural writing and speech talent can be used in an intellectual and professional career. Within the organization, the Virgo Aquarius energy can add thoroughness and detailed accuracy to the business structure. In the mature years, the Air element can bring a strong set of social skills into organizational leadership positions.

If the Virgo/Aquarius combination of energy gets out of balance, self-doubt and gloomy thoughts can hold back the urge for intellectual accomplishments. The precise, critical faculties will slow down any creative innovative thought processes. Getting stuck in critical fact finding can overshadow the airy intuitive, progressive thinking.

This can all lead to a hasty impatience and poor listening skills. A person on the receiving end of this relationship could experience it as undemonstrative and detached. There needs to be a conscious effort to show affection, concern and interest on a personal level with this combination of conflicting elements.

The soul lesson of the Moon in Virgo and Sun in Aquarius is to develop a healthy sense of prudence, practicality, and a love of science and intellectual pursuits. The combination prospers best when in association with others who would provide the initiative or enterprising drive.

Keep moving, Virgo Moon and Aquarius Sun, in a smooth steady flow of divine energy that will utilize an abundance of mental gifts and innovative skills.

Sun in Pisces (Water) with Moon in Virgo (Earth)

"From a shy, hesitant child
to a compassionate, visionary server."

When the Moon is in Virgo and the Sun is in Pisces, the energy flows from the receptive Earth element to the receptive Water element. Since both of these energies are feminine in nature, the transition of growth feels easy with no inner-conflict. Earthy Virgo has a cautious, reserved sense and hesitates to make final decisions. In a complementary balance, Pisces also has that same caution and hesitancy around decision-making. The waning full Moon phase causes a very conscious awareness that there is a push/pull energy in relationships for the combination. These opposing Sun Moon positions create an emotional stress around the give and take in partnering.

When critical thinking Mercury-ruled Virgo is young the child tends to trust factual information and reject the sensing side of Pisces. Instinctive caution and fear can push this soul to hold back any show of vulnerability. Trying new things will be challenging for this one until they begin to trust their sensing side as they grow older.

As Pisces develops in later years, the intuitive, psychic perception get stronger and stronger. Career choices need to involve service and compassionate interactions. This worker is capable of both visionary style and detailed facts. With a strong educational background, this native is capable of great contributions to the world through literature, legal, or medical professions. These contributions would be done in a quiet way without great fanfare and many times without great financial reward.

If the Virgo/Pisces combination of energy gets out of balance, naivety, gullibility, and wishy-washiness can set in. A natural hesitation comes from the mutable, flexible energy of both signs and can push this soul back into the shadows. Fear of criticism also can halt the forward movement for Virgo Pisces. These two signs are pulled toward service and sacrifice for mankind. As long as idealism does not over-magnify the cause, they can be givers without becoming victims and martyrs.

The soul lesson of the Moon in Virgo and Sun in Pisces is to allow the acute mental capabilities of Virgo to bring discernment while the psychic sensitivity of Pisces works with a trust from within. These strengths blended together can become quite inspirational.

Keep moving, Virgo Moon and Pisces Sun, in a smooth steady flow of divine energy toward using this spiritual energy at its highest expression which is service and sacrifice for the highest good of all.

Moon in Libra

Moon in Libra (with all signs)

Each chapter begins with a description of the Moon's purpose for those readers who will want to go straight to a specific Moon/Sun combination.

Imagine a giant mirror reflecting past actions and experiences. According to mythology, the sign that the Moon was in at the time of your birth explains your soul responses in this lifetime. Understanding how the Moon's energy impacts your behavior and emotional reactions is key to understanding your hidden soul pattern and personal timing. You are the center of your own universe and the creator of your own destiny, so you need to understand your gifts and future goals. The eternal questions of the soul are: "Where have I come from?" and "Where am I going?" The most important eternal question, of course, is "Why am I here?"

Moon in Libra (Air)

The energy of Libra comes from the Air element, known to need a large amount of interaction and social exposure. This soul would rather sleep in the middle of a crowd than to be left in a quiet room alone as he prefers to be where the action is. The Libra infant loves to be talked to and held.

The Libra Moon symbol is the scales, so making decisions is not an easy task—even in simple situations such as which food to eat first. This Venus-ruled child does not like loud noises; don't worry, he will not scream and yell for long.

A word of warning about feeding this Libra: the fewer choices you give this indecisive tot the easier life will be for everyone. Make it simple; walk him through the eating and dressing process one step at a time. If you try to rush him, he will give up altogether because he does not want to displease you, but he also does not know what he wants.

The Air signs tend to be quick learners and bright students. This Libra Moon child seldom causes problems at school and doesn't like getting in trouble. His people-pleasing nature makes him eager to help the teacher and fellow students. If he gets in trouble at school, it is usually for talking too much and for being too social. Venus Moon people do not care much for physical labor; they do better in professional fields. So education is vitally important.

As this Libra Moon child begins to grow up, he may not be the first one to stand up and fight for a principle because he does not like confrontation. As an unofficial social organizer, his social groups are very important. He has the ability to see both sides of a situation which is a real asset.

The Libra Moon teenager has a tendency to spend way too much time socializing; it's possible for him to spend all day looking at a cell phone. He is incredibly sensitive to peer pressure, and may take on more activities than he can handle. He really wants romantic relationships and friendships, and may stay in relationships that are not healthy for them rather than be alone. Balance is the key for this maturing Air sign.

The goal of Libra Moon is to use his balancing ability to keep that pleasant, peacekeeping, social side visible to the world. Since he is apt to want to be all things to all people, becoming the social leader in his many groups will allow him to develop into the natural leader he is meant to be.

Sun in Aries (Fire) with Moon in Libra (Air)

*"From a social, people-pleasing child
to a fiery, independent leader."*

When the Moon is in Libra and the Sun is in Aries, there is a natural energy flow is from the masculine, positive Air element to the masculine positive Fire element. Initiating action and forward movement keeps this independent element on track. This Full Moon phase puts relationship issues in full view. There is a natural paradox here between wanting to be liked and accepted and the opposite position of being totally self-reliant and independent. One side of this seesaw wants constant companionship while the other side wants the freedom to go and do without waiting for anyone else. This is a powerful combination because the air of the Libra Moon feeds the flame of the Aries Sun.

The little peacemaker Libra child who strives to keep all situations harmonious does so because they do not like confrontation or disapproval, particularly in friendships. Social acceptance is behind most of their gentle, sweet, polite mannerisms. As this active combination grows up, there will be less focus on what makes others happy and more attention to what makes Aries happy.

One of the greatest tests for this Full Moon phase is finding a comfortable balance in personal relationships. Both sides of this combination love new experiences, so as the Mars nature of Aries gets stronger in adulthood, the entrepreneurial spirit continues to get stronger. This soul should move towards a career that involves people, new experiences, and lots of freedom. Owning a store or running a sales territory would give this individual the perfect opportunity to be in charge of their own time and their own space.

If the Libra/Aries combination of energy gets out of balance, an idealistic innocence may surface that makes the Venus Moon nature want to yield to the will of others to avoid conflict and disharmony. The polite polish of Libra may be a fooler because when it gets down to the bottom line, the fiery Aries warrior will step up with an aggressive stand to challenge any adversaries. Once the Mars energy flashes out, relationships can burn up quickly. Both Libra and Aries love the early exchange in partnering but get bored with long-term interaction. For this combination to remain in a permanent partnership, it would require another person with similar needs for new exchange, action, and interests in sports and art. However, in the end, Libra Moon does not want to live alone, so they will always keep searching for that perfect exciting mate.

The soul lesson of the Moon in Libra and Sun in Aries is to put forth the effort to blend and bond the already compatible Air and Fire energies into a fast-moving, dynamic lifetime. This soul needs to allow their bravery to lead them into entrepreneurial situations where they can use their well developed negotiating skills to create success.

Keep moving, Libra Moon and Aries Sun, in a smooth steady flow of divine energy toward blending that smooth polite demeanor with the Martian fighting energy to create a pioneering, charismatic leader who is willing to step out and take the risks on the front line of life.

Sun in Taurus (Earth) with Moon in Libra (Air)

"From a social, people-pleasing child
to a practical, purposeful leader."

When Moon is in Libra and the Sun is in Taurus, the soul growth energy is moving from the masculine Air element to the feminine Earth element. This shift creates stress because these two elements do not naturally bond and blend. Because the Moon is in the waxing phase, it is working at gathering information to understand the principles of grounding action.

It takes mental awareness to gracefully come from movement-oriented Libra to grounded, stable Taurus. The goal is to develop consistency and security. Beloved lady Venus blesses the temperament of this individual throughout the life. Friendships and social activities will be high on his young ones priority list. Making everyone feel comfortable and included is the name of this your Libras game.

This soul struggles with environments that are not pleasing, such as loud music, loud voices, and unpleasant surroundings. Because this person works at being attractive and charming, there are usually plenty of opportunities for relationships; however, these partners may come and go while Venus looks for that perfect situation. Relationships, love, comfort, security, harmony and balance remain the focus for both goddess signs. When these two energies are combined harmoniously as only lady Venus can do, the individual is capable of great success and comfort in their later years. Libra and Taurus also bring out the ability to make money as well as the ability to manage it. Caution is needed here because too much comfort could get this luxury-lover hooked on the "good life".

If the Libra/Taurus combination of energy gets out of balance, all of the luxury patterns of rich living could cause problems. History proves that too much of any good thing ceases to be good. Whether the obsession is with food, art objects, clothes, or beautiful people, it can spoil the balance in one's life. Venus-ruled people need to be cautious with starches and sweets because it appears that the body does not process them well. So they must guard against storing away both calories and money for a "rainy day". Because this soul is so attached to comfort and harmony, they must guard against telling people what they want to hear to avoid that discomfort of confrontation. Taurus finds it very difficult to give up their comforts, so they dig in their bullish heels and refuse to yield. Stubbornness is not a particularly attractive trait for this earth element to get stuck with.

The soul lesson of the Moon in Libra and Sun in Taurus is to adjust the use of that strong Venus energy toward a lifestyle that supports beauty in all forms. Growth for this combination includes stability in the home life as well as in relationships. It is not hard to attract new friends and partners, but sustaining long-term connections requires deeper commitment. There may be a tendency to be too sweet and agreeable in situations where being direct might be more appropriate.

Keep moving, Libra Moon and Taurus Sun, in a smooth steady flow of divine energy to retain that loving, affectionate disposition while learning to maintain loving, meaningful relationships.

Sun in Gemini (Air) with Moon in Libra (Air)

"From a social, people-pleasing child
to a fast-paced, mentally-quick achiever."

When the Moon is in Libra and the Sun is in Gemini, the energy remains in the positive, masculine Air element where social and mental communication skills are always revered. There is a lack of conflict within the soul because the two lights are functioning with the same energy element. The Moon phase for this combination is waxing which calls for unconscious movement toward expansion and information gathering.

The Libra Moon bestows refinement while the growth into Gemini's mental curiosity only expands their social graces. As children, they charm the world with their warm smiles and polite mannerisms. Because these little people do not like to be scolded, they will need very little discipline or punishment. They may show artistic or dancing talent early in life as Venus gives a sense of color, balance, and dramatic expression. There is such a dislike of confrontation in the early years that this young person can end up looking very indecisive just to avoid disagreement.

As this soul matures, they develop a great love of knowledge that can intensify into intellectual aspirations for a mentally sophisticated career. Business management, sales managers and team leadership are natural tracks for this social butterfly. When combining Libra Moon's strong need to be in relationship with Gemini's need to be mobile, this soul should develop a love of travel with a wide range of social groups. These Libra Geminis are usually charming with a great gift of conversation that makes all social events more fun.

If the Libra/Gemini combination of double air elements gets out of balance, final decisions become hard to make when they relate to people and relationships. Too much planning and too many commitments can overwhelm this airy energy that already scatters their thoughts to too many projects. The appeaser part of Libra may cause them to yield to peer pressure when it comes to choosing priorities. This socializer will talk too much when under stress or ill-at-ease in uncomfortable situations. However, this Mercury Venus person can have a smooth, silver tongue when it comes to charming groups and being convincing. The most difficult challenge for this Libra Gemini air combination is to stay grounded, so they do not create solutions in their head that are never brought to execution.

The soul lesson of the Moon in Libra and Sun in Gemini is to reign in their creative, busy minds, so they accomplish what they plan. It is important for them to use their strong negotiating skills in the business world to manifest positive results. Social groups are very important to the air signs, so friends will come and go as they are connected to current intellectual interests.

Keep moving, Libra Moon and Gemini Sun, in a smooth steady flow of divine energy toward using the strong mental capabilities of the Air element in areas that allow that natural social leadership to shine.

Sun in Cancer (Water) with Moon in Libra (Air)

*"From a social, people-pleasing child
to a nurturing, kind decision-maker."*

When the Moon is in Libra and the Sun is in Cancer, the transition from the masculine, outgoing energy of Libra to the feminine, receptive energy of Cancer does not come easily. The flow is blocked by Air's intellectual approach, so the emotional reactions usually go underground with this combination. The Moon phase is waxing at a point where the soul is struggling to come up out of an unconscious sleep and allow the feeling body to integrate with the mental body of Air.

This sweet, social child has a sense of dependence that needs companionship. There is a definite conflict between the priorities of friends and family. As the Cancer Sun awakens, this combination may become a bit introverted because their emotional nature sets up fears of being hurt or fooled by others. Libra's desire to please creates conflict between trusting others and guarding against having their over-sensitivity damaged.

Both Libra and Cancer are initiators, so as this one grows up, they love finding new adventures and new challenges. They can actually get hooked on new startup programs and forget to complete old tasks and forget to visit old friends and relatives. Since the Cancer reveres the security of home, they need to take time to create a stable nest environment where they can retreat when the overwhelming emotions of the world crash in on them. This nest also needs to be comfortable, well-decorated, and balanced, so the Libra Moon part of them feels harmonious. The instinct here is to leave the family nest early in search of the perfect Libra partner, so they can start their own family and create their own set of traditions and rituals. If the rapport with the parents was good then the urge is to carry on those patterns. If the early experience was not supportive, this soul will branch out to deliberately not mimic the behaviors of their parents and other family members. They will continue to have an overwhelming urge to help others and the need to be fair, the world of business and people is where this action-oriented person belongs.

If the Libra/Cancer combination of energy gets out of balance, there can be extremes in their emotional response that relate to partnerships. There is no more charming suitor than this Venus Moon sign person when they are out and want people to like them but their Cancer moodiness can make them hard to live with on the home front. When Libra is feeling social, everyone is welcome into their home. But when the tide turns and they become overwhelmed and tired, extreme sensitivity and defensiveness can erupt around this normally charming soul. At these times, Libra Cancer needs to head for their private hiding place where they can feel aggressive and work through their deeper feelings alone.

The soul lesson of the Moon in Libra and Sun in Cancer is to learn to balance the social, activity-based urges with the waves of emotional defensiveness. It is important for this one to be able to form emotional bonds and to express those deeper feelings without being in an emotional frenzy. They must avoid the tendency to jump from one social activity to the next always making new friends along the way. The message is to slow down to allow time for deeper commitments and more meaningful conversation. This Moon Venus combination has the ability to charm the world with their smooth speech and winning disposition.

Keep moving, Libra Moon and Cancer Sun, in a smooth steady flow of divine energy toward maintaining your worldly social status while you work to build a strong family circle where everyone is included. A committed love partner should be part of this nurturing picture.

Sun in Leo (Fire) with Moon in Libra (Air)

*"From a social, people-pleasing child
to a fast-paced, outgoing leader."*

When the Moon is in Libra and the Sun is in Leo, the energy flows naturally between these two positive, masculine Air and Fire elements. The waxing Moon phase that is pushing the unconscious soul is struggling to move out of dependency and into self-consciousness. However, the flow should be easy enough to promote success early.

The harmonious, affectionate Venus child desperately wants recognition and approval from both parents and friendships. As they grow, attention and praise become even more important to this expressive, outgoing youth. Leo, as well as Libra, loves to play, laugh, be the center of attention, and be the social leader in all gatherings.

The planetary Sun-Venus rulership creates a refined sense of power in this soul that instinctively can lead with a high spiritual idealism. These leaders excel out in the business world because they know how to negotiate compromise with a pleasant demeanor and fair-minded approach. Their creative ability leads them toward careers involving drama in a colorful life.

If the Libra/Leo combination of energy gets out of balance, an idealistic naiveté surfaces that could lead this soul into a dream world where they are the most important player. A "royalty" complex with a coating of sweet graciousness can become overbearing. Since Venus-ruled Libra is known for falling in love with love, this one can become obsessed with being number one in their lover's world. Being special can really be overdone with this combination. The Leo side of this one will love the drama of romance and create exciting fantasies that cannot be sustained in a real give-and-take relationship. Leo must be careful not to over dramatize their role in their career position because their Libra side does not take criticism well.

The soul lesson of the Moon in Libra and Sun in Leo is to keep the joy and playfulness in your life without becoming overtaken by other people's idea of how life should be lived. By allowing the Leo Fire energy to lead, this individual can move forward in life with ease and enthusiasm. Using a deeply ingrained sense of honor and integrity opens doors in the career world for people to trust and follow this charismatic Leo leader. In love, sentimentality and kindness seem to be more important than passion and ardor. Libra Moon energy must guard against giving up their personal identity to win the hand of the beautiful prized partner.

Keep on moving, Libra Moon and Leo Sun, in a smooth steady flow of divine energy toward using that charm, wit, and heart-warming nature to win over the people in that close circle who will support and encourage success and leadership in your life.

Sun in Virgo (Earth) with Moon in Libra (Air)

"From social, peace-keeping child
to a grounded, analytical problem-solver."

When the Moon is in Libra and the Sun is in Virgo, the element energy goes from positive Air to receptive Earth. This flow calls for a grounding of mental processes into the matter world of earth. Strong mental thoughts here need to find a vehicle for applying that knowledge. The old axiom "knowledge without application is useless" applies to this combination. The waxing Moon phase pushes the energy forward with an impulsive, rushing force that causes spontaneous behavior and responses without much follow through.

The naive, trusting, Venus-ruled Libra Moon wants to create original mental ideas but lacks the ability to execute these visions. These children seek comfort in the attention of others, but the earthy Virgo part of them is shy and holds back from interacting with the group. They are willing to do whatever is asked of them but will never initiate a plan of action on their own. If they are invited and coaxed to participate, they will be a valuable player in any organized activity or personal partnership. Their strong mental problem-solving abilities make them great scholars in school, as they will always conscientiously analysis the information and check out every detail of the process.

As they mature, a great fear of rejection and disapproval emerges, this combination would rather retreat than risk the experience of actual rejection. Groups and organizations may be challenging for this one. There is much creative writing talent with this scholarly mind. This soul might be considered an intellectual snob who would prefer to stay home with a good book than to keep company with individuals who have no love of knowledge. Negotiation and mediation in a legal or business forum are perfect career paths if the education was achieved during their younger more social years.

If the Libra/Virgo combination of energy gets out of balance, this soul can withdraw and detach because of hidden insecurities. Their wants and desires can waffle from desiring friends and partners to wanting to be alone with their work and analytical thoughts. When this combination experiences stress in the relationship arena, their physical health could be affected. Virgos can become over-concerned with the bodies and develop hypochondriac tendencies.

The soul lesson of the Moon in Libra and Sun in Virgo is to maintain a charming smile even when self-doubt is pulling at their subconscious. There is an abundance of creative thinking and writing skills that can be expertly applied through very methodical exacting Virgo processes with this soul. In the business arena, this intellectual works well as second in command. Their sharp mind and pleasant demeanor go far to help them bridge that uncomfortable social gap that they experience within.

Keep on moving, Libra Moon and Virgo Sun, in a smooth steady flow of divine energy toward using all of your social and creative cleverness to work with people who are also determined to methodically move forward with their lives.

Sun in Libra (Air) with Moon in Libra (Air)

"From a social, peace-keeping child
to a quick-thinking, organizing negotiator."

When both luminaries (Sun and Moon) fall in the same sign, the Moon phase may be either New or Balsamic in phase, and both of these call for much self-reflection and self-motivation with the keyword being "Self". With the Sun and Moon in Libra together, the energy focus for the soul is to refine the positive, masculine Air element. This process involves using their acute mental capabilities in a sociable, enterprising manner. The New Moon falls within the waxing phase of the Moon cycle, so the essence of this combination is balance.

The Libra child is usually outgoing, popular, and artistically inclined. They seldom need firm discipline because their strong intuition can pick up the expectations of their elders. The Venus energy makes these children warm, courteous, and cooperative. As they mature, flirting becomes a natural pastime. Relationship will always be a major priority for this double Libra in both their personal and professional life.

Intensity is the focus here to complete the lesson of compromise. There may be too much reliance on others and an inability to move forward spontaneously when others are involved in the decision. Because this combination has a very quick mind, they present themselves socially as charming and humorous. When this air energy has gained their confidence and personal identity, they may be found excelling in the field of the arts, or taking the role of the diplomat, so middle management fits their style as well.

If the Libra/Libra combination of double air energy gets out of balance, it becomes very difficult to make decisions on any front. Indecision and "passing the decision-making buck" is a deep flaw in their character. Actually, Libra can make the hard decision but they would rather not because someone else would then be unhappy. Their wish is for everyone to be happy. This is where the reputation of the "peacemaker" comes from. Because this sign worries about what other people think, they hesitate to follow their own dreams and intuitions. This Venus energy must be careful not to be phony or too sweet in relationships. They must learn to be their authentic self and speak their position in any conflict even in the face of their biggest fear, desertion.

The soul lesson of the Moon and Sun in Libra is to be able to balance their personal needs against a very strong need to be liked. They need to learn to excel, shine, and to lead gracefully. Since Venus has a strong sense of style, dressing for success is not a problem here. Their leadership ability and natural talent for making people comfortable opens the door to high success in the more sophisticated career positions.

Keep moving, Libra Moon and Sun, in a smooth steady flow of divine energy toward growing in personal intuition to tune in to the unconscious to find the true place of peace on earth, within the self.

Sun In Scorpio (Water) with Moon in Libra (Air)

*"From a social, people-pleasing child
to a determined, focused researcher."*

When the Moon is in Libra and the Sun is in Scorpio, the energy flow goes from the positive Air element to the negative or receptive Water element. Going from Air to Water takes the soul from the mental plane to the emotional plane, or from the head to the emotion. The last of the Moon phases in the waning position finds the Moon just behind the Sun in a position of conscious completion of unfinished business.

In childhood, Venus-ruled Libra reaches out to people in a sweet, polite manner with a strong desire to please everyone in their surroundings. However, this soul knows they have come with a reason and that is to make a stand for focusing on the talents of the lifetime. The young Libra loves parties, laughter, and big gatherings; however, as the Pluto energy does not like being around lots of people. As they mature, the intense drive of fixed Scorpio begins to add a more serious side to this soul.

The shift to privacy and secrecy begins around puberty when the hormones activate since Pluto rules the sexual organs and sexuality. Scorpio wants relationship but more on a one-to-one basis with lots of passion and intimacy. There is a strong desire for success that becomes more focused on one objective as the soul matures. This creates an incredible combination for blending people skills with the determination to reach the heights of success. Doctors, surgeons, scientists, investigators, researchers and investment executives could all benefit from this intense combination.

If the Libra/Scorpio combination of energy gets out of balance, romantic passion can take over and shut out any other drives in life. Scorpio's emotional influence can override any of Libra's need for harmony and peace. Obsession with love, sex, power, and the dark forces can overpower the airy softness in the soul and turn this combination to a lustful manipulator. The intense energy of fixed Scorpio must not be allowed to overrun Libra's sense of balance and fairness. If Venus has a strong presence in this person so that kindness and harmony rule, then this energy can be directed into the higher path.

The soul lesson of the Moon in Libra and Sun in Scorpio is to direct their quick mental clarity into a beam of intensified force that will drive this soul to great heights of accomplishment. Staying social and worldly while pushing forward with determination is the mission. Once this soul becomes clear about their destiny, they will dig in and move forward without any need for supervision.

Keep moving, Libra Moon and Scorpio Sun, in a smooth steady flow of divine energy toward blending all of those gracious social skills into a mix with the highly emotional passionate drive that Scorpio adds into an achiever of the highest levels.

Sun in Sagittarius (Fire) with Moon in Libra (Air)

*"From a social, people-pleasing child
to an adventuresome, risk taker."*

When the Moon is in Libra and the Sun is in Sagittarius, the easy flow of energy is from the positive Air element to the positive Fire element. The focus shifts from social communications to action and movement. Because the Moon phase is waning, there is a conscious decision toward shedding old social patterns and moving toward true soul purpose. Both Air and Fire energies act in a positive, masculine out-flowing direction making this combination quite extroverted.

Their instinctive nature as a child is to be polite, subtle, and cooperative, but as they grow, the conscious drive goes more toward direct truth and honesty. There is no maliciousness within the heart of this pattern but there is a strong need to speak their mind and their philosophy without hesitation.

When Venus-ruled Libra and Jupiter-ruled Sagittarius join together, money, grandeur, and extensive travel naturally materialize in their dreams and many times in their lives. Any career dealing with foreign trade, diplomacy, politics, or higher purposes in life. Careers as theologians, spiritual advisors, and counselors will make this person very happy indeed.

If the Libra/Sagittarius combination of fire energy gets out of balance, out of balance, it is easy to over-expand one's budget and capabilities in the name of freedom. Too much socializing and too much excitement could create a wanderer's life where there is no time for the mundane routines of family and career. Philosophy and higher understanding draw this soul out into the bigger world which does not lend itself to staying on task or on the job. Because of the nature of this social butterfly, variety needs to be a part of any lifestyle they choose.

The soul lesson of the Moon in Libra and Sun in Sagittarius is to stay on track to complete their own life mission instead of following others off on an adventure. When Air Fire energy gets confined or unfocused, it can shoot out onto unpredictable and irrational paths. The gift here is a sharp curious mind that loves to read, study, teach, and share their enthusiasm for life. When well developed, this soul expresses dignity, supreme confidence, and sophistication.

Keep moving, Libra Sun and Sagittarius Sun, in a smooth steady flow of divine energy toward staying in awareness and keeping the highest intentions conscious in all actions and relationships.

Sun in Capricorn (Earth) with Moon in Libra (Air)

*"From a social, people-pleasing child
to a responsible, initiating manager."*

When the Moon is in Libra and the Sun is in Capricorn, the energy flow from the positive Air element to the negative/receptive Earth element is blocked in a difficult transition. The waning Moon phase calls for conscious stripping away of old patterns and being willing to share the wisdom gained along the way with others.

As a child, Libra is always willing to please and to sacrifice to keep the peace in the family. Tradition and dignity remain constant throughout the life of this individual. Youth brings a dogmatic drive for success, recognition and fame. If this child is exposed to spiritual beliefs, they may develop a clear intuition and inclination for metaphysical study.

Venus-ruled Libra is always drawn toward romance and marriage, and when Capricorn is involved, the goal of a permanent committed relationship is usually strong. Parenting, family life, and family businesses are all attractive to this energy combination. Although their work may keep them from enjoying the world they have built. These people enjoy careers that follow structured, conservative methods where they are in charge.

If the Libra/Capricorn combination of energy gets out of balance, there can be a tyrannical approach to dealing with employees, partners, and children. Their soft, polite outer demeanor may hide a controlling pattern of intimidation. They can become perfectionists and workaholics who can never be pleased. There is a great dignity within this combination; however, when it gets out of control, it can become haughty and arrogant. Air Earth energy can produce a person who is verbally smooth but inwardly critical. An inner struggle continues within these where one sign says "go be social and fun" while the other half says "be serious, trust no one, and be alone".

The soul lesson of the Moon in Libra and Sun in Capricorn is to be active, outgoing, and responsible. Relationships need to play a big part in their life because the partner brings balance into an otherwise dry, disciplined, routine life. Capricorn must guard against believing that they can do everything better than anyone else. A pompous attitude could destroy the image and the lifestyle that this Saturn-ruled person has worked so hard to build.

Keep moving, Libra Moon and Capricorn Sun, in a smooth steady flow of divine energy toward the maintaining of a balance between partnership and marriage versus career, control, and rigid life patterns.

Sun in Aquarius (Air) with Moon in Libra (Air)

*"From a social, people-pleasing child
to a strong, confident group leader."*

When the Moon is in Libra and the Sun is in Aquarius, both signs hold the positive, masculine energy of the Air element. Social activities and intellectual interactions claim much of their attention. Since the Moon phase falls on the waning side of the cycle, the urge for growth is conscious and pushes to disseminate its knowledge and wisdom. This easy-going, compliant energy usually is quite perceptive with a naturally intuitive mind.

In the early years of development, the youthful attunement to the needs and thoughts of others amazes the family of these children. This one will be the peacekeeper on the playground as well as in the family. As they mature, they value their friends and social activities above everything else. Combining the energies of Venus and Uranus usually stirs up a love of romance, affection, excitement, and eventually marriage.

However, this combo manifests a uniquely independent side that pushes people away if they become too attached or needy. High spiritual expectations in relationships can cause blocks and disappointments in love when people do not live up to Libra's love fantasy. There is innately a keen appreciation of art, music, and literature which can lead to a career where their originality can be rewarded. Any people-based career is attractive here, but it needs to allow room for originality, group leadership and objective problem solving.

If the Libra/Aquarius combination of double Air elements gets out of balance, too much information could cloud the usually exceptional thought processes. The urge is to become distracted by social activities or the inquisitive needs of others through too much conversation. There is a danger of too many facts, too much input, too many options.

All of this mental energy can jam up Air's nervous system so that no decisions can be made. An Aquarian's response to overload is to detach, cool down, and become aloof with people and situations that threaten their independence. Libra's tendency is to go off in search of new friends, relationships, and new lovers. The outcome can be to turn away from the old in search of new horizons. This person needs to be careful not to become fickle with social contacts.

The soul lesson of the Moon in Libra and Sun in Aquarius is to use their broad social skills to lead groups using their intellectual communication talents. The goal is to gather new information which they can use to topple old values and ways of being. If this combination is fortunate enough to find a partner what can also be a best friend, they have a chance to build a truly open, easy love relationship. When they can temper their strong individualistic side and attract harmonious partnerships into their work world, they have the ability to run their own business.

Keep moving, Libra Moon and Aquarius Sun, in a smooth steady flow of divine energy toward applying all those quick mental communication skills at a higher level for a higher purpose that can be used to bring people into the "New Age" of new thinking.

Sun in Pisces (Water) with Moon in Libra (Air)

*"From a social, people-pleasing child
to a compassionate, visionary server."*

When the Moon is in Libra and the Sun is in Pisces, the energy pattern goes from the masculine Air element to the feminine Water element. The soul struggles to incorporate the intuitive, mystical essence of the emotional world. Because the Moon phase is waning, there is a conscious drive to share the wealth of wisdom and spiritual understanding that is so obvious to this one.

The Libra Moon child needs people, affection, and lots of encouragement in their early years, and that pattern does not disappear as this soul gets older. Pisces also searches for safety and protection from the aggressive outer world. Venus-ruled Libra combined with the Neptune vibration of Pisces gives this combination a dreamy nature that falls in love with love.

As they mature, the relationship goal is to appeal to their emotions rather than the intellectual interest. A developed imagination coupled with a strong artistic talent will make all levels of aesthetic creativity possible. A career in the arts, such as music, or in religion would draw out the spiritual universal wisdom of the soul.

If the Libra/Pisces combination of energy gets out of balance, this individual might sink into the fairyland of wishful thinking where one can just sit around hoping that all dreams come true. Pisces always need to stay away from escaping into drugs, alcohol, or sleep as a release from unpleasant situations. Libra energy tends to become impatient and jump into action without forethought while Pisces hesitates to take action in case they change their mind. Worry and fear can stop this one in their tracks if there is any indication of criticism or failure looming on the horizon. Inaction versus jumping too fast presents a quandary for this soul. Avoidance in decision making may be the worst enemy for this combination.

The soul lesson of the Moon in Libra and Sun in Pisces calls for a realistic expectation of relationships and daily life. Strong mental capabilities can combine with the high sensing intuition to allow this soul to function on a very insightful gut level. No matter how much education and information has been garnered on any situation, this Water sign should trust their deeper knowing in the end. Living near water is helpful to this soul because it can heal their buried wounds of the soul. The changing energy of Pisces smooths out when exposed to water, art, music and etheric surroundings.

Keep moving, Libra Moon and Pisces Sun, in a smooth steady flow of divine energy toward blending the social strengths of Venus with the mystical spirituality of Pisces to tune in and become part of the harmonious vibrations of earth.

Moon in Scorpio

Moon in Scorpio (with all signs)

Each chapter begins with a description of the Moon's purpose for those readers who will want to go straight to a specific Moon/Sun combination.

Imagine a giant mirror reflecting past actions and experiences. According to mythology, the sign that the Moon was in at the time of your birth explains your soul response's in this lifetime. Understanding how the Moon's energy impacts your behavior and emotional reactions is key to understanding your hidden soul pattern and personal timing. You are the center of your own universe and the creator of your own destiny, so you need to understand your gifts and future goals. The eternal questions of the soul are: "Where have I come from?" and "Where am I going?" The most important eternal question, of course, is "Why am I here?"

Moon in Scorpio (Water)

The emotional nature of Scorpio comes from the Water element, known to be intense and very quiet. This newborn appears to be totally calm and in control until they really become upset and then their fury can be intense. Naps are not a critical part of this child's daily routine. In fact, this one has incredible stamina when it is required.

The icons that rule the sign of Scorpio are the Scorpion, the Phoenix, and the Eagle. Watch out for the temper of this brooding, sensitive Water baby who may still be in her scorpion stinging phase. With maturity, hopefully there comes the clarity of the eagle. Mars and Pluto, Scorpio's rulers, possess an incredibly strong determination that can become stubborn when pushed. It might be hard to figure out what your little Scorpio Moon child really wants because she will often go into a silent stealth mode until her temper erupts.

The Scorpio Moon child will fight to the death for what she feels is important to her. There will be very little compromise here because this little person will feels deeply and passionately. If you and your child come to a real head-to-head confrontation, you had better be prepared to hold your ground.

Loyalty and honesty rank at the top of her priority list in relationships, and there is no better friend than a Scorpio Moon. Sometimes, it is hard to know what she is thinking because she is a master at hiding her own thoughts. A Scorpio Moon usually knows what others are thinking and when people are lying to her because her Water receptivity gives her incredible intuition. It is very difficult to keep a secret from this one.

As the Scorpio Moon child grows up, it would be a great asset for her to hold on to her tenacity and determination without becoming too quiet, secretive, and mysterious. Being a fixed sign, change does not come easily, so warn this little Water Moon before you change any plan. She might end up withdrawing into a sulky mood if she feels forced to participate in activities that she is not interested in.

This intensely driven soul can either take the high road or the low road. Whichever road the scorpion chooses, there will be no stopping her.

The goal of Scorpio Moon is to use her perception to attain true wisdom, depth, and compassion. Hopefully the Sun sign energy will soften the extremely fixed opinions of this deeply passionate Scorpio fighter.

Sun in Aries (Fire) with Moon in Scorpio (Water)

*"From a quiet, observing child
to a fiery, independent, take-charge person."*

When the Moon is in Scorpio and the Sun is in Aries, the energy flows from the feminine Water element to the masculine Fire element. This brings a forceful shift into the growth pattern because the Moon phase is waning, so it is consciously trying to integrate. Since Mars has rulership over both of these signs, there is much Martian warrior drive and flashing fire action in the persona of this individual. A struggle exists between the Moon/Sun lights as the watery Moon wants to hold back in a "wait and see" mode while spontaneous Fire wants to rush out into new experiences.

The young child appears passive and observant while their mind is questioning and turbulent. They are having a raging battle within but no one sees it. In children, this energy be expressed as sulking or pouting. As maturity sets in, much of that hidden drive and determination becomes more obvious. Their energy begins to give off an aura of competence, control, challenge and independence.

These young people need to receive a good education, so they have a place to channel their strong attracting and assertive capabilities. Intense stares, patient listening, and darting eyes are signs of the deep awakening of growing Scorpio's probing for understanding. In the adult years, this talent for exploration and research works well in careers like investigation, detective work and espionage.

If the Scorpio/Aries combination of energy gets out of balance, the buildup of intense emotion may come out as extreme anger or aggression. Mixing the elements of Water and Fire can stir up and build a powerful head of steam to be used for better or for worse. Mars' fire must always guard against being volatile, excitable and sharp. There is an intense sexual drive in this combination, and they must struggle against possessive and jealous thinking in love relationships. They must also be careful not to choose partners who feed the sensual fires.

The soul lesson of the Moon in Scorpio and Sun in Aries is to direct that assertive, fiery Mars energy in a controlled and focused manner. Because of Water Fire's steamy combination, all of Scorpio's tenacity and determination will be needed. In all kinds of relationships there is no more attached friend than Scorpio Moon. This one will act as the Great Protector whether it is called for or not. Aries waits for no man, but with the steady pace of Scorpio, a constant speed can be achieved so that all projects may be brought to victory.

Keep moving, Scorpio Moon and Aries Sun, in a smooth steady flow of divine energy toward directing all of that high vitality in positive direction which should put you out in front as a winner in the end.

Sun in Taurus (Earth) with Moon in Scorpio (Water)

"From a quiet, observing child to a practical, forceful stabilizer."

When the Moon is in Scorpio and the Sun is in Taurus, the energy flow makes a natural transition from the emotional feminine Water element to the grounding feminine Earth element. Fixity and determination remain a constant throughout this lifetime because both of these signs are fixed and unyielding by nature. This Full Moon phase between the Moon and the Sun awakens the soul from the unconscious to the conscious state of awareness so that struggling to find balance in human relationships becomes a real challenge.

Even as a child this soul can be stubborn and defiant in their way of doing things. Once they are on track it takes time to get this one to make any changes. In early childhood, be extra careful to give them plenty of notice before starting a new game plan. This quiet child becomes much more outgoing and affectionate as they get older. As for being responsible, there is no better person to have the money than the Taurus Scorpio combination. They will keep track of every penny.

However, Taurus loves beautiful things, so they must guard against overspending or over-investing in beautiful art and collectibles as a savings tool. When Mars and Venus are joined together in chart rulership, these planets can create intense charisma. These are magnetic individuals who do have a hidden passion for understanding the deeper meaning of human nature. This combination would do well in financial or scientific career areas where loyalty is a virtue.

If the Scorpio/Taurus combination of energy gets out of balance, the unreasonableness of fixed thinking can be dominant. If that patient, slow moving bull is pushed too far, then the lower stinging side of Scorpio raises its ugly tail. An indecisive, weak personality would not do well in an intimate relationship with this one. It is not wise to get in the way of this fixed sign combination unless it would be another fixed sign but then a stalemate could occur. Because of the deep loyalty felt by this individual, relationships usually last a lifetime; however, if something happens to cause a blow up, it will be extreme and probably permanent. When Scorpio is done, they are done.

The soul lesson of the Moon in Scorpio and Sun in Taurus is to channel that great force and determination in a positive direction toward building something of permanence. Because of their tenacity and patience, they can wait and plan until the time is right, then they will build their program upon solid ground. No combination enjoys the finer comforts of home and food than this one. This is the sign of the true connoisseur. Stability is critical for the career path of this fixed combination whether that be in banking, investments, or manufacturing.

Keep moving, Scorpio Moon and Taurus Sun, in a smooth steady flow of divine energy by combining the water and earth energies to ground the soul to a secure life in a solid relationship with many comforts that can be appreciated and shared with others.

Sun in Gemini (Air) with Moon in Scorpio (Water)

"From a quiet, observing child to a fast-moving, quick, communicator."

When the Moon is in Scorpio and the Sun is in Gemini, the energy flow is struggling out of the feminine Water element into the masculine Air element. It is in the waxing phase of the Moon which indicates an unconscious urge to study and learn the inner-workings of the self.

In their youth, this Scorpio child needs much quiet time with a private place to retreat. They seldom talk about their feelings or their inner-thoughts. As this one matures, they become much more outgoing, social, and even chatty with they are in comfortable surroundings. There is an inborn strength of will and focus that helps the Mercury-ruled Gemini succeed in later years.

When the combined energies of Gemini as a social butterfly and Scorpio's sultry sexuality are working together, this individual can become one sensual, attractive charmer. There is a subtle need to be in control which can cause jealousy and possessiveness to flare in relationships. The career drive will naturally go toward communications through practical business, sales, and management. An artistic or professional career would also suit this combination because the recognition would be more personal.

If the Scorpio/Gemini combination of energy gets out of balance, pent up anger can turn into raging arguments. Most of the time the intellectual, rational side of this one stays detached from deep emotional situations. However, once deeply wounded it becomes very difficult to reason with the closed, fixed mind of their emotional side. Because there is such a sensual attraction to this Scorpio Moon, there may be many sidetracking relationships that play on sex and sensationalism. If this occurs, Gemini's brilliant, penetrating mind may get lost in exciting scenarios that lead to many different adventures but no real substance in life.

The soul lesson of the Moon in Scorpio and Sun in Gemini is to keep a balance between the emotional intensity and the light, airy, flightiness. If the heavy watery energy gets too bogged down in drama, a change of pace such as a little trip or new activity might lighten the mood of this personality. This Mars-Pluto person may get blocked by their own drive for control in their early years and then in later life it becomes difficult to focus on even completing the tasks.

Keep moving, Scorpio Moon and Gemini Sun, in a smooth steady flow of divine energy toward using all of those clever, intuitive, mental abilities to communicate your strong personal message to the world through relationships.

Sun in Cancer (Water) with Moon in Scorpio (Water)

"From a quiet, observing child
to a nurturing, kind, decision-maker."

When the Moon is in Scorpio and the Sun is in Cancer, the soul energy should stay contained within the feminine, passive Water element where the focus remains on establishing deeper emotional commitments and allowing the world to come inside the barrier walls of Scorpio. The Moon phase for the Sun/Moon is waxing which leaves most of the soul drive buried at an unconscious level where it continues to push outward toward being recognized.

In the early years, the Scorpio child holds back and stands in a position of observing. They forget nothing, so they are always comparing their rewards and punishments against their other siblings. Cancer has a strong bond with the mother for better or for worse. This child struggles with feelings of possessiveness and jealousy around the attention and affection of the parents, but mother in particular.

These souls vibrate with a sexual magnetism that attracts relationship opportunities to them often before they are emotionally mature enough to handle them. When they marry early, it is usually because of a strong inner-drive to have a family and build a Cancer nest. In the work world, they need to focus on areas of service where they can nurture and counsel. Whether the career is medicine or teaching or social work, it needs to offer depth with a strong cause.

If the Scorpio/Cancer combination of energy gets out of balance, there can be intense emotional ranting and raving episodes. The Scorpio energy needs to avoid dark brooding that can harbor childhood hurts. If the early pain festers inside, they can become vicious with their anger in later years. Their natural emotional urge is to even the score which never works because it only creates more karma or builds even stronger strings to the original wounding Scorpio. Instead of constantly defending their feelings, they would do better to find someone to talk out their fears, hurts, and frustrations with, so they can be released from the wounds and the buried pain. They need to understand that releasing is a far better solution than shutting down and holding in.

The soul lesson of the Moon in Scorpio and Sun in Cancer is to dig deeper into emotional patterns to understand where these painful feelings began and how they can be healed. When a double water sign energy feels emotionally confident, they can use their experience, wisdom and compassion to lead others through difficult emotional storms. Their ferocious drive to build and create the best of everything may act as an inspiration to other less motivated souls along the path. There is a natural ability to tap into universal guidance and ancient healing techniques that can be used to help others.

Keep moving, Scorpio Moon and Cancer Sun, in a smooth steady flow of divine energy toward maintaining a high spiritual vibration so that the intense passions that flow beneath the surface will not destroy but can be used to lovingly lift others up to higher purpose.

Sun in Leo (Fire) with Moon in Scorpio (Water)

*"From a quiet, observing child
to a confident, strong-willed, outgoing leader."*

When the Moon is in Scorpio and the Sun is in Leo, the element energy is flowing from Water to Fire. The goal is to move from the feminine, emotional holding pattern to the masculine, positive expressive pattern of Fire. A resistance to changing the behavior makes this transition rather difficult because of the fixed nature of both signs. With the waxing phase of the Moon, there is an unconscious push to struggle out of the feeling world into the world of action by pushing forward.

Having both Sun and Moon energies call for stability, and sameness makes letting go of deep patterns to make room for change very stressful. The quiet, observant, intuitive Moon child practices holding in their thoughts and feelings. As the dynamic fiery Leo awakens, the behaviors of pride, drama and leadership come forward with intense force.

It is almost impossible to sidetrack this soul once they have a clear vision of the goal. All relationships or projects with this combination include the qualities of passion, drive and desire. The drive for success and recognition is greater here than with any other sign combination. High achievement can be gained in careers that require tenacity and unyielding determination such as medicine, surgery, science, research, and investments.

If the Scorpio/Leo combination of energy gets out of balance, the need to be right can become brutal. The emotional, passionate influence of the Moon can be quite obsessive when it acts with the positive force of Leo. If these intense feelings are not managed with conscious determination, there is danger of the main life purpose being derailed while seduction and sensationalism take a position at center stage. This double fixed energy can become severely obstinate and demanding if there are no other planetary patterns to soften this dominant nature. Unfortunately Scorpio can hold a tough line to resist change while the Leo struggles with being wrong out of stubborn pride. It is better to offer this combination an alternative choice rather than to expect them to admit outright that they are wrong.

The soul lesson of the Moon in Scorpio and Sun in Leo is to manage the powerful determination that comes in with this soul. It is important to stay on track with the goals of life without staying in the deep rut of habit. Once fixed energy becomes clear about their direction, they can dig in and complete projects without supervision.

Keep moving, Scorpio Moon and Leo Sun, in a smooth steady flow of divine energy toward using the Sun's creative energy in a regal, proper, focused, capable manner to lead and take charge graciously.

Sun in Virgo (Earth) with Moon in Scorpio (Water)

*"From a quiet, observing child
to a grounded, analytical, problem-solver."*

When the Moon is in Scorpio and the Sun is in Virgo, the energy flows naturally from the sensitive, receptive Water element to the grounded, receptive Earth element. By Moon phase, the waxing/growing energy struggles for a consciousness to serve instead of Scorpio's urge to stand back in a secretive observation mode.

This infant starts with a need for stability and routine because of the fixed nature of Scorpio; however, as this little person grows toward adulthood, change and variety become more dominant patterns. This one may have a strong sense of knowing what will happen before it happens. Dreams may be vivid in their young year and continue throughout their life.

Inborn intuition remains a leading force throughout the life while the Mercury-driven Virgo adult prefers to think of themselves as an intellectual. They must avoid shutting down that strong "gut" guidance. With a strong interest in service, precision, health and medicine, this combination does well in the professions of doctor, dentist, nurse, accountant, and economist (both personal and political). When Mars, ruler of Scorpio, blends with Mercury, ruler of Virgo, the mind is detail-oriented, and the tongue may be sharp or direct.

If the Scorpio/Virgo combination of energy gets out of balance, critical thinking can become obsessive and even unreasonable. A deep need for privacy may drive this soul into positions of isolation in work and in the personal life. Because of all of the feminine/yin, receptive energy, self-criticism and criticalness of others can hurt this soul in their drive for power or control in worldly activities. Shyness or illness can become a veil behind which this perfectionist hides. This rational thinker must guard against becoming an over-analytical "Doubting

Thomas."

The soul lesson of the Moon in Scorpio and Sun in Virgo is to strike a balance between the focused, intensity of the Moon and the earthly, detailed practicality of the Sun. This sensitive, perceptive soul has an opportunity to work with others in their journey through the deep times of emotional darkness. Work is a comforting passion for Scorpio/Virgo and allows this combination to overcome buried insecurities while validating the need for work and the need to be of service to others. Being second "in command" allows time for detail and critical thinking. A serious serenity masks a passionate nature making this person much deeper than one would expect at first meeting.

Keep moving, Scorpio Moon and Virgo Sun, in a smooth steady flow of divine energy by combining the Water and Earth elements to ground the soul to a stable life in working, conservative relationships with others so that there can be openness and acceptance in your life.

Sun in Libra (Air) with Moon in Scorpio (Water)

"From a quiet, observing child
to a social, peacemaking negotiator."

When the Moon is in Scorpio and the Sun is in Libra, the shift is from sensitive, receptive Water to detached, mental Air element. It represents the new, waxing phase of the Moon where action is instinctual and rushes out to meet life in a spontaneous manner.

In childhood, this Scorpio needs routine, naps, and quiet time to be alone. Their nature is to quietly observe but hold their feelings close until they feel a sense of trust and security. As Libra matures, social activities and friendship become critically important to them. This youth needs to be drawn out into groups as the mediator or peacemaker which will break the early pattern of solitude. There is an inborn determination that acts as a driving force to move ambivalent Libra to make decisions and move forward with their life.

Because Libra's main lesson focuses around relationships and learning compromise, romance usually surfaces early in the teenage years. The Scorpio sexual drive coupled with Libra's need to partner usually brings marriage or sexual relationships into one's life soul have a penetrating curiosity that makes for a superior student with high ambitions. The career doors may open in many directions from business to science or literature as long as it is progressive in nature. All careers which involve artistic qualities such as, art, dancing, interior design, colors, and harmonious communications suit this combination very well.

If the Scorpio/Libra combination of energy gets out of balance, enthusiasm around intense opinions can wreak havoc in social situations. Libra is learning compromise, so the partner may become the teacher in these heated debate situations. Partners may also come and go as Libra has a fickle side when it comes to partnering with someone who does not want a lot of together and intimacy. These are necessities in Libra's world. A strong ambitious drive can turn the usually charming Venus-ruled Libra into a daunting adversary when they feel their honor or fairness is being challenged. The Scorpio Mars sting should never be underestimated in this combination when it comes to the final hour of decision.

The soul lesson of the Moon in Scorpio and Sun in Libra is to focus the intense drive of ambition in a positive direction where relationships are part of the process instead of being on the sidelines of life. When the heavy water energy gets too focused on outcome, the Libra socialite needs to step back and become engaged with people and partner activities. Communications and strategizing awaken the airy nature and create a balance when obsessive-compulsive behavior is acting out.

Keep moving, Scorpio Moon and Libra Sun, in a smooth steady flow of divine energy toward using all of those social, mediating, and intuitive mental abilities to provide leadership in any arena where you feel passionate about the information.

Sun in Scorpio (Water) with Moon in Scorpio (Water)

"From a quiet, observing child to a determined, focused project manager."

When both luminaries (Sun and Moon) fall in the same sign, the Moon phase may be either New or Balsamic in phase, and both of these call for much self-reflection and self-motivation with the keyword being "Self". With the Moon and Sun in Scorpio together, the same archetypal sign and element, the soul has chosen a cycle focusing on fixed, stable emotional strength.

With both lights occupying the same sign, the goal is to refine the powerful intensity of the fixed water energy. The test here is first to get started and then to move forward with determination without overpowering or destroying others in the process. This young child feels deeper and seldom reacts outwardly so that their emotions are visible. Hiding toys and precious treasures may be a common pastime for this little one. In either case, the drive is to maintain and complete any and all projects and interactions that come into the life path.

As this Scorpio matures, sex, passion, and power need to be used wisely because control will be the challenge. Any profession requiring investigation, exploration, detective work, or healing will intrigue this strong personality as long as it rewards patience and tenacity. The fields of healing, death, wills, and investments also hold an opportunity for success.

If the Scorpio/Scorpio combination of double Water energy gets out of balance, demanding and manipulative behavior could be the result. The stealthy nature of this fixed water sign can go into a stalking mode when focused on a desired possession. They will allow nothing to stop them from achieving their goal. Out-of-control anger can also show up if they are pushed to defend themselves. Even though fixed energy is slow to move, the scorpion can strike with amazing speed and accuracy when pushed too far. It is wise not to push this quiet Scorpio too far.

The soul lesson of the Moon and Sun in Scorpio is to contain that powerful drive and determination so that the energy can be used wisely to accomplish a set plan and purpose. By using their instinctive psychic abilities, they can tap their inner-wisdom and deep understanding of the hidden or esoteric truths of the universe. This soul needs goals and a life plan to actualize their full potential for success while on planet earth.

Keep moving, Scorpio Moon and Sun, in a smooth steady flow of divine energy toward directing that iron will to master your executive abilities while building power and wealth.

Sun in Sagittarius (Fire) with Moon in Scorpio (Water)

"From a quiet, observing child to an adventuresome, risk-taker."

When the Moon is in Scorpio and the Sun is in Sagittarius, the energy flow is going from the feminine Water element to the masculine Fire element creating a movement from sensitive emotion to spontaneous activity. The Moon phase is called Balsamic with the Moon moving behind the Sun in a time of fruition which calls for the soul to pull back into the self by completing many tasks and relationships.

The child part of this soul is quiet, pensive, and observing while the fresh activity created by the flamboyant Sagittarian Sun is outgoing, risky, and adventuresome. Therefore, this combination has two decidedly different behavior patterns which make them exciting and unpredictable. These sign placements are good for health, strong constitution, perseverance, and independence.

Because of the Mars rulership with Scorpio and the Jupiter rulership with Sagittarius, there is quick wit and some sarcasm or combativeness in their nature. This playful spirit attracts relationships quite easily; however, freedom ranks higher on their priority list than partnership, so many hearts may be broken here. This combination needs freedom in their career and may jump around due to their many interests. They won't want to be chained to a desk and chair.

If the Scorpio/Sagittarius combination of energy gets out of balance, it can appear temperamental or self-absorbed. The intense focus of Scorpio looks preoccupied when Sagittarius is flying in their philosophical dream world. When Fiery Sag gets involved in too many interests, the fixed Scorpio tends to become rebellious inside and refuse to move. This soul can resort to running from responsibility because it feels overwhelming to the Fire Sun sign that needs freedom. It is never good for this energy to get into a pattern of "love them and leave them" because it could become a way of life.

The soul lesson of the Moon in Scorpio and Sun in Sagittarius is to be able to maintain that positive attitude and accepting disposition. There is a free and generous aura of energy that makes people feel safe and comfortable. When the spiritual side is activated, there can be great insights into the occult studies with a potential for teaching. Marriage is possible once the Sagittarius is assured that they do not need to give up their freedom. There will be great loyalty and commitment once they decide to settle down.

Keep moving, Scorpio Moon and Sagittarius Sun, in a smooth steady flow of energy toward allowing your far-sighted, intuitive abilities to guide the way in your search for higher wisdom and expansion.

Sun in Capricorn (Earth)
with Moon in Scorpio (Water)

"From a quiet, observing child
to a responsible, organized, successful manager."

When the Moon is in Scorpio and the Sun is in Capricorn, the energy flows from Water to Earth elements in a natural and easy transfer. Both elements call for emotional stability and determination to ground and manifest in the material world. The Moon phase is waning, so the need is for a stripping away of old patterns to allow for better understanding of self. There is a strong will and perseverance that remains in the personality for the entire lifetime.

Even as a child, there is a rigid self-reliance that holds the personality in a serious and cautious posture particularly around strangers. Since Capricorn's urge is to succeed and rule, an attitude of righteous and judgment should be eliminated or at least buried.

Success is almost certain if this soul learns to blend their intensity with some warmth and earnest interest. Honor and integrity are great virtues to build upon with this pattern. There is a natural ability to manage others, so the military and politics are natural fits for this style of leadership. Careers in business management and medicine also allow for success through duty, honor, and loyalty to the creed of the profession.

If the Scorpio/Capricorn combination of energy gets out of balance, a quiet, cold stubbornness can appear that feels very hard and unsympathetic. This intimidating approach can make itself felt without ever saying a word. Bossiness combined with cold criticism can be one of the most unpleasant behaviors when Scorpio/Capricorn feels threatened or unhappy. If this combination gets too carried away with their authority and the need to be right, they may find themselves alone and deserted in later life.

The soul lesson of the Moon in Scorpio and Sun in Capricorn is to channel their need for power and control into positive career objectives where perseverance and objectivity are considered admirable qualities. In a spiritually enlightened soul, mastery over the lower temptations of life can be mastered and leadership achieved.

Keep moving, Scorpio Moon and Capricorn Sun, in a smooth steady flow of divine energy toward achieving your highest goals through discipline and perseverance.

Sun in Aquarius (Air) with Moon in Scorpio (Water)

"From a quiet, observing child to a strong, consistent team leader."

When the Moon is in Scorpio and the Sun is in Aquarius, the energy flow struggles to move from the sensitive Water element to the intellectual Air element. This soul is pushing out from deep emotional intensity into a calm, cool, light demeanor. Since both of these signs have fixed, unyielding qualities, a strong need for stability and consistency follows throughout the life.

However, in youth, this soul is much more quiet and passive, particularly in the classroom where socializing is expected. As maturity comes, the group action becomes easier but total openness still feels like a struggle. There is a worldly consciousness, but it can be too positive, self-assertive or dominating in its delivery.

As the adult shifts more toward intellectual logic, the native becomes more comfortable in the corporate or political arena. Whatever course they set upon, they rarely change it because of a deep need for long-range planning. One of Aquarius' greatest challenges is to break old emotional patterns to make way for a new innovative lifestyle. Once the Scorpio has come out of their shell, organizational leadership is a natural profession for this confident, self-assured Aquarius Sun.

If the Scorpio/Aquarius combination of energy gets out of balance, the Mars need to set up competitive situations can cause real blockages for the Uranus energy that is trying to break loose. This fixed combination can become its own worst enemy by refusing to take action when it is not in the best interest of the soul to stand with heels dug in. Uranus-ruled Aquarius can become sarcastic and shut down emotionally quicker than any other sign. If the emotionally intense Scorpio Moon does not release the need to be in power, the Aquarian Sun energy will never be activated to build a detached position of leadership and thus will not reach its soul goal.

The soul lesson of the Moon in Scorpio and Sun in Aquarius includes dealing with a lifelong need for security and consistency. Friends are particularly important to this developing Air element soul. All of the Air signs have a need to develop strong social skills as a platform on which to practice communications and interactions.

Keep moving, Scorpio Moon and Aquarius Sun, in a smooth steady flow of divine energy that creates a stable pattern that allows for steady expansion into new and exciting situations.

Sun in Pisces (Water) with Moon in Scorpio (Water)

"From a quiet, observing child
to a compassionate, visionary server."

When the Moon is in Scorpio and the Sun is in Pisces, there is a strong pool of energy associated with the Water element and emotional sensitivity. The Moon phase is waning which calls for integration between soul and spirit by sharing knowledge and dispersing wisdom along the way.

This young Water sign will react emotionally every time. You won't wonder what this one is feeling or needing in their younger years. Jealousy and possessiveness may show strongly in the early years. Being around water is important to these souls as it soothes their emotional nature and has a calming effect.

Scorpio Moon can develop a rather harsh intense way of responding to relationships because of the over-sensitivity of the Pisces Sun. In the adult years, professions that involve sacrifice, service, counseling and intuition are natural niches for this strong Water energy. There is also a strong practical, business sense that will support career activity for this mature Scorpio. Many doctors, particularly surgeons and dentists, as well as nurses have strong planetary placements in this element. Music, art, and photography draw out the sensitive, creative part of Pisces.

If the Scorpio/Pisces combination of double water energy gets out of balance, there is much confusion, fear and possibly strong anger involved. It is quite easy for Pisces to delude herself into a fantasy world of dreams and wishes. When that bubble is broken, an extreme reaction can burst out of this vulnerable victim. There is a hidden longing within this soul to escape the bonds of earth and return to higher realms to escape the stress and harshness of earth living. Their over-sensitivity can lead to bouts of depression and frightening dreams. The astral world is quite close to the psyche of this group which may or may not have a positive effect. There is a real danger here of this soul getting trapped by their own fears and imagined dangers.

The soul lesson of the Moon in Scorpio and Sun in Pisces is to use their high psychic sensitivity and artistic talents to their positive advantage in this lifetime. Studying metaphysics, healing, mediumship, and other alternative counseling styles would be beneficial for this one's own personal growth as well as a possible career path. The messages that come from the other worlds should not be ignored because this soul has spent lifetimes developing this ability.

Keep moving, Scorpio Moon and Pisces Sun, in a smooth steady flow of divine energy to draw from your deep emotional well to sustain a focus on spiritual work and selfless service in a difficult time on our planet.

Moon in Sagittarius

Moon in Sagittarius (with all signs)

Each chapter begins with a description of the Moon's purpose for those readers who will want to go straight to a specific Moon/Sun combination.

Imagine a giant mirror reflecting past actions and experiences. According to mythology, the sign that the Moon was in at the time of your birth explains your soul response's in this lifetime. Understanding how the Moon's energy impacts your behavior and emotional reactions is key to understanding your hidden soul pattern and personal timing. You are the center of your own universe and the creator of your own destiny, so you need to understand your gifts and future goals. The eternal questions of the soul are: "Where have I come from?" and "Where am I going?" The most important eternal question, of course, is "Why am I here?"

Moon in Sagittarius (Fire)

The energy of Sagittarius comes from the Fire element, known to bring high vitality, restless action, and a spiritual passion. The soul born with this pattern comes with a need for great freedom and love of adventure. The infant Archer will watch excitedly as people move around him in the nursery.

They desperately need to be free to roam and to experience new adventures every day. Because he loves activity and new faces, Sagittarius Moon will not be happy if he is placed in a quiet corner away from the crowd. Put him right in the middle of the action, and he will happily entertain himself, or sleep right through it all. Don't bother with a playpen for this little one.

You will not find a more open, friendly, optimistic child than this Sagittarius Moon child. Even as an infant, this soul will choose the outdoors and fresh air every time. His happy-go-lucky, expansive attitude makes him a joy to raise as long as you don't mind chasing after him when he wanders off. Since there is a lot of Fire here, he will usually move with a good deal of speed, so be prepared to stay on your feet.

These young seekers will love to talk, question, and talk some more. As soon as they begin to talk quietly, playtime is over. Be careful when you ask them what they think because they may surprise you with a dose of the blunt truth. The Sagittarian child does not think before speaking and will be delighted to share the family secrets with anyone. Please be careful what you tell them. Honesty and openness are his natural traits, and sometimes he will speak without regard for the feelings of others.

The Sagittarius Moon child is not shy and may try to challenge the teacher for control of the classroom. He may not have the patience for school. He will excel in sports where he can use that competitive Fire spirit and be active at the same time. Sports is one place where he can be friendly without getting bogged down in heavy emotional relationships.

Unless the Sun sign energy tames him, it will be necessary to teach this free spirit to save for a rainy day. Their natural instinct is to trust the universe to provide. Faith and higher spiritual understanding will always be a part of this soul's energy. There is probably a large storehouse of spiritual blessings in the spiritual bankbook of this philosophical soul Angels are watching over them.

The goal of the Sagittarius Moon child is to hold on to his positive attitude and faith in the Divine Order that he was born with. To be successful, a strong routine must anchor his day-to-day activities. Look for the crowd at a social gathering, and chances are good there is a Sagittarius in there somewhere.

Sun in Aries (Fire) with Moon in Sagittarius (Fire)

"From an adventuresome, free-spirited child to an independent, fiery pioneer."

When the Moon is in Sagittarius and the Sun is in Aries, both signs are resonating to the high, dynamic, positive energy of the Fire element. Fire energy brings vitality, determination, and the will to take action independently. The natural urge for Fire-Fire is to act, move, and initiate activity. Being in the waning Moon phase of soul development, this combination is being tested in areas of relationship integration and sharing of information and resources.

In childhood, freedom and outdoor activity allow this soul to experience life openly without as many parental restrictions. The more freedom this one has, the happier the child; however, their impulsiveness can get them into unexpected trouble. Enthusiasm gets them through the day and if asked a question, they will respond openly, directly, and more honestly than may be necessary.

Moving into adulthood brings more quick, competitive action and spontaneity to the behavior. The Aries needs to allow their entrepreneurial spirit to have a place to take charge and lead without close supervision. It is the big picture, not the details, that draws out the high philosophical spirit and makes this combination stay engaged without getting bored. If this soul can discipline itself to get the education, there will be many opportunities to be a strong force for good in the world. There can be success in government, the ministry, law, or the fields of reform.

If the Sagittarius/Aries combination of energy gets out of balance, flightiness takes over that pushes this soul to chase new adventures and new experiences without ever finishing the old. Staying on track or staying with any commitment could be a real issue if there is no other fixity in the chart. The speech can be too direct and honest for most other signs, so these people can be considered brash or rude in their social skills. When Fire has no grounding force, it runs out of control looking for freedom. Their big picture philosophy can be an escape from living in reality. Slow, repetitive projects fall outside the range of tolerance for this soul and cause health problems if they get stuck in any routine activity.

The soul lesson of the Moon in Sagittarius and Sun in Aries is to control that high flashing energy pattern, so they can be dynamic without burning out. Using other qualities that the chart provides can allow this fireball to accomplish great deeds. By bringing the world's mental generalizations down to earth, this one can make these ideas realistically significant. The Sagittarius/Aries person is a pioneer, a doer, a crusader for new ideas and lost causes, and an individualist.

Keep moving, Sagittarius Moon and Aries Sun, in a smooth steady flow of divine energy toward directing that incredibly high driving force into success where the effort is self-driven and self-made.

Sun in Taurus (Earth) with Moon in Sagittarius (Fire)

*"From an adventuresome, free-spirited child
to a practical, dependable, stabilizer."*

When the Moon is in Sagittarius and the Sun is in Taurus, the energy flow goes from the masculine, positive Fire element to the feminine, negative Earth element. This growth pattern requires that the fiery activity be grounded in useful, practical projects. However, as the Taurus fixity sets in, a slower pace evolves that creates a need for consistency and caution. The Moon phase for this combination is waning, so it requires integration into compromise and sharing through relationships. This may not be an easy transition for the fiery Sagittarius who instinctively does not want restrictions or structure.

During the early years, there is a tendency toward impulsive action, hasty speech, and an argumentative nature. With maturity comes a strong social sense for mingling with the right and brightest people. Adding the warm, generous humor of Sagittarius to any group makes for excitement, so everyone enjoys this combination as long as they are out socializing.

Taurus has the habit of sticking to routine and not venturing out. If this combination keeps the spontaneity of its Fire energy, then life can still be fun while also taking care of the earthy, practical duties. The Venus energy from Taurus adds a musical talent that may show up as the ability to play by ear without formal training. With age, frugal Taurus should be able to control the flamboyant spending nature of fiery Sagittarius. The career requires some freedom along with strong monetary gain for security, so sales or teaching would be good choices.

If the Sagittarius/Taurus combination of energy gets out of balance, the urge to say what is what in a direct and challenging manner can create problems. When the Taurus bull digs in their heels and Sagittarius feels righteous pious about their belief or viewpoint, even the judge might get an earful of this one's opinion. If the free spirit of Fire gets stuck in the bullheadedness of Earth, there is no corralling this soul to do anything that they don't want to do. Unfortunately, big vision may outrun the capacity for performance.

The soul lesson of the Moon in Sagittarius and Sun in Taurus is to move from a spontaneous, risking pattern into a secure, grounded routine without feeling defeated. This shift may come slowly, so adulthood may come late as this is the sign of a late bloomer. On the positive side, this combination has a love of science, philosophy, and the urge to study the history of religion and behavior. Learning to think in practical, down-to-earth, decisive ways helps with the blending of these two very different energy patterns.

Keep moving, Sagittarius Moon and Taurus Sun, in a smooth steady flow of divine energy by allowing this calm, consistent nature to equalize the adventuresome spirit to create an exciting life where success and financial comforts can be realized.

Sun in Gemini (Air) with Moon in Sagittarius (Fire)

*"From an adventuresome, free-spirited child
to a quick-thinking, changeable doer."*

When the Moon is in Sagittarius and the Sun is in Gemini, the element flow is from positive, active Fire to positive, communicating Air energy. These two elements naturally blend, so the growth process flows easily within the individual; however, both signs fall into the category of mutable flexibility, so it is difficult for this soul to stay on task. The Moon phase is at the Full Moon point, so this soul is moving from the unconsciously driven motive to a conscious awareness that there are choices to be made which show up through relationships. Because both of these elements act in a masculine, out-flowing manner, this soul responds to life in a spontaneous way.

This youth loves to play outdoors and experience life without thought or planning. Too much restlessness makes the early school years difficult unless aspects in the chart allow for a steady thought process. This combination can learn quickly but may not retain the information because of a lack of attention to the deeper reasons for learning. Fantasy novels and stories only encourage this youngster to mentally fly off to never-never land where everything is fun and easy, so this one is better off focusing on factual studies and real life topics.

Since there is a tendency to deliver their opinions with an unexpected bluntness, people need to understand that there is no malicious intent here. The phrase "what you see is what you get" is certainly an appropriate phrase with this combination. The Jupiter-ruled Sagittarian Moon brings understanding of the bigger picture while Mercury-ruled Gemini is learning to communicate that vision clearly and logically. This adult is the "jack of all trades and master of none". So, the career path should allow for hands on applications with much variety and freedom of movement. A career involving teaching, speaking, creative writing, or even travel fits this pattern very comfortably.

If the Sagittarius/Gemini combination of energy gets out of balance, too many ideas confuse this soul in planning a life direction. Remaining flexible is the goal; however, there is a tendency to scatter one's thoughts and actions until nothing actually gets accomplished. Too much action and activity can create a frustrated anxiety pattern that locks up the mental flow of the Gemini energy. There is a habit of making grand and exciting plans, but there is little interest in staying grounded long enough to manifest complex activities. Their flighty nature may appear superficial, so they defend themselves by using intellectual rationale to "explain away" disconnected behavior.

The soul lesson of the Moon in Sagittarius and Sun in Gemini is to be able to keep their mind on track, so they can pursue intellectual learning and retain the information. One of the keys to their learning process is variety and short term exposure. When there are several topics to cover, this mutable thinker is able to jump around without getting bored and losing the train of thought. With this combination, it is better to have some information about many subjects than to try to focus for long periods on only one topic.

Keep on moving, Sagittarius Moon and Gemini Sun, in a smooth steady flow of divine energy toward focusing on current time and using all of the collected knowledge as it is called for spontaneously while continuing to learn and study new ideas.

Sun in Cancer (Water) with Moon in Sagittarius (Fire)

*"From an adventuresome, free-spirited child
to a nurturing, kind, homemaker."*

When the Moon is in Sagittarius and the Sun is in Cancer, the energy flow goes from the positive, masculine Fire element to the receptive, feminine Water element. This is a difficult transition into adulthood because the open, free energy of the child struggles with the instinctual need to be emotionally safe as one gets older. The soul's path as shown through the Moon phase is waxing or growing in light and is still at an unconscious level.

This little person is feisty and will take off running at any opportunity. In youth, this soul has a high-spirited visionary quality that is refreshing yet mystical and outspoken. It is the phase of the student or disciple who is preparing to integrate their ideas and intuitive insight with the flow of the outer world. As the Cancerian qualities appear, there is a softening of the Sagittarian's bluntness because the emotional Moon energy has trouble handling the same abrupt blunt energy coming at them that they are capable of sending out.

If the Sagittarius Moon is able to stay on track with their education, any area of human relations or counseling or teaching would be good for this individual. The Sag/Cancer spirit makes for a good nurturer who can mother and be empathetic with behaviors that reach outside the community box.

If the Sagittarius/Cancer combination of energy gets out of balance, there will be a fiery resistance to being reined in by others or under another's control. This can show up as high rebellion usually aimed at the mother or family. Their understanding of the need to live by conventional values usually only relates to others but not to the self. The underlying entitlement belief is that this one can do exactly as they please. With the Fire and Water elements conflicting, it is hard to decide what the soul really wants and what will make it happy. Sometimes, travel and freedom seem most important and then at other times a beautiful home, a warm family, and secure surroundings are most attracting. For anyone trying to partner with this soul, life can become very complex because the needs change with the cycles of the Moon.

The soul lesson of the Moon in Sagittarius and Sun in Cancer is to direct change and blend it with the need for emotional security. The optimum scenario would be to study high wisdom with occasional world travel while maintaining a comfortable, warm nesting home and family that is stable while the wanderer goes off to seek new adventures. The growth point relates to the home front where it is necessary to be emotionally available to family and friends without disappearing when the emotional levels get overwhelming.

Keep moving, Sagittarius Moon and Cancer Sun, in a smooth steady flow of divine energy toward nurturing your intuitive feminine side while you allow the masculine adventurous side to seek universal understanding that can be applied to the act of living a meaningful family life.

Sun in Leo (Fire) with Moon in Sagittarius (Fire)

"From an adventuresome, free-spirited child
to a fast-paced, outgoing leader."

When the Moon is in Sagittarius and the Sun is in Leo, the positive Fire element rules the soul energy bringing high enthusiasm, excitement, and flamboyance into the life pattern. This soul feels happy with itself as the transition from Moon to Sun is harmonious in nature. The Moon phase supports unconscious willingness to move forward and bud out into a colorful life.

As a child, there is a strong love of adventure, with a restless edge that keeps pushing this high energy soul forward even through high risk situations. A spiritual spontaneity loves the risk of seeking higher learning and broader visions of the world.

With maturity, the goal here is to anchor this free spirit into a fixed plan of action that will bring forth leadership by using this knowledge for the good of the planet. Great goals can be accomplished if the scattered Sagittarius seeker can use self-restraint to focus on the task and allow the fixed good-hearted disposition of Leo to set the course of action and then follow it. Any career that allows for utilizing the spiritual or serves the greater good of the group will be good for this combination. Philanthropic and humanitarian careers attract this high energy outgoing Leo as long as people and fast-paced activity are present.

If the Sagittarius/Leo combination of double fire energy gets out of balance, no one can measure up to the special expectations of this one. Arrogance, drama, and pride in behavior can hold would be friends and lovers at arm's length. If the Sagittarius wanderlust continues to rule the life, there may be many romances but never any serious commitments because there may be something better just around the next mountain. Even though Jupiter-ruled Sagittarius acts as though everything is wonderful, never embarrass this Leo stubborn energy in public or they will be gone for sure. There is some fickleness that needs to be grounded and willing to make commitments.

The soul lesson of the Moon in Sagittarius and Sun in Leo is to stabilize that highly motivated, exciting energy of this Fire duo by directing the focus toward leadership. They will use their talents by instilling spiritual principles and positive outcomes for the whole group, whether that group be in work, church or family. This growth also involves learning to make a deep level of commitment in relationships in all areas of life.

Keep moving, Sagittarius Moon and Leo Sun, in a smooth steady flow of divine energy toward a finer attunement of the highly spiritual Fire element using your developed leadership abilities to shine out in world through success and joyfulness.

Sun in Virgo (Earth) with Moon in Sagittarius (Fire)

*"From an adventuresome, free-spirited child
to a grounded, analytical worker."*

When the Moon is in Sagittarius and the Sun is in Virgo, the energy flow struggles to shift from the positive, active Fire element to the negative, receptive Earth element. Starting out with a high spirit, full of adventure and daring, this soul needs to shift the focus to grounding the activities in routine life matters where service and work can be accomplished. The Moon phase in this relationship is waxing and indicates a struggle of the soul to break out of the unconscious, impulsive pushing phase and begin to reach for goals. Both of these signs represent a flexible, changeable instinct that makes for a restless behavior style.

The Sagittarius child approaches life from a free-flowing, exciting, philosophical attitude. A natural love of learning inspires this soul to work on gathering knowledge for the purpose of using it in some form of service. As this soul matures, it can become difficult to commit to one career or place to live.

Variety continues to nag at this person because both Sagittarius and Virgo are mutable or changeable in nature. A love of spiritual wisdom combined with a literal ability to process and analyze information should provide an ability to teach, inspire, preach, and guide other souls along the higher road of life. Careers that are constantly changing work well for this one or teaching at higher levels where travel and exploration increase the expertise are favorable. They do best in the second position because they don't care for being first in line.

If the Sagittarius/Virgo combination of energy gets out of balance, the inner-impulsive nature is prone to making hasty judgments while the grounded nature wants to analyze and process all of the details before acting. When both patterns activate, a stalemate is created

253

where nothing happens because fire energy wants to go and earth energy wants to wait to be cautious. The Jupiter-ruled Sagittarius can cross swords with Mercury-ruled Virgo and then many things may be said that could have been left unsaid. Too much honesty can become an arrow aimed to hurt another.

The soul lesson of the Moon in Sagittarius and Sun in Virgo is to develop a well-organized plan and then to stay with it until it is completed. It would be a natural flow of progression to hold a high office of guidance in some institution. Moving into later life metaphysics can play an integral part in provided extended growth for this information seeking combination.

Keep moving, Sagittarius Moon and Virgo Sun, in a smooth steady flow of divine energy by setting the soul intent to include adaptation to the higher teachings and universal laws that become more clear with deeper study.

Sun in Libra (Air) with Moon in Sagittarius (Fire)

*"From an adventuresome, free-spirited child
to a social, balanced mediator."*

When the Moon is in Sagittarius and the Sun is in Libra, the energy flow goes naturally from the positive, masculine Fire element to the positive, mental Air element. The waxing Moon phase brings an instinctive push outward for the soul to continue its growth with an unconscious drive to expand. The active fiery Moon behavior ultimately needs to be refined and smoothed into a Venusians' graciousness that perfects the social qualities of these two signs.

The young child begins by rushing out into the world with wild innocence, speaking quickly and with great honesty. Their warmth and openness makes everyone receive them as a fresh breath of air; however, that direct, truthful speech can become a bit aggressive or adversarial when they want to do things their own way. This one will have a keen interest in learning early, so start early with reading them book.

As they grow and Venus applies her magic, this free spirit becomes more refined and ready to become a real leader in their own social world and beyond. The planet Jupiter brings open flow, and Venus adds charm and grace, so this combination can create a warm, romantic individual who succeeds on their personality attributes, particularly in business or in law. An ability to see things in a broad perspective gives a prophetic quality and lends to spiritual study in the areas of religion, philosophy, and science. Sales talent, in any industry, is natural because of this ability to see beyond the small situation to bigger arenas.

If the Sagittarius/Libra combination of energy gets out of balance, "too much of a good thing" can take hold of this adventuresome soul. Pleasure and travel may take precedence over the drudgeries such as work and routine responsibility. If the pride and independence get too strong in this combination, they are hard to approach or get close to. It would be easy to see this soul running from place to place and relationship to relationship without attaching too long to anyone. Variety needs to be a part of life but only a part.

The soul lesson of the Moon in Sagittarius and Sun in Libra is to stay in balance and not get carried away with the dreams of the moment. Fire and Air energies have a fantastic overactive drive to move, do, and go. So it is wise for this one to get the education early while the Sagittarius need for learning is so strong, then any career involving people and organizing people becomes an easy task. This is an easy person to like, for as long as they are around.

Keep moving, Sagittarius Moon and Libra Sun, in a smooth steady flow of divine energy toward staying committed to the task and the relationship currently in your life because there are no greener pastures out there for the conquering. Use all of your quick wit and social gifts wisely.

Sun in Scorpio (Water) with Moon in Sagittarius (Fire)

*"From an adventuresome, free-spirited child
to an intense, focused project person."*

When the Moon is in Sagittarius and the Sun is in Scorpio, the energy is moving from the positive outgoing Fire element to the feminine, receptive Water element. With the Moon phase waxing out into new growth, this soul begins life with an impulsive, pushing action that can overpower their caretakers.

This free-spirited child loves the outdoors and particularly loves playing alone in an imaginary world. The conflict between being open to the adventures of life and the feelings of needing to be guarded against those who would intrude on their privacy and expose their secrets makes this soul difficult to understand. Even as a young person, this one has definite ideas about their beliefs, philosophies, and political opinions.

There is an unpredictable pattern here that is attractive and provocative yet guarded and unreachable at times. There is a natural secretiveness here around sexual relationships and also a great attraction to intrigue. Careers involving exploration, adventure, investigation, and mystery draw the best of both patterns from this individual.

If the Sagittarius/Scorpio combination of energy gets out of balance, a secretiveness about their adventuresome escapades can shut other people out. With this combination of Mars ruling Scorpio and Jupiter ruling Sagittarius, extremes are possible with aggressive, combative behavior occurring when this one is crossed. Anger seldom surfaces, but when it does it can be ruthless and destructive. Jealousy and possessive can surface once this one actually settles on a mate. But if rejected, this free-spirit is quickly out the door without a word.

The soul lesson of the Moon is Sagittarius and Sun in Scorpio is to remain flexible with a positive attitude while learning to stabilize their life patterns. Flitting from adventure to adventure will not allow the deep emotional needs of Scorpio to bond with others in meaningful relationships. Once the spiritual search begins, deep occult study will draw this soul into higher enlightenment with the opportunity to teach universal truths. Marriage and commitment can be very positive once the philosophical Sag finds a way to maintain a sense of freedom while allowing them to become intimately and passionately inner-twined with their partner.

Keep moving, Sagittarius Moon and Scorpio Sun, in a smooth steady flow of divine energy toward allowing your passionate, focused will to take hold, so you can soar with the eagles and flow with divine vision.

Sun in Sagittarius (Fire)
with Moon in Sagittarius (Fire)

*"From an adventuresome, free-spirited child
to an open, direct wandered."*

When both luminaries (Sun and Moon) fall in the same sign, the Moon phase may be either New or Balsamic in phase, and both of these call for much self-reflection and self-motivation with the keyword being "Self". With the Moon and Sun in Sagittarius together, there is a strong concentration of energy in the positive, masculine, active Fire element. The Moon phase relates to the soul's growth, the lesson here lies deep within where understanding of self and higher purpose reside.

As a child and as an adult, this adventurer needs to be able to escape. Because of this self-focus, relationships take a secondary position in this lifetime. An intense love of freedom and independence pushes this young child into a reckless and sometimes verbally rebellious behavior.

Sports and outdoor activities that require a quick mind and quick physical responses allow this fireball energy to shine even in competitive situations. From childhood through adulthood, travel, adventure, philosophy, religion, science, and law, all hold the attention of this seeker of knowledge. A philosophical mind enjoys standing back and observing the big picture. With a strong natural talent for persuasive speaking, any career involving the inspiration of others is a good use of this native's gifts.

If the Sagittarius/Sagittarius combination of double fire element energy gets out of balance, the need for new horizons pushes this soul out into the world as a wanderer or gypsy traveler. In their search for deep spiritual meaning, they can become self-righteous or religious fanatics. There can be extremes in temperament because of the mutable, flexible nature of this Fire sign. Duality is part of the nature but if it gets unstable, nervous tendencies can become a real challenge that creates a lack of mental focus. Sag can become a radical thinker or revolutionary if they are not careful.

The soul lesson of the Moon and Sun in Sagittarius strong pattern is to maintain stability in their beliefs and learn to live by the creeds which they espouse. A warm, outgoing nature provides a welcome environment for open spiritual debate which is their greatest passion. There is a tendency to shift directions without finishing the job, so the greatest challenge is to harness the expanded mind to focus and apply all of that acquired knowledge.

Keep moving, Sagittarius Moon and Sun, in a smooth steady flow of divine energy toward inspiring others to follow the higher path by setting a courageous example of being open to new and honorable principles.

Sun in Capricorn (Earth)
with Moon in Sagittarius (Fire)

*"From an adventuresome, free-spirited child
to a responsible, organized traveler."*

When the Moon is in Sagittarius and the Sun is in Capricorn, the positive, masculine Fire element is flowing toward the feminine, receptive Earth element. The goal is to ground and utilize the high fiery drive in a process of building structure on this plane. The Moon phase is waning, so the purpose is to complete lifetimes of scattered projects and unfinished relationships.

Even though this child is open, playful and clever, there is a serious side that always makes this little one appear to be an adult. An ambitious drive to succeed remains ever present in all of their actions. The restless need for movement pushes this achiever to complete a multitude of tasks to experience a feeling of success.

Throughout the life, there is a love of travel and adventure, but it must have a purpose and a recognizable result. Saturn-ruled Capricorn grounds flighty Sagittarius to make every activity worthwhile and purposeful. On the professional front, business success is always a part of the process, but there should be strong emphasis on counseling, organizing, and duty. Commerce, business, and financial management, or church hierarchy are areas where this far-thinking organizer could use their many gifts.

If the Sagittarius/Capricorn combination of energy gets out of balance, inner-conflict between expanding outward and pulling inward, or growth and cutting back, causes great stress and nervous tension. Jupiter's push toward optimism crosses with Saturn's need for caution and limitation. The result may be that this native runs away to follow their own dreams, or they stay and throw themselves into their work to accomplish a feeling of control and success. This soul must learn to relax, or they will never find peace because they are always searching for the side of themselves that they are not utilizing. There is a touch of intellectual snobbery here that makes this individual demanding of self and critical of others who are not using their mental powers wisely.

The soul lesson of the Moon in Sagittarius and Sun in Capricorn is to use the adaptability and flexibility that this soul was born with and blend it with the practical, dependable, responsible grounding that Saturn insists upon. Any career that utilizes critical thinking skills and represents an ambitious challenge will hold the attention of this broad-spectrum thinker.

Keep moving, Sagittarius Moon and Capricorn Sun, in a smooth steady flow of divine energy toward anchoring the clear thinking in a responsible position where positive recognition and high success are possible.

Sun in Aquarius (Air) with Moon in Sagittarius (Fire)

*"From an adventuresome, free-spirited child
to an open-minded, objective thinker."*

When the Moon is in Sagittarius and the Sun is in Aquarius, the positive outward energy flow goes from the Fire element to the Air element. Since these two patterns are complementary, the process of growing up feels natural and flowing. The waning Moon phase calls for a stripping away of old ways and fixed thinking to make way for the soul journey back to inner-peace.

This child is highly energetic and full of innovative ideas with strong opinions. In youth, their overly independent attitudes appear rebellious but they consider themselves to be open, objective and reasonable. There is a broad visionary scope within this soul that fights courageously on the side of fundamental truth. It is hard to change their opinion on the intellectual front particularly when they become righteous about their truth and honor.

This combination is inclined to be abrupt and impulsive in their speech but still manages to attract a large number of friends and acquaintances. High intellectual thinking combined with strong organizational skills brings this native great opportunities at the executive levels of large organizations. The Jupiter and Uranus planetary combination creates a pattern of broad, progressive, humanitarian attitudes that are good in personal relationships also.

If the Sagittarius/Aquarius combination of energy gets out of balance, detachment and abrupt speech can cause all kinds of social problems with friends as well as family. A "know-it-all" attitude can freeze people in their tracks if they dare to challenge this one's intellectual opinion. Compromise is a tough struggle for this combination, particularly in personal relationships where feelings come in to play more often. This native's high individualistic drive to do things their own way causes real issues in the group setting also. Learning to express in a warm and non-combative manner would help this one's soul growth tremendously.

The soul lesson Moon in Sagittarius and Sun in Aquarius calls for the integration of their higher mind with their strong social skills to bring people together in group cooperation. Using their personal magnetism wisely will allow for many opportunities to come to them without much effort. Once the Sagittarius free spirit settles down, there can be a very rewarding, loving partnership based on honesty and friendship.

Keep moving, Sagittarius Moon and Aquarius Sun, in a smooth steady flow of divine energy toward taming that impulsive instinct to charge forward into a smooth, steady, deliberate forward movement capable of handling multiple high-level tasks successfully.

Sun in Pisces (Water) with Moon in Sagittarius (Fire)

"From an adventuresome, free-spirited child to a sensitive, compassionate server."

When the Moon is in Sagittarius and the Sun is in Pisces, the energy must struggle to shift from the positive, outgoing Fire element to the receptive, feminine Water element. The waning Moon phase indicates a need to strip away old systems and look deep into the soul patterns to see what needs to be dissolved. There is a mutability in both of these signs that allows for over-activity and sense of becoming overwhelmed by a deep need for duty and sacrifice.

In childhood, imagination and creativity run high to support a strong intuitive, progressive thinking process but they may also get lost in abstractions and generalities. As this soul matures, they may develop extraordinarily broad thinkers. It is important for this combination to narrow their interests to one field and set about mastering it.

The ability to perceive and understand symbols may be one of this soul's greatest gifts. Relationship may come and go with the combination because one-on-one pairing is not the primary goal. They should choose a mate who is self-sufficient, so there is a separation of priorities. Success can come through service, the social sciences or literature because all of these professions would utilize these compassionate and perceptive skills.

If the Sagittarius/Pisces combination of energy gets out of balance, a lack of concentration and instability become overwhelming. All of this flexible, mutable energy can appear a bit naive or confused, so people may not understand the depth of this soul's awareness. Too much nervous tension can turn this changeable individual into a real chatter box which is not their normal pattern. This soul combination must guard against frittering away their time and energy of superficial projects and sacrificing missions. Staying on task is the most difficult challenge for this "now" based Jupiter Neptune energy.

The soul lesson of the Moon in Sagittarius and Sun in Pisces is to focus their high intuitive, spiritual awareness into a profession or talent where it can be used. The soul understanding of the symbols of the universe can be used in many ways to broaden the world's spiritual knowledge. This gift needs to be shared with one or one thousand, but the energy needs to flow out to allow for connection with other spiritual souls. If this soul will honor their higher call instead of getting caught up in the busy work of everyday life, there are opportunities for real contributions.

Keep moving, Sagittarius Moon and Pisces Sun, in a smooth steady flow of divine energy toward allowing the spiritual pace of the universe to carry your soul to a clearer vision and higher understanding for universal good.

Moon in Capricorn

Sun in Aries (Fire) with Moon in Capricorn (Earth)

*"From a serious, responsible child
to a fiery, independent pioneer."*

When the Moon is in Capricorn and the Sun is in Aries, the blocked flow of energy is from the feminine, receptive Earth element to the positive, active Fire element. This is the waning cycle of Moon where conscious integration and stripping away of old ways and patterns is called for. Relationships provide an arena for minimizing the strong leadership qualities of both of these signs; however, the real battle is with the self.

The early childhood is experienced more on an adult level because planet Saturn rules this Capricorn child. Responsibility and proper behavior are part of the natural persona for this one. Since Aries is always representative of independence, these two signs together produce a very controlled and productive young person. No one needs to do much scolding in this situation; however, the parents may feel the disapproval from their child if they are not acting responsibly.

Ambition and leadership are magnified by an impatient drive to be first, so there is a strong competitive nature that does best when tied to a structured environment or career. This Saturn Mars native prefers to do things for themselves because of a very strong independent streak. So, any position that allows them to be independent makes them happy. Sales or a top leadership position work well for this person.

If the Capricorn/Aries combination of energy gets out of balance, the urge to initiate action but not follow through can become a problem. Their perfectionist nature is quick to point out any weak points in other peoples personality, but this combination does not take criticism well. In fact, they can become quite the intimidator when they have some authority over others. Saturn-ruled Capricorn rules time and being on time may be an issue with this one because whatever they are doing is more important than anyone else's schedule. Usually this combination controls their anger, but when they become irritated their remarks are quick and burning.

The soul lesson of the Moon in Capricorn and Sun in Aries, two cardinal signs is to learn to maintain a steady pace in the work and personal activities, so they do not burn out. Their quick mental energy allows them to establish a strong initial plan, so they do best when they set up the plan and then delegate the completion of the project to someone else. Because of a deep need for tradition and commitment, marriage usually works for this one particularly if they can be the one in charge.

Keep moving, Capricorn Moon and Aries Sun, in a smooth steady flow of divine energy toward a strong, enterprising, leadership position where your courage and organizational skills can be honored.

Sun in Taurus (Earth) with Moon in Capricorn (Earth)

"From a serious, responsible child
to a practical, dependable stabilizer."

When the Moon is in Capricorn and the Sun is in Taurus, the Earth element rules the soul and the personality in a grounded, realistic, receptive way. The waning phase of the Moon calls for growth in conscious integration with others through sharing knowledge and resources. There is a strong, serious nature that is very apparent even when this child is quite young.

They may learn at an early age how to give orders and have others do their bidding. However, as they mature, they will develop a consistency of pace that encourages them to set goals and then manifest them. The strong Earth influence brings a stable, plodding work ethic that allows this soul to acquire an abundance of material possessions as well as a high position in their career life.

Any profession that deals with money, investments, and business organization will allow the practical side of this one to shine. In relationships, there is a soft, affectionate nature under that proper exterior that people can count on. A successful Saturn Venus will always take care of family and be a devoted loving parent; however, they may appear to be a bit fixed and authoritarian in their discipline style.

If the Capricorn/Taurus combination of double earth Element energy gets out of balance, there can be a lot of procrastination about getting started on any project. Comfort is a high priority for Taurus, so they can get a bit lazy and think of many reasons not to initiate the plan. Caution and practicality may squash any playful spontaneity particularly if there is any sense that one's security is at stake. This one can definitely get bogged down in duty and responsibility if they are not careful. They must guard against using intimidation and disapproval to get their own way or to control the actions of those close to them.

The soul lesson of the Moon in Capricorn and Sun in Taurus is to be consistent without being to dry and cold. Success is a natural pattern of development here, so it is only required that this soul make a strong organizational plan and then stick to it. Possessions are important to this one, so they need only to remember to take care of their precious collections once they get them.

Keep moving, Capricorn Moon and Taurus Sun, in a smooth steady flow of divine energy toward using that strong, practical temperament wisely to nurture those you love and encourage them to become as responsible and reliable as your nature allows you to be.

Sun in Gemini (Air) with Moon in Capricorn (Earth)

*"From a serious, responsible child
to a fast-paced, mentally quick achiever."*

When the Moon is in Capricorn and the Sun is in Gemini, the flow of the energy goes from receptive, feminine Earth to positive, masculine Air. An adjustment is required in this maturation process where the grounded, earthy thought process must become lighter in nature and more open to ideas and new thinking. The Moon phase is still unconscious and struggling to study and learn in preparation for the next cycle of integration.

Being a strong student is critical to the development of this serious, loner child. Not only information but the ability to communicate that information and interact comfortably in social settings is part of the school learning game. A literal learning style needs to be broken, so the student can learn to create outside the box and become a more open-minded free thinker.

A conventional lifestyle demanded by Saturn covers up a strong urge for mental freedom. A professional career in the business world provides the most comfortable arena for this thinker. Relationships may get put on the back burner until this native feels secure in their outer world. Because of their disciplined work style, good memory and solid mental talents, a career in civil service or government would work here. Since this combination has a strong mental temperament, there should be a strong focus on science and invention.

If the Capricorn/Gemini combination of energy gets out of balance, the tendency is to pull within and shut out other people's thoughts and opinions. They may even make business commitments that they never follow through with. Completing tasks represents a real challenge for mutable Gemini. Saturn and Mercury together can become heavy which opens the door to depression and deep worry about the "what-ifs" of life. In relationships, this combination can become detached and little cold if people interfere with their "work" time. The Capricorn Goat can surprise the world with their astute ability to make hard decisions and cut the emotional cords if required.

The soul lesson of the Moon in Capricorn and Sun in Gemini is to open up to innovative ways of thinking and living. Being confident around organizational abilities and work ethic will provide this Gemini with a great platform for success. Their strong mental talents will serve them well to envision the future.

Keep moving, Capricorn Moon and Gemini Sun, in a smooth steady flow of divine energy toward expanded thinking to embrace new horizons while the grounded part of the soul gets fed by a secure work position that forces routine and follow through of projects.

Sun in Cancer (Water)
with Moon in Capricorn (Earth)

"From a serious, responsible child
to a nurturing, kind decision-maker."

When the Moon is in Capricorn and the Sun is in Cancer, the shift from the receptive Earth element to the receptive Water element requires a deliberate action of balance. The Moon phase is Full in Capricorn meaning that the Sun and Moon are in opposition at the time of birth, creating an imbalance of emotional energies that could act cold and practical. Integrating emotions into the decision-making process is the key.

Relationships with family provide a needed secure nest where this little one can grow while feeling safe and loved. Parental influence plays a critical role in this child's development because their nature is to follow the behaviors and traditions established by the tribal family. Executive skills appear early in life as this one willingly takes charge of the responsibilities within the home.

Even as a young adult, this combination is actively engaged in initiating new opportunities to accumulate wealth and position out in the business world. A naturally shrewd negotiating sense allows them to drive a hard bargain with a smile and a sweet demeanor. All relationships need to be traditional as a deep need for home and family drives a strong need to marry and have children. Career can consume this one when they make their business associates their friends leaving no time for outside interests. This pattern could be very boring for the partner when they do not fit into that business world.

If the Capricorn/Cancer combination of energy gets out of out of balance, too much action and not enough down time could be a problem at home. Unexpected mood swings could occur during Full Moon periods and upset the normal controlled, self-contained disposition of this cool Capricorn.

The soul lesson of the Moon in Capricorn and the Sun in Cancer is to develop a warm, safe environment where the Cancer Crab feels safe and secure. Family responsibilities and commitments ground this individual and bring the soft, nurturing side which does not often show out in the business world. A deep love of homeland and security should keep this soul close to their birthplace.

Keep moving, Capricorn Moon and Cancer Sun, in a smooth steady flow of divine energy toward building strong business relationships that can support the family and traditional lifestyle that is so important to the inner-peace of your soul.

Sun in Leo (Fire) with Moon in Capricorn (Earth)

*"From a serious, responsible child
to a fast-paced, outgoing leader."*

When the Moon is in Capricorn and the Sun is in Leo, there is an energy flow from the negative, receptive Earth element to the masculine, active Fire element. This shift requires inner adjustments within the soul that break the solid, hard-core, grounded patterns of Saturn-ruled Capricorn. The Moon phase is waxing which creates an instinctive, pushing action that struggles with getting in position to take action.

As a responsible, mature child, this soul starts taking control of the show at an early age. There is power here that is harnessed in a controlled, determined pattern that is driven to succeed. The child may become spoiled because they expect the best and usually create a dramatic scene if they do not get what they want. On the other side, Sunny Leo can be quite fun in a comfortable, structured setting.

This soul's ambitious drive will place them at the top of whatever profession they choose to go after. A desire to climb the mountain of success and be the ruler does not leave much time for casual relationships, so anyone in their life is there for a reason. Powerful friends and influential people naturally come forward to help this over-achiever reach their lofty goals. Relationships can work if the partner is willing to let this king or queen reign in a benefic manner.

If the Capricorn/Leo combination of energy gets out of balance, a demanding ego can roar and scare away those who might have been supportive. Power struggles and bossiness can make personal friendships difficult to maintain over time. As long as the partner supports this one's financial goals, there will be a strong bond. Intimidation is a dangerous weapon that this soul possesses and should avoid using because of the karmic price.

The soul lesson of the Moon in Capricorn and Sun in Leo is to use that powerful drive in a responsible fashion so as not to damage other souls on the climb up the mountain. There is an old saying "be careful who you step on on the way up because you will meet them on the way down". This is sage advice for this soul. Because play and relaxation are important for balance in life, this combination needs to practice working hard and then taking time to play. In the well-developed soul, great leadership abilities surface early in the life and provide opportunities for prominent positions in high places.

Keep moving, Capricorn Moon and Leo Sun, in a smooth steady flow of divine energy toward building a strong foundation that will support great success and honorable rewards for you and your family.

Sun in Virgo (Earth) with Moon in Capricorn (Earth)

*"From a serious, responsible child
to a grounded, analytical problem-solver."*

When the Moon is in Capricorn and the Sun is in Virgo, the receptive, feminine Earth element rules over the grounded focus of the lifetime. The waxing Moon phase makes growth an unconscious drive to push out to gather the nutrients necessary to build a solid, successful life plan.

Even as a child there is a fine mind with critical thinking skills that draws out their analytical nature. Problem-solving expertise begins early and stays dominant throughout the life. This serious young person is always working toward building a solid business or professional career that will allow then to be in charge of their own destiny. Even with the shy tendencies of Virgo, this is not a journey that requires inner-struggle, so this soul enjoys their own company.

Relationships need to be of a practical nature with other serious-minded people. Business or science is the most natural mediums for growth with this calculating mind. Any career requiring organization and detail will be successful.

If the Capricorn/Virgo combination of energy gets out of balance, too much work can make this individual a bit dull and boring. If their naturally astute and critical mind is turned on to friends and loved ones, the receiving person could feel picked apart and severely criticized. Hidden under that confident exterior, there lie deep levels of insecurity and self-doubt. By always appearing in control, this Virgo protects their vulnerable side. In emotional situations, this Earth combination can become very hard, cold, and dry especially if a Water sign comes along and throws in muddy water.

The soul lesson of the Moon in Capricorn and Sun in Virgo is to apply their strong, reasonable, practical senses to the personal relationships in their life, even though most of their relationships probably have come from connections in the business world. Follow through in both personal and professional relationships can be a challenge, so this earthy energy needs to use their take-charge ability to delegate the details to others.

Keep moving, Capricorn Moon and Virgo Sun, in a smooth steady flow of divine energy toward blending the two strong archetypes of Earth into a solid, pleasant, supportive, as well as successful lifestyle that is good for both you and your family.

Sun in Libra (Air) with Moon in Capricorn (Earth)

"From a serious, responsible child
to a social, quick-thinking negotiator."

When the Moon is in Capricorn and the Sun is in Libra, the energy flow struggles to make the shift from the receptive Earth element to the positive, outgoing Air element. The Moon phase pattern is waxing unconsciously as it struggles to push out from its contained space into a place where it can take action.

This quiet, serious child automatically takes responsibility for self and others as soon as they are able to talk. In the early years there is not much talking, but that changes as airy Libra begins to grow up and make friends with everyone they meet. The natural instinct is to keep the emotions controlled and tucked away so there is no vulnerability.

However, there is great sensitivity to the needs of others and it is important that others think well of them. There is a gift for managing people and negotiating business deals that comes from a strong sense of being purposeful in reaching a satisfactory outcome. This combination does not like to leave business or personal relationships in limbo. Because of the naturally ambitious nature here, selfishness can show up when success is within sight.

If the Capricorn/Libra combination of energy gets out of balance, an attitude of over-confident cockiness can be overbearing to others. Usually Venus-ruled Libra can mask the bossy, domineering side of Capricorn, but when Venus can't have peace and harmony, they will go for all out war, and they usually win. Too much action and too much business eats up all their time, and there is no time left for relaxing.

The soul lesson of the Moon in Capricorn and Sun in Libra is to use their outgoing, organizing skills in a purposeful way that will benefit others around them. Sharing is one of Libra's major lessons in this lifetime, so achieving a balance of work and play is important for family values. It is important for this Saturn-ruled person not to get into a routine where there is no time for socializing with people other than the mate. Libra needs friendships to keep them on an even keel.

Keep moving, Capricorn Moon and Libra Sun in a smooth steady flow of divine energy that supports a balanced exchange between the business world and the personal world, so that Venus charm can reach out to people and be warm and delightful.

Sun in Scorpio (Water)
with Moon in Capricorn (Earth)

"From a serious, responsible child
to a determined, focused researcher."

When the Moon is in Capricorn and the Sun is in Scorpio, the energy flow goes from the receptive, feminine Earth element to the feminine, receptive Water element. This is usually a smooth transition for the soul as it grows and matures. The waxing Moon phase instinctively pushes this soul to rush out and experience life in an unconscious drive to experience. Both signs bring emotional stability and a firm grip on the ambitious drive.

Even at birth no one is going to control this little soul. This one knows how to demand attention and has the courage to back it up. The Saturnian sense of duty and discipline is strong even in the child, so it does not take much discipline to raise this one. When this youth becomes a teenager and the sexual energy opens up, this one will make her own decisions and then keep her secrets deep within.

There is definitely a "Don't Tell and Don't Ask" policy with the private life here. Because this soul knows their own worth, she will demand recognition for her talents in the business world and can succeed wherever she chooses. Tenacity will be the driving force. Careers in business management or surgical medicine are natural outlets for that incredible focus.

If the Capricorn/Scorpio combination of energy gets out of balance, a very hard, no-nonsense attitude comes out as cold stubbornness. This can be an icy energy that she shares with no one. The sexual drive and the sexual charisma can bring the soul many temptations and have a major impact of lifelong decisions when choosing a partner. When this watery energy feels threatened, they will throw cold criticism out as a defense. If this Scorpio/Capricorn energy gets too carried away with

285

the need to be right, they may find themselves alone and deserted in later life.

The soul lesson of the Moon in Capricorn and Sun in Scorpio is to use their intensity, the sensuality and determination wisely. Such power as this soul possesses should be monitored and trained in positive directions to create good for all instead of safety for one. Duty, honor, and loyalty are the highest that this combination can offer to the world, and they can do it with a great presence.

Keep moving, Capricorn Sun and Scorpio Moon, in a smooth steady flow of divine energy in a flexible, consistent manner that allows for ambition and drive to carry you all the way to the top of the ladder.

Sun in Sagittarius (Fire)
with Moon in Capricorn (Earth)

"From a serious, responsible child
to an adventuresome, risk-taker."

When the Moon is in Capricorn and the Sun is in Sagittarius, the energy flow goes from receptive, feminine Earth to the positive, masculine Fire element. The New Moon waxing phase instinctively drives this soul out into the world to experience it on a fresh, spontaneous basis.

With a serious, responsible emotional base, this child follows the rules and naturally takes charge of duties within the family. Commitments to parents are taken very seriously, so there is not much rebellion, at least outwardly, shown here. As this young person matures, the enthusiastic, fiery, free spirit of Sagittarius gets stronger and wanderlust sets in. Many Jupiter-ruled people end up living far from their birth place because it permits a stronger sense of independence.

A determined ambition, a quick mind and solid common sense support any career, but the highest interests will be in business, church or law. Higher spiritual purpose pushes this one towards making a difference in an orderly fashion. This could be the life of the crusader. Any career that allows for expansion and feeds the ambitious spirit of this combination will hold their attention which naturally brings success.

If the Capricorn/Sagittarius combination of energy gets out of balance, the urge will be to break loose and travel the world. However, the Saturn influence pulls back demanding caution with limited boundaries. A push-pull energy pattern can result in high nervous stress that can go into depression. Jupiter-ruled Sag has trouble staying on track and tends to scatter their attention and their clothes while good old Capricorn knows the life should be orderly with everything in its proper place. Saturn is a great guilt builder, so this soul may spend much time guilty about what is not happening instead of enjoying what is happening. If intellectual snobbery comes into play, this individual could become quite judgmental of others as well as of themselves. If this happens, Sagittarius can become more outspoken and direct than is necessary.

The soul lesson of the Moon in Capricorn and Sun in Sagittarius is to follow the high road to new horizons by using their strong organizational skills and management talents to build their own dream. When this energy makes a partnership commitment, they will stick it out to the bitter end or to the heavenly end because their word is their bond. As the Jupiter nature expands in later life, fun, laughter, adventure, and travel pull at this responsible soul's heart strings.

Keep moving, Capricorn Moon and Sagittarius Sun, in a smooth steady flow of divine energy toward expanding your spiritual vision beyond the limits of the tribal family to a success that includes recognition, creativity, and true joy.

Sun in Capricorn (Earth)
with Moon in Capricorn (Earth)

*"From a serious, responsible child
to a grounded, initiating manager."*

When both luminaries (Sun and Moon) fall in the same sign, the Moon phase may be either New or Balsamic in phase, and both of these call for much self-reflection and self-motivation with the keyword being "Self". With the Moon and Sun together in Capricorn, there is heavy influence on the pattern of the initiating Earth element. Both of these lunar phases call for the personal growth to focus on self, both within and without. Discipline, responsibility, duty, and success all drive this soul to manifest solid results in their life.

Even in childhood, this little person seldom needs to be disciplined by their parents; however, their urge may be to take control of the household and become the boss. The key word for this combination is "refinement" of responsibilities.

Success can come in the business world or the professional world, but having a position of power is crucial to this soul. Respect and recognition rank high on their needs list, so a relationship must provide these qualities or it will not last. A strong need to work alone by a strict schedule limits the free time for snuggling and romance during the week. However, commitment is a primary quality for the Earth element, and it is at its strongest here. A strong ability to take charge and get things done makes double Earth a real mover in their field. Family will never suffer under the protection of this determined soul; however, no one else may need to do much either which may or may not be a good precedent to set.

If the Capricorn/Capricorn Combination of double Earth energy gets out of balance, a heavy concern over the smallest details can consume this earthy individual. The perfectionist nature can set such high standards that this soul never feels that they have accomplished their very best. Depending upon the other energies in the chart, this trait may or may not stop this achiever from continuing to climb the mountain or just give up feeling that their best is not good enough. A reserved, cool appearance can intimidate others while this guard was really created to protect the insecure softness that the Capricorn Goat tries so hard to protect. Saturn's influence must guard against melancholy and the battle with self-control.

The soul lesson of the Moon and Sun in Capricorn is to stand confident in the knowledge that they have truly given their best to live by the law and obey the rules. There is a lesson in surrender here to the idea that there are rules and regulations set by the community and society that they must live by. Thinking out of the box and off the grid is not the way for this structured Capricorn. Allowing patience for the self as well as others will bring a more relaxed approach to living which will permit time for play and travel. When on vacation, this soul feels the most at ease of any time in their life because the feeling relates to being off duty.

Keep moving, Capricorn Moon and Sun, in a smooth steady flow of divine energy toward accomplishing your life goals in a way that allows time for the joy of family and friends to provide a well-rounded happy lifestyle where you feel empowered by your own choices.

Sun in Aquarius (Air) with Moon in Capricorn (Earth)

*"From a serious, responsible child
to a objective, confident group leader."*

When the Moon is in Capricorn and the Sun is in Aquarius, the energy flow goes for the receptive, feminine Earth element to the positive, masculine Air element. The soul is moving from a grounded, traditional pattern to a progressive, mental thought process. Because the Moon phase is Balsamic, there is a need to go within to process outside events and not allow the world to influence the thinking. Strong, capable organizing skills are available to be used by this forward-thinking Air sign.

As a child, this one behaves as an adult with strong reasoning powers and clear opinions about the process of getting things done. There may be some early head-strong behaviors that make this youth appear obstinate and unyielding when the family pattern does not mesh with theirs.

By the time this strong personality reaches adulthood, forethought, fearlessness, and a fundamental honesty make worldly success easily attainable. This energy ties strongly to the American or United States birth chart which represents freedom and justice for all. Many famous patriotic Americans have found their fame using the same humanitarian qualities that built this country. Whether the success is in the political sector or the private sector, it is available to this goal-driven Air sign.

If the Capricorn/Aquarius combination of energy gets out of balance, a cool, detached attitude can hold loved ones at a distance. Their critical-thinking skills which are usually their greatest asset can become a real liability if this normally confident soul feels threatened. They can produce a sharp, cutting sarcasm that could freeze anyone in their tracks. Isolation is always Capricorn's main line of defense.

The soul lesson of the Moon in Capricorn and Sun in Aquarius is to maintain a steady course of achievement toward their highest humanitarian goals. A strong inborn common sense guides the life journey of this individual to lofty heights where they can make a real difference unless a lack of self-worth inside them stops the flow. This soul is learning the needs and blessings of having good friends. They are also learning to be a good friend as well. It is these social support systems that will help them along the road to their particular brand of success.

Keep moving, Capricorn Moon and Aquarius Sun, in a smooth steady flow of divine energy toward utilizing all of the disciplined characteristics that can support a consistent climb up into the world of doers and decision-makers where you can fulfill your honorable dream.

Sun in Pisces (Water) with Moon in Capricorn (Earth)

*"From a serious, responsible child
to a compassionate, visionary server."*

When the Moon is in Capricorn and the Sun is in Pisces, the energy flows easily from the grounded, receptive Earth element to the emotional, receptive Water element. With the Moon phase waning in an integrative fashion, there is a call to look deep in the soul and strip away any blocks that would hinder a core understanding of true motives.

This responsible, quiet child seldom breaks the rules or speaks out of turn. Holding most of the ultra-sensitive feelings inside seems prudent to this reserved young person. Their intense ambition forms a strong determination to overcome all fears that surround being out in front of people in a leadership role.

Taking charge when responsibility is called for is a natural here. As this young person matures, there is a natural draw to service, whether in the private or the public sector. Commitments always come easily to Saturn people, so marriage with a willingness to serve or sacrifice should be part of the life experience.

If the Capricorn/Pisces combination of energy gets out of balance, too many hurt feelings and buried resentments can make this person appear cold and disconnected. Shutting down and dealing only the facts is one way this very sensitive soul can protect itself. When really out of phase, this one could shut down and go into their own fantasy world where no one can emotionally reach them. If this occurs, counseling could help this native process and sort out deep vulnerable feelings that may not appear rational on the surface. Family expectations have a dramatic impact on this soul's self-esteem.

The soul lesson of the Moon in Capricorn and Sun in Pisces is to create a safe personal space where outside influences cannot destroy their sense of security. Because of Pisces fear of the unknown, the Capricorn influence needs to create a structure and schedule in their life. The high imagination of the Neptunian influence can blossom and produce beautiful surroundings when it feels safe. A creative, artistic touch should soften the practical environment of earthy Saturn. There is a gift here to be able to make structured objects gracefully charming.

Keep moving, Capricorn Moon and Pisces Sun, in a smooth steady flow of divine energy toward staying focused on childhood dreams and adult capabilities to create a beautiful warm space where you can enjoy the rewards of your hard earned efforts.

Moon in Aquarius

Moon in Aquarius (with all signs)

Each chapter begins with a description of the Moon's purpose for those readers who will want to go straight to a specific Moon/Sun combination.

Imagine a giant mirror reflecting past actions and experiences. According to mythology, the sign that the Moon was in at the time of your birth explains your soul response's in this lifetime. Understanding how the Moon's energy impacts your behavior and emotional reactions is key to understanding your hidden soul pattern and personal timing. You are the center of your own universe and the creator of your own destiny, so you need to understand your gifts and future goals. The eternal questions of the soul are: "Where have I come from?" and "Where am I going?" The most important eternal question, of course, is "Why am I here?"

Moon in Aquarius (Air)

The energy of Aquarius comes from the Air element, known for strong intellectual responses to emotional issues. This soul was born with a sense of higher values and clear awareness. This baby Aquarian already does his own thing at his own pace.

It is very easy for this Aquarian Moon child to entertain himself, because he is not particularly needy. He can disengage from whatever activity is going on around him. He will survive quite well in a hospital nursery, emotionally detached from the other babies. A strange sense of not belonging begins with the early family and more particularly with the mother.

If this child is not given a great deal of freedom, he may shut down emotionally and end up having to search for approval for his unique style outside of the family. It really is not necessary to be overly protective of this Uranus-ruled child, as he will go off by himself to work on a new project or to dream up inventions. Many Aquarian Moon children are charming and brighter than their siblings, so they may experience criticism for standing apart and being their own person. The young Aquarian Moon approach is to stand back and be safe; as such, their family needs to make an effort to ensure this Water-Bearer feels like they belong in the family.

This little organizer needs to be allowed to be social so that he can practice his team-building skills at an early age. In school, if their non-conformist intellectual talents are rewarded, the Aquarian will excel and make a difference in the scientific world. If the intellectual talents are stifled, this independent student will probably rebel and not achieve his highest academic potential. Young Water-Bearers tend to do well at organized sports, because they can be competitive and lead others.

As this Uranus-ruled Moon sign gets older, there seem to be more opportunities for them to shine. Independence becomes more acceptable as he becomes an adult. This soul seems to focus more on the group than on one individual.

The goal for Aquarius Moon is to maintain a strong sense of self without holding people at arm's length because he feels that he cannot trust them. Hopefully, these natives can stay open and objective while developing other spiritual qualities of sensitivity as they grow into their Sun sign energy.

Sun in Aries (Fire) with Moon in Aquarius (Air)

*"From a social, detached child
to a fiery, independent leader."*

The energy of Aquarius comes from the Air element. People born with this fixed Moon are very social. Intellectual thinking and strong opinions are what stand out for this casual friend. A soul that chooses this waning Moon placement has the urge to integrate life experience and eliminate anything that keeps this one from the goal.

This detached, independent child needs a place to be alone where he can isolate and do his own entertainment. He likes people but only for a while then he will disappear to a quiet place that allows him to be creative and original. A strong love of learning makes this one hungry for new in-formation and mental stimulation. Young Aquarius can be detached from the family activities, so this nonchalant teenager may disappear from the home scene during those puberty years.

The erratic energy of Aquarius needs social interaction, so friends rank high on their priority list. However, being affectionate is not very important to them, because too much emotional involvement slows them down. This combination cannot endure being controlled or limited in any way, and they will go to any lengths to be in charge of their own lives. Courage and independence can blend to make this individual a strong leader in the corporate or the political front.

If the Aquarius/Aries combination of energy gets out of balance, a streak of rebellion can appear out from behind that smooth, friendly exterior. Mars-ruled Aries has a tendency to flash fire when frustrated or irritated, so when this is combined with the Aquarian ability to be brusque and combative, there can be trouble. There is no lack of self-confidence with Aquarius Aries, so they do not mind standing out as unique or even a little different and a little cocky.

The soul lesson of the Moon in Aquarius and Sun in Aries is to unite their quick mental prowess with their humanitarian attitudes to make a difference on the larger world front. This soul loves to fight for the higher cause, so there is no better advocate for change than this one.

Keep moving, Aquarius Moon and Aries Sun, in a smooth steady flow of divine energy toward using all of the blessings and education that have been accumulated in your experience to make a difference in whatever circle you may find yourself. Maintain your fiery drive to make a difference in the world.

Sun in Taurus (Earth) with Moon in Aquarius (Air)

"From a social, detached child
to a practical, dependable stabilizer."

When the Moon is in Aquarius and the Sun is in Taurus, there is a difficult transition from the masculine, positive Air element to the feminine, receptive Earth element. Since the Moon phase is waning, the soul lesson is to integrate with the outside world while analyzing the inner-motives.

The friendly, outgoing, social child has a strong touch of caution woven into their character. A need for comfort and refinement adds gentleness to this individual that is not usually found in Aquarians. Because of the fixity within both of these signs, change seldom happens quickly and then not without resistance and planning. Venus-ruled Taurus can be calmed through touch and stroking.

As an adult, higher education will be important because their mental quickness can combine with a Taurean's thorough ability to study in depth and complete many levels of academic excellence. Education or finance is both strong fields for this determined long-range achiever. With maturity will come a settling from the individualistic need to be different into a more stable life pattern that includes security and material comforts. A natural gift of planning, scheduling, organizing, and blending gives this a natural ability to be a social leader.

If the Aquarius/Taurus combination of energy gets out of balance, a bullheaded reluctance to conform can block the natural progression of growing up. If this one becomes rebellious, it is difficult to get them to listen or understand why they should change their ways. Only time will show them why it is necessary to develop a routine and get an education. As friends in their social circle begin to acquire expensive toys and houses, this observer will figure it out and make the shift on their own time. When Aquarian energy detaches, they have trouble hearing any alternative solutions.

The soul lesson for Moon in Aquarius and Sun in Taurus is to remain willing to learn from others and listen to suggestions with an open-mind so that the hard knocks of life do not always need to be their teacher. This combination definitely needs people and loving relationships in their life.

Keep moving, Aquarius Moon and Taurus Sun, in a smooth steady flow of divine energy toward using all of that determination and creative originality to bring groups together and to build a solid foundation for all of your family to be secure.

Sun in Gemini (Air) with Moon in Aquarius (Air)

*"From a social, detached child
to a fast-paced, curious achiever."*

When the Moon is in Aquarius and the Sun is in Gemini, the energy flow stays in the positive, outgoing Air element. Social interaction and communication remain the focus throughout the whole lifetime. The waning Moon phase calls for integration with others through sharing knowledge and wisdom. There is a strong desire to disseminate information.

Even as a child, this soul never meets a stranger. Busy, busy, busy, with lots of activity; it sets the pace here. Study, reading, people interaction, this Uranus-ruled energy has a strong individualistic aura that shows high independence. Strong opinions stand out even at an early age.

As this soul matures, there is actually a more engaging attitude than in childhood. An original and inventive thought process brings a natural turn into a lifelong study of multiple levels of metaphysical studies. All cutting edge studies keep this high energy soul excited and engaged.

If the Aquarius/Gemini combination of energy gets out of balance, all of that mental energy can become so frenzied that nothing gets completed. Because of the flexible nature of the Gemini sign, enthusiasm can cause them to start too many projects and finish none. On the personal front, when this soul gets nervous or uncomfortable, the tendency is to talk too much and repeat a point over and over. Keeping the concentration under stress situations creates a real challenge for this airy person.

The soul lesson of the Moon in Aquarius and Sun in Gemini is to combine their strong people skills with their creative talents to interact with friends and provide leadership in any group setting. A fascination with universal movement makes science a natural study for this perpetual student. Any personal relationship with staying power will require humor, strong communication, openness, and plenty of activity, so boredom does not set in.

Keep moving, Aquarius Moon and Gemini Sun, in a smooth steady flow of divine energy toward building a strong educational support system that will allow all of your dynamic mental talents to flower and bloom in a progressive group setting.

Sun in Cancer (Water) with Moon in Aquarius (Air)

"From a social, detached child
to a nurturing, kind, decision-maker."

When the Moon is in Aquarius and the Sun is in Cancer, the soul must make adjustments to move from the positive, outgoing Air element to the receptive, feminine Water element. The waning phase of the Moon calls for relationship integration through sharing information and knowledge with others.

This young child is born with an engaging smile and a friendly disposition. A natural objective intellect and a scientific mind make schooling an adventuresome experience. Because of a high need for socialization and adventure, there will be many opportunities to take leadership during the education years.

When this combination reaches adulthood, there is a new attraction to public life and large groups of people as opposed to experiencing small intimate groups that require emotional vulnerability. The water influence of Cancer draws out a cautious attitude that protects their highly vulnerable emotional side. If the Cancer sensitivity is willing to be exposed, great warmth can come forth to reach out to less confident people and lift that insecure soul up to their best potential. Social leadership is a natural for this individual.

If the Aquarius/Cancer combination of energy gets out of balance, a detached, nonchalant attitude can blanket their feelings which make this one appear disinterested in other people's lives. There are two extreme patterns within this soul that can show up under stress – one is a cool, aloof separation from the current situation, and the other is an over-emotional, defense reaction that overflows without warning and drives this Cancer Crab back into their shell where they feel safe. The only way to break this pattern is to think about how their withdrawals is affecting the people they love. A very soft heart is hidden under that casual appearance.

The soul lesson of the Moon in Aquarius and Sun in Cancer is to risk close relationships where there can be safety in friendship and service to family. Natural leadership qualities allow this gentle soul to lead, guide, and teach higher levels of thinking that expand the group consciousness into broader understanding. This one belongs out in the world where they can impact the larger population.

Keep moving, Aquarius Moon and Cancer Sun, in a smooth steady flow of divine energy toward maintaining an expanded mental perspective while bringing that broad vision down into a personal level of interaction that allows you to create a warm and nurturing home and family.

Sun in Leo (Fire) with Moon in Aquarius (Air)

"From a social, detached child to a confident, fast-paced, outgoing leader."

When the Moon is in Aquarius and the Sun is in Leo, the energy flow goes from positive, masculine Air to positive, masculine Fire. This Full Moon phase calls forth an emotional energy that feels the need to integrate a strong individuality into relationships. This may not be an easy task for this powerfully strong independent identity.

As a child, this one is good natured, sociable, and independent. They will consider school a comfortable place school because of Aquarius' interest in mental challenges and social leadership. During the teenage years, a sense of rebellion may lead this one to venture into unusual studies and draw unusual friends who are also dramatic and creative.

These experiences will satisfy the broad-minded curiosity and need for challenge that remains a part of this one's adult personality. Warmth, charm, and a dramatic charisma will permit this soul to achieve great things if they can harness their ego and focus it on humanitarian goals that will serve the greater good. Leading groups is a natural gift for this high energy person. This one needs to allow their Sunny disposition and generous nature to shine and carry them into a high leadership position where their self-confidence is dignified.

If the Aquarius/Leo combination of energy gets out of balance, a strong need for attention can push this one into behavior that appears bizarre or over-dramatic. If their pride feels challenged, this fixed energy can shut down, become aloof, and isolate from the group. If these behaviors appear extreme, they are because there is an inborn stubborn determination that can become totally unyielding when challenged. It is more rewarding to be a friend than a family member with this combination because Aquarius always reaches out to friends first. Friends tend to make them feel the most important.

The soul lesson of the Moon in Aquarius and Sun in Leo is to hold their position without becoming unreasonable or ground into doing things their own way. When this combination stays focused, they can have great success in the political world as well as in marriage and friendship.

Keep moving, Aquarius Moon and Leo Sun, in a smooth steady flow of divine energy toward accomplishing high goals using the strong leadership qualities and smooth demeanor that you brought into this lifetime.

Sun in Virgo (Earth) with Moon in Aquarius (Air)

"From a social, detached child
to a grounded, analytical, problem-solver."

When the Moon is in Aquarius and the Sun is in Virgo, the flow of the energy must adjust from positive, masculine Air element to the receptive, feminine Earth element. A scale-down is required during this lifetime from the big humanitarian picture to the specific details of personal action in the Earth environment. The waxing phase of the Moon unconsciously calls for information and study to move the soul growth forward.

This friendly, little observer has a shy reserve that protects them from being rolled over by strong leader types. This detached persona carries over into adult life and gives this soul the ability to stand back in crisis situations and make sound logical decisions.

Because there is a natural scientific thought process with this combination, any career involving medicine or crisis management fits their talents well. This analytical observer has great intuitive faculties also which supports any level of diagnostic work from metals and engineering to medical. Since the sign Virgo rules small animals, any vocation tied to veterinarian medicine would also be a good fit.

If the Aquarius/Virgo combination of energy gets out of balance, there is an instinctive caution that blocks any spontaneous flow of affection and makes this one appear a little too aloof and cool. When the strong, analytical thought processes get stuck in higher mind and higher outcomes, the world of theory and "What If" can hold their total attention, and they will be tempted to live in their head. Being considered a poor listener is part of this detached scenario. A partner on the receiving end of this preoccupation could feel left out and invisible at times. It is really difficult for this one to be flirty, snuggly, and spontaneous in romantic situations unless there are other supporting strong planets in the chart.

The soul lesson of the Moon in Aquarius and Sun in Virgo is to be open to change both in their public and private life. Being born with a developed scientific, intellectual thought process, the gift here is to be able to apply these talents to a career where they can share their insight and intuitive gifts as well. Shyness can be the most difficult hurdle in stepping out as a strong force. Education may well be the best environment for this soul to find a level of comfort which will allow for high advancement and true success.

Keep moving, Aquarius Moon and Virgo Sun, in a smooth steady flow of divine energy toward using the great mental gifts that you were born with to create a specific niche where the earthy, analytical nature of Virgo will feel comfortable.

Sun in Libra (Air) with Moon in Aquarius (Air)

*"From a social, detached child
to a peace-keeping, fast-thinking negotiator."*

When the Moon is in Aquarius and the Sun is in Libra, the easy flow of energy within the positive, masculine element of Air makes this lifetime one of growth within harmony. Social experiences and intellectual interactions occupy most of this busy soul's time. The waxing Moon phase calls for the gut instinct to guide the process of getting in touch with the intellectual thought process to create a solid path for development.

High intuition and critical thinking skills combine to make this airy socialite capable of forming groups and moving people into the right positions for a successful outcome. Even in childhood, this easy-going little person creates a harmonious atmosphere around them that dissipates competitive, disruptive attitudes. As this one grows up, friends and family enjoy the warm, undemanding nature of this Libra people pleaser. Schooling should not be a problem for this child or any child born with Aquarius logic unless other factors intervene.

Lofty, idealist expectations in love can cause problems if this romanticist chooses a partner without spiritual depth and social skills. Any corporate training, science exploration or sales position is attractive to this combination as long as it allows opportunity for originality and group leadership.

If the Aquarius/Libra combination of energy gets out of balance, too much socializing could detract this "chatty Cathy" from completing goals. Other people's questions can easily get this easy talker off line from the project at hand. With a highly inquisitive mind, this soul always gets caught up in too many facts, too many options, and too much information. The expected overwhelming calendar also provides a deterrent to getting projects accomplished.

Unfortunately, when Air signs get bogged down in too much information their nervous system usually takes the physical hit and then all kinds of anxiety ailments can occur. A naivety and idealism around love leads Libra blindly into relationships that do not fit their lifestyle. Then fickle Libra may flit off to a new excitement instead of trying to work on the problems they need to face.

The soul lesson of the Moon in Aquarius and Sun in Libra is to project the best of their light, intellectual traits in a way that attracts other strong, open, progressive individuals into their circle. This is a lifetime opportunity to apply their natural broad social skills in a leading position where others can benefit and share in their higher humanitarian goals. If they are fortunate enough to attract a spiritual friend as a partner, then this soul could experience a true soul mate relationship.

Keep moving, Aquarius Moon and Libra Sun, in a smooth steady flow of divine energy toward blending all of the best communications skills from the Air element into a smooth delivery style that will magnetize exciting opportunities and people with high integrity into your inner-circle.

Sun in Scorpio (Water) with Moon in Aquarius (Air)

"From a social, detached child
to a determined, focused, researcher."

When the Moon is in Aquarius and the Sun is in Scorpio, the energy flow struggles from the positive, masculine Air element to the negative, feminine Water element. The Moon phase is waxing with an unconscious urge to push forward to get a plan of action. Determination is prominent in this pattern.

This youngster is an independent thinker and a good student. Even in the younger years this fixed sign combination has strong opinions that he is willing to fight for. As a social leader, this one can mold the opinions of those around them and create enough pressure to make a difference. Because the Aquarius Moon individual considers himself to be broad-minded, he struggles even with his own intolerance. This explains a great deal of the soul's inner-struggle transitioning from the Air to Water elements.

There are strong executive leadership qualities in the combination along with a natural assumption that they are right. The Scorpio's intensity and focus keeps them on track once the plan is set. Double fixed signs seldom change directions in mid-steam once that long-range vision is established in a career path. That same commitment usually holds in relationships also.

If the Aquarius/Scorpio combination of energy gets out of balance, obstinacy can stop them from accomplishing that bigger goal. There is a tendency with fixed combinations to dig in their heels and miss some of their most promising opportunities. Uranus-Mars energy can come across as biting and sarcastic when cornered in an argument, quicker than any other planetary pattern. If the Aquarius Moon type decides to drop back and "do their own thing", the Mars sexual drive may sidetrack the individual and then they spend their whole life defending that decision and miss the mark completely.

The soul lesson of the Moon in Aquarius and Sun in Scorpio is to establish a long-term plan of accomplishment and then stick to it with a flexibility that allows for divine adjustment. A quiet reserved nature hides great passion for whatever relationship or humanitarian project happens to grasp your attention. Friends and sweethearts may not readily see the kind, gentle side at first but when they get close that deep caring is there.

Keep moving, Aquarius Moon and Scorpio Sun, in a smooth steady flow of divine energy toward using all of that perceptive intuition and psychic nature to plow forward to achieve your loftiest goals while maintaining a focused drive to fulfill your deepest desires.

Sun in Sagittarius (Fire) with Moon in Aquarius (Air)

*"From a social, detached child
to an adventuresome, free-spirited seeker."*

When the Moon is in Aquarius and the Sun is in Sagittarius, the energy flow goes smoothly from the positive, masculine Air element to the positive, masculine Fire element. With the Moon in the waxing phase, the soul urge is to push instinctively outward struggling to break loose and be independent. This action makes the Aquarius Moon child eager to be on their own and do things their own way.

As a social, young person, friends and acquaintances are very important because this is where a lot of debate and intellectual challenging can occur that allows this one to usually be in the superior position. The crusader identity continues into adulthood where a highly idealistic approach may push this combination to take on broad social causes to fight for the higher good.

Any career, whether it be in public life or the private sector, that allows for high intellectual discussion and looks toward the big picture is a natural for this Air/Fire energy. Marriage and partnerships usually come a little later in life because this fireball needs to learn to hold back with some of their opinions and be more accepting of other people's priorities.

If the Aquarius/Sagittarius combination of energy gets out of balance, a chilly detachment can turn people off who do not agree with this one. Those who have the same religious beliefs are in and those who do not are out. Sagittarius can become quite challenging and direct if they feel that their cause or their personal position is being compromised. The rebellious teenager that lives inside never gives up their rabble-rouser nature. One of the hardest things for this combo to do is to grow up and settle into a routine lifestyle where there is space for a true partner.

The soul lesson of the Moon in Aquarius and Sun in Sagittarius is to focus their broad humanitarian understanding on projects that can realistically make a difference in the world. A tendency to travel out into the world crusading for altruistic causes that will not serve the larger whole can sidetrack their own life purpose. Once this highly intellectual wisdom seeker learns to be non-combative in their speech they have the natural ability to rally groups together for a common cause and to truly make a difference.

Keep moving, Aquarius Moon and Sagittarius Sun, in a smooth steady flow of divine energy toward applying all of your inborn talents in literary arts and intuitive perception to blend groups of people to make a difference on a greater scale. Guide others to "seek" with you.

Sun in Capricorn (Earth) with Moon in Aquarius (Air)

*"From a social, detached child
to a responsible, take-charge manager."*

When the Moon is in Aquarius and the Sun is in Capricorn, the combining of the masculine Air element with the feminine Earth element is not a natural flow. Air energy focuses on the intellectual learning process while earthy Capricorn must ground information to make it useful. This waxing New Moon phase instinctively nudges this soul forward in a spontaneous way but always with purpose.

As a young student, mental challenges and social groups with a cause are attractive because this over-achiever will not bother with people or activities that do not bring a practical advantage. Achievement is one of the main lifetime goals, so any program that strengthens their organizational abilities will get their attention. There is talent here for big business undertakings and financial management. However, relationships may struggle without that personal, affectionate touch unless there are softer energies that support the birth chart.

If the Aquarius/Capricorn combination of energy gets out of balance, hard-core determination can become coldly competitive and ruthless. There is a strong, healthy self-respect that does not waste time on useless causes or stupid people. This detached energy can become withdrawn and success-driven if there is not a loving, warm partner in the picture to bring out their protective side. They always need to be on guard not to use their natural talent for cutting sarcasm when they feel the need to justify themselves.

The soul lesson of the Moon in Aquarius and Sun in Capricorn is to achieve high attainment in the business world without being totally absorbed by their own importance. Persistence is the strongest in-born trait and it should be applied to both the career and the surface, becoming an additional tool in the personality tool box.

Keep moving, Aquarius Moon and Capricorn Sun, in a smooth steady flow of divine energy toward utilizing all of the mental and business skills that you were born with in a responsible occupation while you hold onto the warm, friendly side of the airy Moon by including people in your life.

Sun in Aquarius (Air) with Moon in Aquarius (Air)

"From a social, detached child
to a objective, confident group leader."

When both luminaries (Sun and Moon) fall in the same sign, the Moon phase may be either New or Balsamic in phase, and both of these call for much self reflection and self-motivation with the keyword being "Self". With the Moon and Sun together in Aquarius, the soul purpose is to focus on a positive, masculine Air element expression with a sense of higher values and clear awareness.

Even as a young person this soul shows strong individuality with the urge to handle their own decisions and the own choices. This one could be the rebel who wants to topple old traditions and bring in new thinking. In school, social leadership is a positive use of this one's urge to bring innovation into their world.

Because of their quick-witted, objective, original thinking style, professions that demand creativity and reward far-sighted vision work well for this intensely fixed Air person. Some career possibilities would be: marketing, public relations, scientist, inventor, or possibly astrologer.

If the Aquarius/Aquarius combination of double Air energy gets out of balance, eccentricity and isolation can become a social problem. When in a position that does not honor their mental worth or make them feel special, this one can become demanding with unpredictable behavior. There is a deep fixity in this soul that can make then a little crazy when they over-focus on a situation or an outcome that they expect or want. There can be a fear of intimacy if there was pain through the family during childhood.

The soul lesson of the Moon and Sun in Aquarius is to use their knowledge wisely by participating in groups that have the power to create social change. This soul has come in with a refinement that includes discretion, discernment and careful thought, so any activity to which they choose to apply themselves will benefit greatly. Behind that charming and sympathetic nature is a noncommittal soul who loves being alone.

Keep moving, Aquarius Moon and Sun, in a smooth steady flow of divine energy toward becoming a humanist or reformer that is part of making the great changes in our society. By developing the observer position, the goal should be to rise above the emotion of the masses and make an independent assessment of what innovations would be helpful in the world where you have an impact.

Sun in Pisces (Water) with Moon in Aquarius (Air)

"From a social, detached child
to a sensitive, compassionate visionary server."

When the Moon is in Aquarius and the Sun is in Pisces, the energy flow moves from the positive, outgoing Air element to the receptive, feminine Water element. The waning phase of the Moon is Balsamic which calls for the soul to share its collected resources and complete unfinished business.

During childhood, this soul learns quickly how to make friends, enjoy acquaintances, and endear themselves to the world around them. Being the defender of social cause starts early, so this young person may lead out the reformers and be the persuasive writer or speaker who heralds social change.

All intellectual and humanitarian pursuits catch this broad-minded Air sign's interest. A missionary spirit can find positive outlets in the religious arena or the counseling field. Careers that serve the people and the higher purpose work best for this world-server. In their personal life, a sensitive, compassionate side acts to reach out and protect those they love and cherish.

If the Aquarius/Pisces combination of energy gets out of balance, a temperamental, aloof attitude can emerge that holds the world at a distance. If this one becomes too confident around their acquired expertise, a holier-than-thou attitude can develop that places them above everyone else. When other people disagree, the Pisces nature can quietly slide away and brood privately. This one will not stay down long because too much domestic home stability becomes boring very quickly.

The soul lesson of the Moon in Aquarius and Sun in Pisces is to apply their perceptive humanitarian observations to a career that will impact the larger group. They are usually willing and eager to serve the public unless there are restrictive aspects in the chart that block socializing. In the private life, there is a strong calling to be a good citizen and pillar of the community who is loved and respected.

Keep moving, Aquarius Moon and Pisces Sun, in a smooth steady flow of divine energy toward using all of your inborn business sense and strong intuitive vision to build that group who will make a difference to your highest cause.

Moon in Pisces

Moon in Pisces (with all signs)

Each chapter begins with a description of the Moon's purpose for those readers who will want to go straight to a specific Moon/Sun combination.

Imagine a giant mirror reflecting past actions and experiences. According to mythology, the sign that the Moon was in at the time of your birth explains your soul response's in this lifetime. Understanding how the Moon's energy impacts your behavior and emotional reactions is key to understanding your hidden soul pattern and personal timing. You are the center of your own universe and the creator of your own destiny, so you need to understand your gifts and future goals. The eternal questions of the soul are: "Where have I come from?" and "Where am I going?" The most important eternal question, of course, is "Why am I here?"

Moon in Pisces (Water)

The Pisces energy comes from of the Water element, known for its emotional sensitivity, psychic intuition and fear of the unknown. This soul may have trouble separating their goals from those of other people. The Pisces Moon infant arriving on earth with this strongly developed emotional system may have trouble shutting out the feelings and thoughts of the people around them.

Many times, this baby is crying because of outside tension in the room, or someone close to this Fish is upset. This little soul must learn how to handle the unseen emotions in her environment.

One of the more difficult traits of this Pisces Moon child is that she does not like routine. The young watery Moon can develop a whiny disposition when she gets too tired. Instead of yelling and screaming, she will cry and complain until you put her to bed. Sleep seems to be an issue with Pisces Moon children. They either want to sleep too much or they can't sleep at all. It depends on what is bothering them.

Since the Watery Pisces energy is attached to the astral world, these children usually have very prophetic dreams and tend to go off by themselves to play in this other reality. It is not uncommon for them to dream about relatives who have died or to receive a message from one who is preparing to die.

As young children, they may see the elves, fairies, gnomes, and dwarfs who live in the middle kingdom. Most of the time they call these little people their friends and playmates. Don't be too quick to judge these kids, this unseen kingdom is open to the young Water element souls.

When this sensitive little Pisces Moon goes to school, encourage them to participate in school plays and music classes. They will have a natural talent for the arts. It may be drawing, painting, playing an instrument, or acting. It is important to encourage these gifts when they are still young because their innocence will fade as they get older. They will be hesitant to show these gifts as they become more self-conscious. It does not take much disciplining to keep this gentle little one in line. She is quite aware of what other people expect of her. Count on her to defend the underdog at school or share her lunch with someone who had no lunch money.

This Pisces Moon may end up trying to please their parents rather than following their own dreams. As a teenager, it is important to have a stable environment for this Fish so they don't get over influenced by peer pressure or get lost in their dream world. Many extremely sensitive Pisces Moon souls become guarded and withdrawn as they get older to protect themselves,

The goal of Pisces Moon is to try to hold onto the kind, gentle love of humanity that was prominent in her as a child when she matures emotionally. Hopefully this creative soul will not shutdown, but integrate, their intuitive gifts into their outer-world life.

Sun in Aries (Fire) with Moon in Pisces (Water)

*"From a sensitive, emotional, intuitive child
to a fiery, independent warrior."*

When the Moon is in Pisces and the Sun is in Aries, the natural flow of energy goes from the receptive Water element to the positive, outgoing Fire element. The waning Moon phase calls for the soul to integrate many lifetimes of study and then share their knowledge with others.

This intuitive little child who is born with a sensitive heart and a compassionate demeanor also has a very independent, quick response to energy coming toward them. When they try to blend their watery emotions with their fiery attitude, sometimes they just sit there and steam and sometimes unpredictable responses occur. The extremes of their behavior may go from pouting and whining to fighting back like a little warrior. It is more productive to coax this little fireball than to try to force them into submission. As a young person, this combination may turn into a victim or martyr due to family situations beyond their control.

When this scenario occurs, the Aries survival influence nudges them to pull away impulsively, taking rash and sometimes unwise actions on their own. If there is no strong spiritual influence in the early years, this soul may wander out into the world feeling lost and unloved. Once their fiery Aries independence takes hold, a terrific survival strength kicks in that pushes them into their power. Any successful career for Aries needs to utilize their strong creative talents as well as a high level of independence.

If the Pisces/Aries combination of energy gets out of balance, there can be a lot of brooding, worry, and temperamental feelings. Because of the idealism of the Pisces, that first partnership may not end up to be what they thought they were getting. Then if the martyr complex sets in, they could stay in the relationship long after the love has died. If the damage from relationship is deep, this romanticist may draw back into solitude to heal and then stay there where it feels safe. On the other hand, Aries may develop a pattern of always "taking the bull by the horn" and becoming too aggressive.

The soul lesson of the Moon in Pisces and Sun in Aries is to allow their intuition and inner-guidance to guide them out into the world of risk where new experiences can be their teacher. There are two extremes of activity here. One extreme represents too much activity with no time to rest, and the other extreme is to withdraw with no social activity at all.

Keep moving, Pisces Moon and Aries Sun, in a smooth steady flow of divine energy toward using that inborn intuitive sense to remain attuned to the feelings of others while permitting that pioneering spirit to allow you to take risks while being open to new insights and new experiences.

Sun in Taurus (Earth) with Moon in Pisces (Water)

"From a sensitive, emotional, intuitive child to a practical, consistent stabilizer."

When the Moon is in Pisces and the Sun is in Taurus, the energy flow moves easily from the feminine, passive Water element to the feminine, grounded Earth element. The waning integrative phase of the Moon calls for the soul to shed off any old fears or patterns that do not help in soul growth.

There is a sensitive, tender, affection that this Pisces infant brings into this world that will remain with them throughout this lifetime. The child has strong psychic intuitiveness that may show up as imaginary friends and angels. The gifts of the artist appear early in the development as natural musical or drawing talents. The urge of the young person may be to retreat into the sweet world of the inner mind where all of these other world activities can be strong. A kind, pliable disposition allows this combination to get along well socially and have many friends; however, their nature to be too giving may bring disappointment and hurt.

In maturity, this one needs to focus on a career that provides security and financial stability because these become more and more important in later years. A good marriage, good living, and peaceful surroundings – all of these make for a very happy Pisces Taurus combination.

If the Pisces/Taurus combination of energy gets out of balance, isolation and fantasy can capture their thoughts and preoccupy them. The Venusian rulership of Taurus can bring in a prudish nature that gets carried away with being offended by crass behavior. Because of the dreamy Neptune influence, this one could enter blindly into that perfect romance wearing those "rose-colored glasses". If once hurt, then the Pisces fear mechanism turns on and this one has to struggle to get out of the wounded victim syndrome.

The soul lesson of the Moon in Pisces and Sun in Taurus is to tap into that wealth of artistic talent that lives within the Pisces imagination and use it to paint a beautiful life. Financial security ranks near the top of the list along with comfortable surroundings and artistic collectibles for this combination, so they should make an effort to create a soft, warm and elegant home.

Keep moving, Pisces Moon and Taurus Sun, in a smooth steady flow of divine energy toward bringing forth the creative energies and using them to become financially solid while you stay connected to your strong spiritual intuitive side that will bring peace to your inner self.

Sun in Gemini (Air) with Moon in Pisces (Water)

"From a sensitive, emotional, intuitive child
to a social, fast-paced communicator."

When the Moon is in Pisces and the Sun is in Gemini, the energy struggles to move between the feminine, receptive Water element and the masculine, outgoing Air element. With the Moon phase waning, integration is called for with the world where one searches deep in the soul to see what is real and what is not real.

This infant is born into a sensitive body that is naturally vulnerable to the feelings of everyone around them. Because they associate their feelings with those of other people, they are easily overwhelmed and frightened by crowds. Throughout their younger years, they live in their own make-believe world where they dream of the unattainable and perfect life. As the mental curiosity of Gemini gets stronger, this young person becomes very inquisitive and loves to travel or just be on the go.

A deep restlessness makes this soul a seeker of knowledge and experience, so the educational field naturally attracts them. Being both psychic and resourceful opens the door to any career that combines both the imagination and the logical side of the mind. Writing, art, music, or speaking could be avenues to utilize these creative talents. There is also a strong need to participate in the human services by voluntarily helping others along the way.

If the Pisces/Gemini combination of energy gets out of balance, the inquisitor and "Doubting Thomas" comes out to question anything that is one does not intellectually understand. A doubting attitude holds people at a distance; this one's behavior could be read as negative or fearful which keeps solid friendships from developing. With all the mutable energy of Pisces Gemini, this person can become fickle, jumping from relationship to relationship and job to job. A superficial interest in their surroundings makes deep commitments more difficult.

The soul lesson of the Moon in Pisces and Sun in Gemini is to use their highly tuned intuition to guide them as they develop strong logical, practical mental skills. Learning to use their strong Mercury-ruled Gemini communication gifts will open new doors in the commercial sales industry or in the field of drama. Overcoming fear of failure marks a significant growth point for this soul. Living near the water will also help this restless spirit to settle into a stable lifestyle.

Keep moving, Pisces Moon and Gemini Sun, in a smooth steady flow of divine energy toward blending the inner world with the outer world where all of that quick wit and fun fantasy can come out in a tactful way so that all those artistic communication skills can be applauded.

Sun in Cancer (Water) with Moon in Pisces (Water)

"From a sensitive, emotional, intuitive child
to a nurturing, kind, homemaker."

When the Moon is in Pisces and the Sun is in Cancer, the energy focuses on the feminine, receptive Water element. Sensitivity, feelings, and emotion remain at the top of the list as the waning Moon phase soul works to integrate their nurturing talents into a life work that allows them to share their understanding.

This shy, overly sensitive child hides in the shadows to protect themselves from challengers. However, within the family circle, this soul will show their creative, warm, social side. Since Pisces is a flexible sign, this young person loves novelty and is always ready to try something new and different by going with the flow. A well development mediumistic gift keeps this soul in tune with the other side of the veil by making them always conscious of the presence of their angels and guides.

As the Cancer energy activates, this easy-going combination awakens to a call to relate to the world in some area that will allow them to be a loving nurturer. Their role could be the ultimate mother or it could bring them into a career where nurturing is the key to success. Water element individuals are naturally drawn to the service industry where their instinctive talent for quickly tuning into the emotional and mental processes of others is considered to be an asset.

If the Pisces/Cancer combination of energy gets out of balance, emotions may come pouring out as fear. When their defensive walls go up, it becomes difficult for this one to be able to listen to reason. Caution forces an emotional shutdown when feelings are running high and there is nowhere to hide. Dramatic tears could be a means to an end when things are not going their way. This one needs to be careful with drugs and alcohol as an escape or a means to relaxation because it is all too easy to slide into that cozy fantasy world. Sleep can also be a great escape for the Pisces emotional Moon energy.

The soul lesson of the Moon in Pisces and Sun in Cancer is to blend that unconscious intuitive sensing radar with the responsive, perceptive nature of fast-acting Cancer. This receptive Moon quality opens many doors for the dynamic achiever. Personal relationships in family, work, or a strong social environment always hold the first priority for this soul who is learning to integrate their life with others. Whether the bonding is with the tribal family or the larger spiritual family, being a part of the larger whole remains the major theme of the lifetime.

Keep moving, Pisces Moon and Cancer Sun, in a smooth steady flow of divine energy toward using all of the sensitive, dramatic, creative talents in a way that will open your life to exciting relationships with dynamic people who will love being nurtured.

Sun in Leo (Fire) with Moon in Pisces (Water)

*"From a sensitive, emotional, intuitive child
to a creative, dramatic leader."*

When the Moon is in Pisces and the Sun is in Leo, the energy flow struggles to make an adjustment from receptive, feminine Pisces to masculine, outgoing Leo. The waning Moon phase calls for integration of the talents through building personal relationships.

The young, sensitive Pisces energy child responds cautiously to the outside world. Their feelings float close to the surface, so they develop a guardedness that continues to protect, and this person begins to develop an outer world confidence that does not necessarily feel valid from within. Both signs have a strong talent for blending color with a creative flair which could lead to a career in interior decorating, design or painting.

An instinctual pull to work safely behind the scenes conflicts drastically with the Sun's call to step out in the limelight and be seen. With maturity, there is a strength that surfaces that draws this one into leadership but the career needs to have a strong cause. Strong presentation skills as well as good organization abilities open the door to many different professional paths. In personal relationships, early partners may not last because there is a very definite shift in their needs from idealism to excitement and passion.

If the Pisces/Leo combination of energy gets out of balance, pride and personal righteousness can become overbearing. Because of the over-sensitivity of their emotional nature, a strong offense may be hiding a defensive, insecure position. A childish reaction to being pushed into being in a service position may be to respond as a victim or martyr. The opposite negative reaction is to leap out like a lion and attack from the offense. This is not an easy combination to keep the emotional balance from degenerating into dejection or depression.

The soul lesson of the Moon in Pisces and Sun in Leo is to bridge the gap from the emotional responder to the dramatic, outgoing leader. The theater would be a natural place to develop these talents positively while maintaining a safe environment for the experience. Pisces has a fearful side, so adventures that involve too much risk are not comfortable for this one who needs to know what is coming next. There needs to be time to allow the instinctive intuition and spiritual understanding that came in with this soul to continue to flourish as part of this lifetime's growth.

Keep moving, Pisces Moon and Leo Sun, in a smooth steady flow of divine energy toward harmonizing the two very different sides of yourself into one powerful presence that can show their vulnerable, spiritual, creative side to your family and the world.

Sun in Virgo (Earth) with Moon in Pisces (Water)

"From a sensitive, emotional, intuitive child to an analytical problem-solver."

When the Moon is in Pisces and the Sun is in Virgo, the energy flow goes across the chart from the receptive, feminine Water element to the receptive, feminine Earth element. The Full Moon waning Moon phase calls for a balance of extremes that can be integrated through developing personal relationships.

This watery, emotional child hides behind the protection of the family because their instinct is to feel frightened and vulnerable. It is hard to keep the attention of this little dreamer since a deep inborn restlessness pulls them because they are seldom paying close attention to what is coming next. Imaginative dreams and creative visions occupy most of their time.

As the Virgo creative thinking skills awaken in maturity, the combination of intuition and analytical processing can bring out hidden inventive talents that really come from being attuned to the collective unconscious. Leadership is not for this behind-the-scenes worker. This one prefers the flexibility that a backup position allows. In relationships, this very flexible energy does best with strong take-charge individuals. It keeps this soul from having to be the final decision maker. Any profession that involves service from the compassionate social worker to the wise, astute doctor works for this insightful sensitive person

If the Pisces/Virgo combination of energy gets out of balance, a fear of making decisions can throw this one into a state of paralysis. If they have not built a strong inner faith, their tendency is to over-analyze and over-ponder every decision keeping them from moving into positions of authority. A consistent hesitancy to commit holds this soul back in the shadows where they may be the most comfortable.

When they are in charge, a critical attention to detail makes this worker not only self-critical but also a nit-picker with their fellow workers.

The soul lesson of the Moon in Pisces and Sun in Virgo is to use that Neptunian intuitive vision alongside the grounded, logical abilities of Mercury to serve mankind in some way that helps with the healing of the soul or the body. When this soul is able to handle their own sensitivities in a positive manner, then they can begin to help others through the healing process.

Keep moving, Pisces Moon and Virgo Sun, in a smooth steady flow of divine energy toward blending those compassionate qualities with a developed attention to detail that allows life to flow smoothly in a meaningful direction that result in happiness and personal satisfaction.

Sun in Libra (Air) with Moon in Pisces (Water)

"From a sensitive, emotional, intuitive child to a social, peace-keeping negotiator."

When the Moon is in Pisces and the Sun is in Libra, the energy is trying to flow from the feminine, receptive Water element to the masculine, outgoing Air element. An adjustment is required to make these two parts of the soul compatible. The Moon phase is waxing which calls out an instinctive urge to gather information and knowledge as a disciple of wisdom.

Childhood is filled with dreams and visions that may only play out in the inner-world because this one lacks the courage to risk failure unless other patterns are present in the chart. Just as the child nature is cautious, so is the Venus-ruled Libra energy. Even though there is a strong psychic nature, this soul should avoid spending too much energy here because it could keep the attention in the world of illusion instead of allowing the strong mental processes to develop through practical, intellectual activities.

In relationships, this young romantic may get caught up in the dream and then find themselves in a very unbalanced relationship. Any career dealing with people is a natural here for there are strong diplomatic skills that do well in negotiations as well as a sincere demeanor that puts people at ease.

If the Pisces/Libra combination of energy gets out of balance, a fairytale fantasy may occupy their time so that they never move out into the real world to actually manifest their dreams. A strong fear of being hurt keeps this delicate soul out of risky situations; however, it also keeps them out of the mainstream of activity and social situations that they need to grow. Indecisiveness is a chronic problem with the Libra nature because they do not want to be responsible for hurting anyone else. Between the huge need to avoid conflict and the fear of being wrong, this combination seldom speaks out honestly about their feelings or their position on any subject.

The soul lesson of the Moon in Pisces and Sun in Libra is to learn to take risks by stepping out and taking action in a balanced and fair way. This one needs to develop a realistic expectation in relationships and also in their daily life. They also need to expand their conscious learning by acquiring formal education because the Air element needs mental stimulation for soul growth. Careers that deal with the arts, beauty and communication bring out the very best in this social combination.

Keep moving, Pisces Moon and Libra Sun, in a smooth steady flow of divine energy toward using all of the spiritual, intuitive gifts that came in with you and then combining them with newly developed people skills that allow you to interact on a high social scale with all levels of successful people.

Sun in Scorpio (Water) with Moon in Pisces (Water)

*"From a sensitive, emotional, intuitive child
to an intense, driven, researcher."*

When the Moon is in Pisces and the Sun is in Scorpio, the energy flow stays comfortably within the feminine, receptive Water element where the natural focus is on the refinement of the emotional nature. The waxing Moon phase calls for an instinctive pushing outward to prepare to take action out in the world. This individual has a deep intuitive gift that was there at birth. Water energy is a conduit for spiritual messages from the other side.

Even as a child this sensitive soul has a great imagination and a true love of the arts. There is an intensely romantic nature that is protected in idealism, so if this soul is ever hurt in love the instinct is to shut down and exist within their safe protected world. There is the capability to see through people and situations even better than they feel comfortable with. Any career that uses this uncanny insight such as, medicine, counseling, investments, and inheritance would be rewarding for the water reflector.

If the Pisces/Scorpio combination of energy gets out of balance, a hypercritical attitude can cut people at their most vulnerable spot. There is a knack for showing disapproval without ever saying a word. It is all communicated through facial expressions like shrugs, gestures, and or the deadpan look. If the Pisces fear gets activated, this one's imagination can drive them into a real state of anxiety where it concerns their security or their family. Nerves can become locked up with is combination when the Scorpio tenacity refuses to let go of the apprehension. Explosive anger may end up being a release for all of the pent up emotion.

The soul lesson of the Moon in Pisces and Sun in Scorpio is to cultivate that mystical intuition and sensitivity into a clear channel so that spiritual wisdom can be brought through in the counseling work that is chosen. There should be benefit through children with this combination. As long as this one is not pulled to the negative side, there will be many occasions where this soul can positively guide those who are attracted to them.

Keep moving, Pisces Moon and Scorpio Sun, in a smooth steady flow of divine energy toward allowing the spiritual forces above to use your open channel in a way that will benefit our brothers and sisters on the planet.

Sun in Sagittarius (Fire) with Moon in Pisces (Water)

*"From a sensitive, emotional, intuitive child
to an adventuresome seeker."*

When the Moon is in Pisces and the Sun is in Sagittarius, the energy flow struggles to shift from the receptive, feminine Water element to the positive, masculine Fire element. The waxing Moon phase calls for an instinctive unconscious push to establish a plan of action.

The demure sensitivity of the small child suffers under harsh demands from the family or the world. Since both of these signs are mutable in nature, anxiety and worry build up under pressure. Even as a young person this one does not feel confident to take charge and assume a position of authority. This one lives mostly in a private inner world of their own personal thoughts, ideas and ideals. There is a rather detached attitude to life that does not pull this soul into close relationships early in the development.

With maturity comes a much more adventuresome spirit and a philosophical attitude. Since there is no great interest in the material things in the world, this broad thinker does not fit in the business world but must find a profession where there is higher purpose and a principle of higher values. Intense relationships are not easy for this combination because of their abstract view of universal purpose and a preoccupation with the larger picture.

If the Pisces/Sagittarius combination of energy gets out of balance, too much activity causes instability which keeps anything from getting completed. This one must fight becoming distracted from the current project and even from the current conversation. Serious anxiety can build up if the Sagittarius philosophy of flow is not applied. Too much nervous energy can stimulate the need to talk and over-explain a particular point or principle. This mutable combination must guard against frittering away their time and energy on superficial projects and sacrificing missions. Because of a highly sympathetic nature, this soul could be easily be taken advantage of and then painfully discarded.

The soul lesson of the Moon in Pisces and Sun in Sagittarius is to become more stable in their daily routines and more apart of earthly living. The understanding of high spiritual principles occupies most of their waking hours, so religion and professions of service work best on the career front. A great gift of non-judgment has been bestowed upon this one which allows healing energy to also become stronger in later years.

Keep moving, Pisces Moon and Sagittarius Sun, in a smooth steady flow of divine energy toward making a difference on the planet by using your ability to see the big picture along with a mystical sense of higher purpose.

Sun in Capricorn (Earth)
with Moon in Pisces (Water)

"From a sensitive, emotional, intuitive child
to a grounded, responsible manager."

When the Moon is in Pisces and the Sun is in Capricorn, the personal energy flow moves between the feminine, sensitive Water element and the feminine, receptive Earth element. The waxing phase of the Moon indicates an instinctive urge to rush out into life and push forward from the nest to find the soul's own way in life. This young adult individual is comfortable in their own company since the life time theme remains inwardly based.

In childhood, this one seeks to serve their family willingly and quietly. Because this is a loner personality, the intuitive messages come through very clearly during those formative years before the high achievement drive sets in.

With maturity comes a strong, responsible drive to succeed in the material world of business or the power world of the high-ranked professional. Either one of these positions brings the same control and recognition as the king at the top of the mountain. No sign is more duty bound and set to standards than the initiating earth energy of Capricorn. Determined concentration brings the persistence to drive projects to completion. Relationships take a back seat to their work schedule, but when they commit they are usually loyal with strong responsibility to the family.

If the Pisces/Capricorn combination of energy gets out of balance, a joyless sense of drudgery and depression can come over this one when their deepest fears of failure show up. This combination experiences a sharp separation between their feeling side and the action side of the personality. A cold, restless melancholy can take over when the sensitive inner-child feels threatened. There is no more withdrawn energy when hard times hit than this one.

The soul lesson of the Moon in Pisces and Sun in Capricorn is to nurture that sensitive, warm emotional soul energy that is so visible in the early years and combine it with the determined strength of the Capricorn Mountain Goat. By allowing the inspirational Neptune influence to add intuitive creativity to your life, many original ideas can be born that will contribute to producing better ways to do things. If greed and power take over, the innate intuition shuts down and the joyful sense of accomplishment goes away.

Keep moving, Pisces Moon and Capricorn Sun, in a smooth steady flow of divine energy toward using that grounded persistence to make a contribution not only to the business world but also to the charitable institutions of the world.

Sun in Aquarius (Air) with Moon in Pisces (Water)

"From a sensitive, emotional, intuitive child to a social, confident, group leader."

When the Moon is in Pisces and the Sun is in Aquarius, the energy flow reluctantly moves from the feminine, receptive Water element to the masculine, outgoing Air element. As this is a waxing New Moon phase pattern, the instinctive urge is to unconsciously push out into new experience.

When this little soul arrives into this world, they feel vulnerable and shy. Because of their emotional gullibility, they can easily be imposed upon and taken advantage of. Instead of becoming angry, their instinct is to become hurt and victimized.

As maturity sets in, a broader, more objective perspective awakens the higher consciousness of the Aquarian mind. In the adult years, this compassionate soul aims for the high road which removes them for the material drives of the masses and forces them into their own belief system. With education, the objective mental faculties will develop, but there will always be that mystical leaning toward the other worlds and hidden kingdoms of life.

If the Pisces/Aquarius combination of energy gets out of balance, a victim/martyr complex can set in that drives this extremely sensitive sacrificer into real withdrawn depression. When others disagree with their opinions, they may act nonchalant, but chances are they will quietly slide away and brook in private. When this combination goes into withdrawal, the deep past life feelings of inferiority will rise up and torment them. There is definitely a fear of deep relationships where one can be taken advantage of. A cool, detached, noncommittal attitude can protect that soft side out in the world.

The soul lesson of the Moon in Pisces and Sun in Aquarius is to combine the intuitive, perceptive qualities with the objective, mental clarity of the air element to produce a friendly, warm, spiritual self-contained individual who sets their own standards and follows their own path. The soul has an uncanny understanding of the symbols of the universe can use them to become a strong mystic, psychic, clairvoyant, or an excellent spiritual astrologer.

Keep moving, Pisces Moon and Aquarius Sun, in a smooth steady flow of divine energy toward growing beyond the limitations of fear-based Pisces into a progressive mental understanding that will allow you to reach new heights as a contributor to the greater New Age Aquarian movement by sending positive energy out into the universal collective. Prayer and meditation are two ways to do this.

Sun in Pisces (Water) with Moon in Pisces (Water)

*"From a sensitive, emotional, intuitive child
to a creative, visionary artist."*

When both luminaries (Sun and Moon) fall in the same sign, the Moon phase may be either New or Balsamic in phase, and both of these call for much self-reflection and self-motivation with the keyword being "Self". With the Moon and Sun together in Pisces, the feminine, receptive, flexible essence of the Water element is the lifetime focus. Whether the Sun Moon relationship is New Moon or Balsamic in nature, there needs to be a conscious awareness of the self and what it is here to accomplish.

The early childhood brings out the anxious, naive, innocence of the Pisces idealist. As this one grows, they maintain a close connection to the astral world where their imaginary friends and angels guide and amuse them. A mediumistic nature opens the door to all levels of spiritual work if the soul is inclined to use their creative talents in the area of service. This strong imagination could just as easily be developed in the world of music and art.

Any field that offers opportunities for creativity, fantasy, art, imagination, or service could provide a valuable platform for growth. Because of their dreamy nature, double Pisces may struggle with the real world of real relationships, so they tend to fantasize about being in the perfect relationship until they get older and into the middle of their life. In fact, this one will spend much of their life sacrificing for others. It is important for them to be sure they are sacrificing for the right cause.

If the Pisces/Pisces combination of double water energy gets out of balance, this one can become a pitiful victim who fights with bouts of illness or depression. The hardships of life on earth can overwhelm this sensitive soul and make them yearn to be free on this human body.

This chameleon can put on a charming facade that can fool the most astute observer into thinking that all is well here when it may really not be at all. There can be a fairytale delusional piece to this personality that fools the world into seeing them however the occasion calls for. They must also be careful not to fall in love with their own illusion.

The soul lesson of the Moon and Sun in Pisces is to become clear about their life goals and then stay on track to accomplish the necessary steps to get to the finish line. It is important to use the inborn mystical vision wisely as a part of the profession or chosen career. The most important step is to set a life goal, for that is not easy with mutable signs. Being an idealist, this one can follow the spiritual path, the political path, or the path of fantasy and fame in the theater.

Keep moving, Pisces Moon and Sun, in a smooth steady flow of divine energy toward making those dreams come true in the outside world where other people can benefit from your sacrificing nature and your giving disposition.

Continuing on Your Soul Life Path

Continuing on Your Soul Life Path

"Knowledge without application is useless to the soul."

Once awake, the soul can steer their life vehicle toward an expansion that reaches out for love, harmony, and inner-joy.

The purpose of this book is to expose the possible choices that a soul must make during this lifetime for growth or stagnation. When the conscious mind recognizes old patterns and becomes aware of new options about ways of being, living, interacting, and succeeding, then, one can see their life choices. Then they can become actively engaged in manually overriding old habits to create different situational results.

As conscious beings searching for a higher purpose, the conscious mind is always processing incoming data. There is an unconscious selection process that continually screens incoming images. The question that stands out is "How does the soul recognize pertinent data that resonates with this life experience?" As an individual reads about their unique etheric patterns that join together to make up their behavior traits, they should ponder the bigger question that arises, which is "How does one capture the vision of their planetary pattern and then follow that path of their personal life soul journey?" The saying that "Knowledge is Power" shows that information brought to the conscious mind awakens the inner person to take action in the outer world.

Information must be ingested and then experienced (to take action) before it can be woven into the fiber of the soul and incorporated into the soul pattern. Then experiences become part of the vibration of the music of one's Spirit.

Astrological symbols are part of universal geometry so the soul's unconscious recognizes these patterns and responds to them. As the individual reads about themselves, hidden wisdom is awakened from the shadows to be processed in the conscious world of thought. By recognizing and studying about one's lifetime symbol pattern, the alpha mind grasps the bigger picture and begins to formulate the Soul's Life Path.

The journey begins in earnest when one's personality joins with the unconscious memory of the astrological pattern that needs to be accomplished in this lifetime. Once awake, the individual can focus on overcoming challenges, dissolving blockages, balancing extreme behaviors, and utilizing soul talents and gifts. This information is all registered in the person's Natal or Birth chart which is calculated using the exact planetary positions at the date, time and location of birth. The positions of the Sun and Moon are the primary indicators of the Life Path; they are supported by all of the other planets, fixed stars, asteroids and sensitive points relating to a native's unique picture. The natal birth chart represents one's spiritual DNA or distinct fingerprint for this time on earth.

Going Further

Since astrology helps us learn more about who we are, there is always more to learn. The natal birth chart shows information about your life's purpose. There are also deeper patterned charts that reflect soul accomplishment. The Draconic chart, based on a nodal zodiac, shows developed gifts. The Esoteric chart provides guidance for focused spiritual development. When a seeker is ready to dig deeper, these charts can be consulted along with the person's natal birth chart. As a certified astrologer, I and the gifted astrologers who have graduated from my school are happy to help you on this journey.

Please do contact our office (pam1gallagher@gmail.com) if you feel the call in your gut to take your study further, or if you have any questions about the steps on the path or the content in this book. Congratulations on finishing this book. Enjoy the journey, for the chart unlocks a map, and it is up to you to continue to embrace and explore the path.

CPSIA information can be obtained
at www.ICGtesting.com
Printed in the USA
FFHW021658031019
55369833-61117FF